LET THERE BE LIFE

For Violet Klenov
we are all stories in the making and your
career helps to bring new stories to life.
Best wishes Roger Gosden
September 2019

LET THERE BE LIFE

An Intimate Portrait of Robert Edwards
and His IVF Revolution

Roger Gosden

Jamestowne Bookworks, Williamsburg, Virginia

Roger G. Gosden is currently affiliated at William & Mary and lately a professor and research director at Weill Medical College of Cornell University.

Jamestowne Bookworks, Williamsburg, Virginia
©2019 by Jamestowne Bookworks
All Rights Reserved. Published 2019

ISBN 978-0-9975990-4-6 (print edition)
ISBN 978-0-9975990-5-3 (digital edition)

Let There Be Life by Roger Gosden
Biography and memoir of a scientist
History of In Vitro Fertilisation
Social History of 20th century Britain
Law and Ethics of Fertility Treatment and Embryo Research
Gallery of Images

Jamestowne Bookworks LLC
107 Paddock Lane
Williamsburg, VA 23188
https://www.jamestownebookworks.com

Cover image: Robert Edwards in the 1980s at his Bourn Hall office in Cambridgeshire, leaning over a desk covered with pictures of IVF babies. (Corbin O'Grady Studio/ Science Photo-Library)

Bob Edwards inspecting his tree plantation in 2008.
(Courtesy of Rita Basuray)

Endorsements

Robert Edwards changed the world, bringing life, hope, and joy to millions of people. I owe him everything—**Louise Brown**, World's First IVF Baby

Thanks to Robert Edward's vision, determination and dedication, countless women like me have the children we longed for — **Grace MacDonald**, mother of Alastair, the first IVF baby boy

This is a tale of true scientific courage. As an infertility advocate and Board member of RESOLVE, I see the life-changing value of IVF every day. In this stirring first-hand retelling, Dr Gosden brings to life the untold story of Dr Robert Edwards, the pioneer behind this essential therapy. Anyone who has created a family via IVF should read this book — **Lee Rubin Collins**

Bob's extraordinary and spirited life journey changed the social history of the world: this thoughtful biography will inspire generations to come — **Kay Elder**, Senior Research Scientist at Bourn Hall Clinic

Roger Gosden has done a magnificent job in producing this biography of a remarkable man. His research has provided us with much new material about Bob Edwards' life, and this new information is integrated in a compelling narrative that I could not put down. He describes in terms entirely comprehensible to the lay person the scientific aspects of Bob's work, set in the wider context of Bob's life and personality — **Martin Johnson, FRS**, Cambridge University

I can think of no one better than Roger Gosden to do justice to Bob's exceptional life and work — **Mike Macnamee**, Chief Executive at Bourn Hall Clinic

An incredible journey of a true pioneer, who not only changed the field of reproductive medicine but also the social fabric of today's world—**Zev Rosenwaks**, Weill Medical School of Cornell University

Bob Edwards' vision and struggles to apply basic embryology to solve the pain of human infertility, penned beautifully by disciple Roger Gosden—**Alan Trounson**, Monash University

Gosden's engaging book about the most gripping biological discovery of the past 100 years, equivalent in biology to relativity and quantum mechanics in physics, focuses on a single heroic biologist, Dr Robert Edwards, who single-handedly changed the lives of despairing infertile couples, despite the naysayers — **Sherman Silber**, Infertility Center of St Louis

I consider myself one of Bob's disciples, learned a lot from him in science, literature, and life—**Mohamed Aboulghar**, Professor, Cairo, Egypt

To the unknown patients whose perseverance and sacrifice helped to make a medical revolution with timid hopes for themselves

Your children ... are the sons and daughters of Life's longing for itself. Kahlil Gibran: *The Prophet*

Sing in me, Muse, and through me tell the story of that man skilled in all ways of contending, the wanderer, harried for years on end. Homer: *The Odyssey*

The Author

Roger Gosden is a British and American scientist whose career began as a research student and fellow in Cambridge, England, supervised by Robert Edwards. After a Population Council fellowship at Duke University, he moved to Edinburgh Medical School in 1976 where he worked for 18 years, subsequently a professor and research director at Leeds and McGill Universities, and the Howard & Georgeanna Jones professor of reproductive medicine at Eastern Virginia Medical School. In 2004, he moved to Weill Cornell Medical College in New York City, joining on the faculty his wife Lucinda Veeck, the embryologist for America's first IVF baby. They live in Williamsburg, Virginia, where he is a writer, naturalist, and visiting scholar at William & Mary.

Table of Contents

Preface

This is the story of a miner's son who brought a revolution to medical science. It is the life of Robert Edwards, an affable Yorkshireman called "Bob" by his friends and colleagues and hailed around the world as the "Father of In Vitro Fertilisation" (IVF). He dismissed the flattering tribute, saying that a team of relay-runners is needed to finish a long race, but his leg of the course demanded the most stamina and dogged determination. It took more than brilliance and Edwards' luck; the winner needed character, charisma, and the gift of a robust constitution.

The history of his career is a list of "firsts" — the first fertilisation of human ova in vitro, first test-tube baby, first embryonic stem cells, and first genetic testing of microscopic embryos. After those achievements he didn't sit back for accolades and awards but rolled up his sleeves again to apply science for people with the heartache of infertility or family histories of dreaded disease or disability. In opening the first IVF clinic in the world, he became a biomedical entrepreneur, a role added to an overfilled life as a university teacher, globe-trotting lecturer, politician, scientific publisher, hobby farmer, and proud family man. His energy was as legendry as his legacy.

He didn't come from a privileged background, except for the immense advantage of a mother's ambition for her son and loyal helpers, many of them women. It is not surprising, then, that his work would eventually benefit women's health and family building, but there were no other indicators that his arrow would fly. At university he nearly failed his degree but enjoyed soft landings afterwards at research centres under eminent mentors in

Edinburgh, California, and London, before finally settling in Cambridge. His greatest luck was to marry Ruth Fowler, and he was lucky — or visionary — to collaborate with Patrick Steptoe and appoint Jean Purdy as an assistant, but it wasn't an easy race to his goal, and after golden years there were tragedies.

It was an uphill struggle to study human embryos against the gravity of political, scientific, and theological opposition. Some authorities called him crazy, others said he was a murderer. The problem of "Generation" had tantalised some of the greatest minds in the history of science, including Aristotle and William Harvey. They wanted to know where babies come from, said by some to be sacred knowledge that should be off-limits to research, so when Bob came along hoping to create embryos in his Petri dish, he was accused of playing God. Branded Dr Frankenstein, it was a foolish label that did not stick because IVF is a cooperation between nature and medicine to help struggling life to flourish. He was first to lay groundwork for the ethical care of human embryos in vitro, and to urge responsible research before clinical application. These were foundations for the social acceptance of a controversial technology and legislation for a booming baby-making industry in the future.

It took passion, but was it a narcissistic ambition or did it have deeper roots? Bob wore his celebrity status lightly. He grew up in a family and community that had experienced hardship and world wars, and had observed conflict and suffering first-hand, although never a victim himself. It was natural for an optimistic young man in the post-World War 2 generation to admire science, justice, and equality as hallmarks of a progressive era. By chance, he landed in a field ripe for development and close to that dearest hope of humanity — raising healthy children. IVF was his great gift and noble achievement, borne out by five million births in the year of his death, and will soon double in number. His two closest colleagues never lived to see so much flourishing, and for him the fulfilment of patients' hopes was the greatest reward because the acclaim of a Nobel Prize and knighthood from H.M. the Queen was almost too late.

Not every nobelist deserves the attention of a biographer, but Bob left a legacy to society that has diversified the meaning of "family" through one of the great scientific breakthroughs of the last century. Planned as a life story, this book has fanned into a broader narrative because the man and IVF are braided histories. It has required forays into social history and politics to understand the character that drove endeavour, and what a character! Until his final illness, he never stopped pressing forward to new goals, fighting for reproductive liberties, and when the toil of laboratory and clinical work was over, he became an innovative publisher to democratise scientific knowledge.

To be an intimate witness is a huge advantage for a writer, and this one had to beware of letting objectivity slacken or sliding into sentiment from familiarity and fondness for his subject. When Harvey Cushing wrote a magisterial *Life of Sir William Osler* in 1925 about his mentor it was easy for reviewers to accuse him of being partisan and making the great doctor a saint. History is too precious and important to compromise, and this author has made strenuous efforts to avoid sanitising Edwards' life. He was a brilliant and charismatic man guided by a sensitive conscience, yet no angel for he could be stubborn and infuriating.

Although prepared with a scholar's care, this book is not primarily for academic libraries but intended for readers who want an accessible story about the history of IVF and the men and women who brought the revolution. The young generation today who regard IVF as standard treatment will be amazed how hard it was won, and that without Bob and his colleagues we might still be waiting.

I have taken occasional liberties to create internal reflections to reveal the goals and fears of people as faithfully as possible to the actors I knew (indicated where I use their first names). I have neither concealed my enthusiasm for their dazzling successes, nor hidden reservations about what the future holds. This is a contentious field and there are bound to be readers who disagree with my review; some people still regard IVF as abhorrent and dread the prospect of more spin-off technologies. I respect differences of opinion and conscience about matters of deep gravity, yet I won't apologise for my own convictions. Bob Edwards never would. The writer Kingsley Amis is reputed to have said that "if you can't annoy someone there is no point in writing".

A Fellow of the Royal Society of London, reflecting on an association with Bob Edwards over 40 years, told me he still didn't understand what drove the man. A biographer's responsibility is to declare and explain his or her subject. I have struggled to demystify the man by using biography as the heart, memoir the lungs, and history the blood of his story. Bob was singular in many ways, and his openness, conviviality, and high state of excitement concealed as much as it revealed about the man within. In a famous book that most avid readers like Bob have read, Viktor Frankl claims the search for meaning is fundamental for the contemplative mind, finding gratification in doing something significant (work), caring for something or someone deeply (love), and boldness in challenging times (courage).[1] They are aspirations widely felt, certainly not the exclusive property of men and women with outstanding talents, but I believe they account for a remarkable life and achievements described in the following chapters.

Roger Gosden

July 2019

Publisher's Note

This book has found a natural home nested among others about reproductive biology, medicine, and surgery at Jamestowne Bookworks (see page 347). A momentous story that transformed millions of lives around the globe and impacting society and legislation might be expected on the list of a famous publishing firm or a university press, but commercial realities give low priority to biographies of scientists and doctors. But the loss of marketing muscle in an independent press is compensated by greater freedom for authors. A life story can be crafted as they think fit, without steering the content and style to surf a popular wave. Bob would understand as he was a man who chose his own path.

It is expected that a book generated in the United States would be written in American English. The product is in British English (*The Economist* Style Guide), not for the ease of the author who originally came from the UK, but because clinical IVF began in England, closely followed by Australia. It quickly became a global story and American readers can feel proud that the first tentative steps were on their soil and learn why it was barren ground before it blossomed.

Finally, considering an intended broad readership, the text is not speckled with references to support every important fact and quotation, like purely academic books, but has selective endnotes and suggested further reading to satisfy curiosity and provide information that may be unfamiliar to readers outside British Commonwealth countries.

Jamestowne Bookworks
Williamsburg, Virginia

Acknowledgments

I am immensely grateful to Bob and Ruth Edwards' daughters for the honour of writing his biography. Caroline, Jennifer, Sarah, Anna, and Meg shared their family history, arranged for research in residence at Churchill College and at Broadrake in Yorkshire. They introduced me to people I needed to interview and were always responsive to enquiries.

The book has leaned on the scholarship of my former colleague Professor Martin Johnson, FRS of Christ's College, Cambridge. No one has reviewed Edwards' life and scientific contributions more deeply. The series of papers he co-authored with my friend Dr Kay Elder of Bourn Hall Clinic based on laboratory notebooks at Oldham has uncovered a lost history.[2] Caroline and Jennifer and daughter Amy, Kay, and Martin read a draft of the manuscript, offering many helpful suggestions, but any remaining errors or omissions are my responsibility alone.

The following people shared memories and information, their names listed alphabetically without professional or academic titles. Mohammed Aboulghar (Cairo), Ricardo Asch (Buenos Aires), Barry Bavister (New Orleans), the late Michael Bedford (NYC), Rachel and Mike Benson (Chapel-le-Dale), the late John Biggers (Boston MA), Caroline Blackwell (Cambridge), Benjamin Brackett (Georgia), Peter Brinsden (Devon), Daniel Brison (Manchester), Louise Brown (Bristol), Liz Budd (Cambridge), Jacques Cohen (NYC), Alison & Joanna Cook (Burford, Oxon.), Paul Cook (Oldham), the late Ian Craft (London), Alan Dexter (London), Nancy Edmondson (Yorkshire), Dean Edwards

(Ontario), the late Gordon Falconer (Manchester), John & the late Anona Fallows (Oldham), Mary Fowler (Cambridge), Sir Richard & Lady Wendy Gardner (Oxford), Brian Gosden (Devon), Alan Handyside (London), Geraldine Hartshorne (Warwick), Outi Hovatta (Finland), Colin Howles (Geneva), Howard Jacobs (London), Eric Jauniaux (London), Jenny Krapez (Melbourne), William Ledger (NYC), Henry Leese (Windermere), Richard Lilford (Warwick), Bruno Lunenfeld (Florida), Grace MacDonald (Stirling), Angela & Steve Markham (Cambridge), Mike McClure (formerly at NIH), Rajvi Mehta (Mumbai), Shirley Middleton (Skipton, Yorks.), Robert Moor (Cambridge), Sarah Norcross (London), the late John Purdy (Ely), the late Barbara Rankin (Cambridge), Carol Readhead (Pasadena), Doug Saunders (Sydney), Joseph Schenker (Jerusalem), Joe Schulman (Maryland), Ann Silver (Cambridge), Roger Simons (Bourn Hall), John Slee (East Lothian), Chris Smick (Maine), Andrew Steptoe (London), Pat Tate (Cambridge), Patrick Taylor (Alberta), James Alexander Thom (Bloomington, IN), Alan Trounson (Melbourne), Eurof Walters (Cambridge), the late Baroness Mary Warnock (London), John & Barbara Webster (Nottinghamshire), Susan White and Batley History Group (Yorkshire), David Whittingham (Monmouthshire), and Peter Wright (Cambridge).

Several people listed above have died since I interviewed them. There are others who predeceased my research but who contributed nonetheless through recorded or recalled conversations: Tim Appleton, Colin ("Bunny") Austin, Gordon Dunstan, Howard Jones Jr, Anne McLaren, Jean Purdy, Patrick Steptoe, and, most of all, Bob and Ruth Edwards.

Edwards and Steptoe jointly published a concise autobiography in 1980, providing a unique source of facts and quotations up to the birth of Louise Brown.[3] It is the great responsibility of a biographer to be faithful to history, and readers feel uneasy if they notice conflicting records or memories, sometimes between equally authoritative sources. This author does not claim the accuracy of every fact, only that he has made an honest attempt to weigh evidence for the most probable truth and seek verification whenever possible.

Mike Macnamee of Bourn Hall Clinic and Kamal Ahuja of the London Women's Clinic, both former associates of Edwards, kindly gave access to archives at the hall and filled gaps in my knowledge about its history and publishing enterprises. The director and staff at the Archive Centre of Churchill College, Cambridge, provided guidance as I perused the personal papers of Edwards, Barbara Rankin, and Enoch Powell. I received generous cooperation, too, at the British Library, the Royal Society library, Edinburgh University library, Manchester City library, Bristol Archives, Archives of the California Institute of Technology, Center for the History of Medicine at Harvard University, and the alumni offices and archives of Bangor and Edinburgh Universities.

I am deeply grateful to Cambridge alumna Lauren Barr for careful copy-editing and helpful remarks.

Finally, I thank my wife Lucinda Veeck Gosden for patience during the lengthy project and sharing memories of Edwards in the early days of IVF in America. She was my first reader.

Roger Gosden

Profit from royalties will be donated to the Edwards-Steptoe Research Trust (UK) and RESOLVE, the National Infertility Association of America.

Glossary & Abbreviations

Aneuploid: describes a cell with a missing or extra chromosome (i.e., 45 or 47 chromosomes in humans)

Blastocyst: the stage of embryonic development when a ball of about 64 cells expands into a "cyst" before implantation (*q.v.*)

Corpus luteum: a structure formed from a collapsed follicle (*q.v.*) after ovulation; it produces progesterone and oestrogen (*q.v.*) until the end of the menstrual cycle or continues in pregnancy

Diploid: a balanced pair of chromosomes of maternal and paternal origin (46 in human cells)

Embryo stem cell: a transitory, pluripotential cell (*q.v.*) in blastocysts (*q.v.*) which can be maintained indefinitely in vitro or induced to generate all the cell lineages of the body

Epigenetic: changes of form or function caused by altered expression of genes without mutations in the DNA sequence

Fallopian tubes: the tubes that convey sperm from the uterus towards the ovaries, and embryos in the opposite direction

Fibroblast: a widespread cell type producing collagen and other fibres in connective tissue

Follicles: unitary structures in the ovary responsible for fertility (ova) and hormone production (oestrogen and subsequently progesterone); they are depleted around the time of the menopause

FSH: follicle-stimulating hormone from the pituitary gland stimulates the growth and secretion of follicles (*q.v.*)

Gamete: the sperm or unfertilised ovum

Haploid: a single set of chromosomes remaining after germ cells divide by meiosis (*q.v.*)

HCG: human chorionic gonadotrophin, a protein hormone secreted by trophoblast (*q.v.*); used to test for pregnancy; since it is more abundantly available than LH (*q.v.*) (which it resembles), it is injected to trigger ovulation for fertility treatment

HMG: human menopausal gonadotrophin, a hormonal product (*q.v.*) of menopausal women's urine rich in FSH and LH activity; originally used for fertility treatment (e.g., commercial *Pergonal*)

Implantation: the process in which a blastocyst (*q.v.*) attaches to the uterine wall where it forms a placenta

ICSI: intra-cytoplasmic sperm injection, the artificial injection of a sperm into an ovum (*q.v.*) for fertilisation

Inner cell mass: a minute patch of cells inside the blastocyst (*q.v.*) containing embryo stem cells (*q.v.*)

IPPF: International Planned Parenthood Federation

IPS cell: induced pluripotent stem cell, a stem cell with similar potential to embryo stem cells (*q.v.*) created by reprogramming the genome of somatic cells (*q.v.*)

IVF: in vitro fertilisation, a laboratory procedure in which ova and sperm are combined in a dish; often used as a generic term for assisted reproductive technologies (ARTs)

LH: luteinising hormone, a protein secreted by the pituitary gland to trigger ovulation and stimulate progesterone (*q.v.*) from the corpus luteum (*q.v.*) (also stimulates testosterone from the testes)

Meiosis: two special divisions in germ cells in which genetic material is swapped between chromosomes to create novel combinations and split the double set to make them haploid (*q.v.*) for fertilisation

Morula: a ball of cells grown from a fertilised ovum but not yet at the blastocyst stage (*q.v.*)

Oestrogen (estrogen): the female sex hormone, a steroid produced by follicles (*q.v.*) and the placenta

Ovum: the unfertilised egg, technically known as the "oocyte"

Parthenogenesis: production of offspring from an ovum without fertilisation ("virgin birth")

PGT: Preimplantation Genetic Testing, a procedure in which one or two cells are extracted from an embryo to test for aneuploidy (*q.v.*) or mutations in DNA (formerly abbreviated as PGS and PGD, respectively)

Phagocytes: cells that ingest, and often digest, foreign particles and bacteria

Pituitary gland: a gland the size of a pea between the brain and the palate which produces several protein hormones, including FSH and LH (*q.v.*)

Pluripotential: a term for embryo stem cells and IPS cells (*q.v.*) expressing their ability to produce every cell type in the body (except placental cells)

PMSG: pregnant mares' serum gonadotrophin, a protein hormone produced during equine pregnancy with FSH and LH potency (*q.v.*)

Polyploid: a cell containing an extra set(s) of chromosomes either from the ovum after failing to eliminate a polar body (*q.v.*) or a supernumerary sperm (e.g., a triploid human cell contains 69 chromosomes)

Progesterone: the dominant steroid hormone of pregnancy

Pronuclei: the nuclei in fertilised eggs, usually one male (from the sperm) and one female, each containing a haploid (half) set of chromosomes (*q.v.*)

Quantitative genetics: a branch of genetics concerned with continuous variation from multigenic effects (e.g., physical stature)

Somatic: adjective for cells other than ova and sperm

Trophoblast: outer cells of the blastocyst that become precursors of placental cells at implantation

Zona pellucida: the clear protein shell around the ovum

Prologue

An Uncommon Don

The platform sign glided across the window as the train from King's Cross crawled into the station. I stood among passengers closing smart phones and slinging backpacks on their shoulders, bracing for the halt and the doors to open. On my first visit to Cambridge 40 years earlier, I stepped out of a smoky diesel carriage onto the platform to breathe crisp winter air crossing the fens from the North Sea. Heading for the exit, I jostled among students in duffel coats, a woman pushing a stroller, and a man in tweeds sucking on a pipe whom I took for a university don. I was then walking into a future I hardly imagined, and now I could look back through the lens of memory at faces and places that became familiar. Coming there as a student barely 21 years old, I had a newspaper cutting in my pocket that prompted an application for graduate study with a Dr Robert Edwards at the University. It announced a breakthrough in human embryology that promised new life where there was only sterility, yet the man at the centre was condemned and mocked. I came as a novice for scientific adventure and careless of the controversy, and now returning to say thank you and goodbye to my mentor.

We poured into the station yard. The mainstream flowed towards a file of taxi cabs pulling into the street past wobbling cyclists and students plodding to their colleges. I gazed around for a friendly face. There was a woman with light brown hair and a black jacket waving over the heads of passengers and greeters.

We plunged forward into an embrace. It was my friend Kay, a doctor at Bourn Hall, the ancient manor house that found a new identity as the first clinic for in vitro fertilisation, or IVF as it is universally known.

"Welcome back, Roger," she whispered. "Will America soon have a black president?"

"Maybe. What's our plan?" I was eager for local news and glad to leave American politics behind for a break.

She drove us to Grantchester village along country lanes bordered by grassy verges and hawthorn walls. Through gaps in hedges I glimpsed at flat fields stretching to the horizon, but Bourn Hall was further down the road than our destination. The Jacobean manor house of red brick and lofty chimneys was once the home of aristocrats, a miniature and more ancient version of Downton Abbey. Bob Edwards and Patrick Steptoe converted it to a clinic that became the engine of a fertility revolution that would have stunned earlier residents. Thankfully, they didn't sacrifice its stately presence at the hub of an ancient village. The clinic still offers a thriving service, if quieter now and seldom in the news. Treatment that was sensational has become conventional, the pioneers have gone, and test-tube babies are no longer rarities. And, yet, the technology still breaks ground in genetics and stem cell science, and in making babies in new ways it continues to impact society.

We turned into the village along a shaded lane of horse-chestnut and beech trees. Across the green, behind a gatekeeper's cottage, the crenelated bell tower of a gothic church watched over a row of thatched cottages. The clock over the narthex was out of sight, but its hands are stuck at ten to three in my mind, thanks to Rupert Brooke's poem I learnt at school.[4]

Kay noticed I was checking my wristwatch. "Yes, it's tea-time."

2

At the Orchard tea garden, we wandered across a lawn splashed by sunlight pouring through the canopy of gnarled apple trees. Late wasps circled over apples browning in the grass. Kay sank into a green canvas deckchair to reserve our table while I joined a queue of Americans decanting from a coach tour of English churches and cathedrals. We had all come for a traditional cream tea.

The Orchard opened in the Edwardian Age. I imagine gentlemen in striped blazers and boaters puffing on pipes, and ladies in long dresses and silk gloves chatting from under floppy hats. The proprietors claim it is still a magnet for celebrities, and over the years one might have spotted Virginia Woolf, Alan Turing, James Watson, Steven Hawking, Prince Charles, and others whose names, if not their faces, you know. I expect Ernest Rutherford came there, the famous physicist who wisecracked that, "All science is either physics or stamp collecting". His young granddaughter, Ruth, would come along with him or her father, Ralph Fowler, an eminent Cambridge mathematician.[5] I wondered what those men would have thought of Bob Edwards, the working-class man and scientific "stamp-collector" who helped to create millions of new lives, surely a legacy as vast as Lord Rutherford's?[6] And what would those two men have thought if they knew Bob asked Ruth to marry him?

His parents never brought him to the Orchard when it was a redoubt of privilege. He grew up in a council house in the industrial north of England where his father was an ex-miner and his mother worked in a cotton mill. But anyone can sit at the Orchard now. Ahead of me, a teenage girl with tattooed arms stood beside her pink-haired boyfriend, preferring a faux silver tea service to quicker service in town at Starbucks. I, too, visited the Orchard as a humble student, sauntering across the cow pasture from college, or punting against the slow current on the river. Those were my formative years, and I wondered if their lives would also unfold in unexpected ways.

Bob's own story is an instance of how hard it is to predict life's arrow. Most personal histories shoot straight from the bow without getting far aloft. Some misfire and quickly fall to the ground, but occasionally one soars into the blue.

As the line crept forward, I noticed a gate opening to a cricket pitch beside the river and mused if the lovely scene had inspired Roger Waters to compose "Grantchester Meadows" in the 1960s for Pink Floyd. He was a pupil at the same school as my old colleague Barry Bavister. Barry was a graduate student ahead of me whose "magic fluid" helped Bob to achieve an historic breakthrough by uniting ova and sperm in a dish to make human embryos. Jean Purdy was another member of the team. She attended the girls' school, located then a safe distance from the boys near the hospital where she trained as a nurse. None of them was marked for distinction, but both shot a high arrow.

At the end of the queue, I carried a tray back to Kay to unload a teapot and scones with strawberry jam to enjoy over conversation. It was time to catch up with news about the Hall and Kay's embryology book, but the conversation soon turned to Bob. I was anxious how our meeting would go.

"He's no longer the man you remember," she said. "When I called ahead, Ruth told me he was having a better day." I never really knew what ailed him.

"He was recently in a public ward at Addenbrooke's," she continued. "When I asked if I could see Professor Edwards the nurse looked blank at me. She didn't know what kind of professor he was, and no one else was wiser. Bob was unknown in his hometown, yet still lionised around the world. Can you believe it?"

Fame is ephemeral but my memory of first encounter never faded.

I arrived at Bob's office in the physiology department on a blustery day in February 1970. His assistant Jean Purdy greeted me with a grin, then feigned a hard knock on his door to show how to get attention. There was the sound of scraping chair legs inside before the door suddenly flung open and I was face to face with "Dr Frankenstein", as the media dubbed him then. He offered a crushing handshake and screwed his face into a broad smile. The greeting was over in a flash as he plunged out of the lab, leaving me to wonder why this friendly man with dark floppy hair was so vilified. This was my introduction to his signature dynamism.

I overheard him in another room. "Bunny, Roger's here," he said in a northern accent. He reappeared with a courtly older man with an Australian twang. This was "Bunny" Austin, the laboratory chief and most beloved figure I ever met there. He earned a place in the history of embryology for discovering a mysterious process of sperm maturation that Bob feared was an obstacle to IVF.

"Ready for a pub lunch, Roger?" Bob asked as he suddenly reappeared in the doorway.

This was a stunning offer for a student expecting Cantabrigian formality, even wearing his tie and jacket that day. How would my pitch for a scholarship go down in a bar? Instead of a gruelling interview, I felt like a visiting nephew, and the dissonance confused me. I did, however, notice an easy-going atmosphere in the lab where faculty and students were on first-name terms, and sorry to learn that informality was not the general rule across the campus, although much more so today.

We stepped outside into winter sunshine to find The Fountain, a watering hole favoured by academics. Bob leaned on the bar as the landlord siphoned pints of bitter and exchanged a joke. He never missed the opportunity to chitchat.

"Can you drink at lunchtime?" he asked, as he laid a frothy glass on my beer mat. He was teasing me, for no student needs to be asked.

If my application was successful, I guessed he would give me a project on animal embryos or a favourite molecule to forge a career, as many scientists have from a smart choice. There were Cambridge men who made great reputations from a single molecule, and it was my impression the more arcane the better, and the less utility the greater the prestige. It was scientific puritanism in the city of Cromwell, but to Bob it was topsy-turvy thinking, and he would have none of it. He was an uncommon don, striding from molecule to man before translational science became mainstream. He fervently believed in science working for human good and relieving suffering.

My newspaper cutting reported he had fertilised human eggs in vitro. This was the real thing after a long history of false claims. He was collaborating with Patrick Steptoe who had a gynaecology practice in the north, and the only senior doctor who would collaborate with him in those days. They were a match in gritty determination for a goal that was nothing less than the holy grail of reproductive medicine.

The media sensationalised their endeavours with silly warnings about a brave new world that distorted the honest goal of helping nature back to health. Mavericks and heretics always enthralled me, so the prospect of working with Bob had the attractive frisson of danger. The condemnation he bore for over a decade from public figures and his own profession would have disheartened a less heroic figure. But didn't Arthur Schopenhauer say that truth passes from ridicule to violent opposition to a third state when people accept it as self-evident? That is a fair summary of the history of IVF.

Throughout what passed as my interview, Bunny sipped his beer quietly. He was Bob's greatest advocate at the University. A perfect pair innocent of academic jealousy, they listened to the unformed theories of freshmen, and treated janitors and academic grandees with the same grace.

When the bartender collected our glasses, Bob cast a glance at the clock. I still didn't know how my application stood. I looked for a nod or a wink as we stood up, but Bunny mildly asked, "Does October sound ok?" Lives turn in bewildering moments, and his signal was as sweet as the aftertaste of ale. My compass started spinning for a project, but I learned that Bob's students followed their own star, through clouds of obstacles and uncertainty if necessary, as he had. He had an optimism grounded in faith that no philosophy was surer of its way than science.

The sun still shone as Kay and I left the Orchard to stroll over to the churchyard and meander between memorials over clipped lawns to find Jean Purdy's grave. It was easy to miss her grey slab, and we eventually found it in a corner near a yew tree close to her mother and grandmother. A posy of plastic flowers was the only sign someone remembered Jeannie; there was nothing engraved on her headstone to record a notable life. It was a setting worthy of Thomas Gray's elegy for people who in other circumstances might have achieved lasting notice, like Cromwell and Milton, two Cambridge men in the poem. Jeannie helped Bob and Patrick to make an extraordinary legacy, but her name was missing in the story. If Rupert still resided at the Old Vicarage, he would wander down to compose an ode for her.

"I heard it was a dreich day." Kay nodded at the slang intended to convey a bleak image of people gathered at the graveside to mourn a life ended prematurely. It was only a few years after the first test-tube baby was born and long before IVF became the standard of care for infertility. Three years later, more people came to bury Patrick not far away at Bourn parish church. Patients still stroll down from the hall to pay respects at his graveside, but no one makes the pilgrimage to Jeannie's tomb.

The churchyard was empty apart from a pair of woodpigeons strutting in downy clerical collars and a magpie that watched like a warden. But it was hard to be gloomy in a place that stirred memories of the trio and other colleagues who helped people realise their dreams of children, and so I left with an urge to tell their story.

As we drove to another village, I tried to rehearse in my head some final words for Bob, the man who launched a medical revolution and many careers besides my own. Nothing I thought of expressed how I felt. We approached his farm along a narrow lane of overgrown hedges, entering a courtyard where a row of ducks on a wind vane announced Duck End Farm.

Ruth was waiting at the farmhouse door, her hair trimmed straight across the brow like a veil over her thoughts and now snowy white. She was a hidden woman in the story, an energetic multitasker like her husband, the lioness who raised their five daughters, managed the farm, and was an accomplished scientist in her own right. She was Bob's muse and his most loyal supporter. I wondered how she coped, and if the late calm in their lives was her reward, because she would never receive the glittering accolades heaped on her husband. She was his best prize.

8

She led us to the conservatory where he sat in a wicker chair beside a window and laid aside a journal on his lap when we approached. He always had his head in a book or was writing one when he wasn't doing physical work outdoors.

"Hello, Kay," he said, ignoring me. "Who did you bring this time? Ruth, do you know that man?"

The teasing confirmed the old Bob was still with us. After a brief exchange of news, Kay and Ruth withdrew to another room and I had him to myself. I expected he would look frail at 82 years old, worn out by constant activity and unimaginable pressures, but he still looked hale under a vigorous crop of grey hair. He wanted to get past pleasantries to talk about science, and not dwell on past achievements as many elderly VIPs do. He had a fresh topic.

"Roger, you know about salamanders. They're like newts in our pond." He spoke as fast and low as ever, which forced closer listening. "You know Spallanzani studied them."

I felt like his student again. He talked and I nodded. I knew nothing about Padre Lazzaro Spallanzani when I joined the lab in 1970, but I learned he was an 18th century scientist when knowledge was settled more by authority than objective evidence. Bob was ahead of his time, too, and could be a reincarnation of the man, except he could never be a Jesuit priest.

"He fertilised frog eggs in vitro," I chipped in, "and was first with artificial insemination". I thought Bob wanted to talk about reproduction, so I added, "I think it was a spaniel," to sound scholarly, but there was something else on his mind.

"Here's the thing," he said. "Salamander tails and limbs self-repair after amputation. Internal organs too. They grow from a mixed bunch of stem cells in a blastema."

Since we warm-blooded creatures have lost that ability during evolution, I assumed he was leading me up the garden path to embryo stem cells, his promising lead for regenerative medicine.

His eyes brightened, shedding a decade as he recalled a famous discovery. "I remember the shock when we saw those cells in our dishes. They divided so often they seemed immortal. Some turned into blood, heart, and nerve cells. We wondered what the hell's going on and if they could be used as transplants."

"Didn't you worry the cells could grow explosively?" I asked.

"There's a cancer risk, of course, but we may not need them after all."

He hadn't changed a bit. Even before stem cell science had crested, he was looking for a new wave. He revelled in scientific voyages through uncharted waters and would have ridiculed a "theory of everything" as a false hope of a final, all-encompassing cosmology, a disappointing end to the boundless quest for knowledge.

He picked up the journal again, flipping over pages with a licked finger to a picture of a mouse ear.

"A Philadelphia researcher thought her technician forgot to punch ear marks to identify the animals. But when she made a new set of holes they closed over and healed. You might say, so what, because pierced human ear lobes grow over without earrings, but she found some internal organs can regenerate from injury."

He implied that if organs can be repaired in mice so, too, can ours with help from technology. The genetic tweaking would involve some occult DNA code that has lain dormant since our amphibian ancestors crawled out of a Devonian swamp. This was not the first time his theorising left me turning in bed at night, wondering if it was science fiction. It was never safe to call Bob barmy because we had seen some of his wacky ideas come true.

He raised a finger. "Chop it off in a fetus and it grows back, but not after birth. Our ability to repair organs apart from skin goes underground, so we need to find the genes and switches involved."

I was more cheered at his passion than by the lesson. Instead of resting on his laurels, he was leaving yesterday's triumph with embryo stem cells for a new obsession, and it helped to know about the old Jesuit's salamanders.

The conversation was briefly interrupted by a question at the open door. I turned to look out the window at the weeping willow tree laying its tresses on the lawn and a perky blackbird that had forgotten its summer song. Beyond the garden I imagined the woodland that Bob had planted with his own hands, transforming the naked landscape and now in glorious fall colours. He was a man of many parts.

When I turned back, Kay winked from the doorway. It was time to go. He stood up, no longer as agile as when we first met, but instead of leading us to the front door he beckoned to a side room. Kay shrugged. We mustn't tire him.

There were two illuminated glass cabinets displaying a collection of honours, awards, and prizes. There were shields and plaques, certificates and medals, a model of the Rod of Asclepius, a metal cast of a mother and child, and much more. On top of the cabinets, a row of inscribed silver plates sparkled in a spotlight.

It was a glorious record of a life's achievement, but I felt a twinge. Two of the most endearing things about him were modesty and self-deprecating humour; I never knew him proud and pompous, even when he became a celebrity. He was always the Yorkshireman who loved to chat with great and small, but the exhibition revealed a heart I never knew, and was sorry.

Afterwards, I felt churlish. Every hero deserves honour after sailing home from an odyssey. Bob was always generous with credit, flattering protégés with authorship of important papers and giving opportunities and privileges before we earned them. Sometime later I realised my misapprehension because the exhibition was not his idea at all. His eldest daughter urged the family to display his awards so everyone can enjoy them, and they had to excavate cupboards and under beds to find the treasure. So that explained it, and I was relieved.

He darted a finger back and forth to point at cherished objects. There was the Lasker Award, said to be America's Nobel Prize, the King Faisal International Prize from a region with a special place in his heart, the star and ribbon of a Chevalier of the Legion d'Honneur conferred by the French President. But as he recalled that ceremony his demeanour seemed downcast. He might have been tired, but I suspected something on his mind. Something was missing.

There was no Nobel Prize after years of nominations. We hoped he had the consolation of knowing the greater tribute from ordinary people who were grateful for his gift from science. We wanted history to be fairer to him and his colleagues and pay them the homage they deserved.

Struggling for something positive to say at the farmhouse door, I dreaded closure. The most heartening words I could think of sound frivolous now, but they seemed apt and I still believe our greatest legacy is our family, and students if we have them, as they fertilise the future. I thought he would like the pun, but he never smiled, and I doubt he got my meaning.

After the door latch snapped behind us, I knew I would never see him again. From the empty yard I looked at the closed door as one may glance at the cover of a book after reading an absorbing story. It was unimaginable in the first pages, and we hardly guessed the daring and brilliance needed for the great endeavour, or that a stubborn streak was required.

The story began inauspiciously when Bob was a young teenager working as a farm hand after he was evacuated to the Yorkshire Dales during the war. The wild district inspired the urban boy. He could look over a stone wall across the fields to trains steaming over Ribblehead Viaduct, an awesome span supported by pillars like giant arms reaching up from Batty Moss. The smoke would remind him of his mother in danger in the Manchester Blitz and his disabled father labouring with bad lungs in a nearby railway tunnel. Did the world have to be so grim? Could a strong-willed, idealistic lad on the threshold of manhood make a difference? What did his vision portend, and to what end would it lead? A later generation would be stirred by stories of young wizards crossing a viaduct to Scotland, but Bob knew that real endeavour calls for a journey of action and sacrifice. One day he would find a hole in the wall to crawl through to bring an impulse to the world it could not resist.

1

REAL GRIT

Who can say what goes through a soldier's mind as he waits in a muddy trench with a bayonetted rifle, waiting for the whistle to send him over the top? Whatever Private Samuel Edwards witnessed as he ran into the din and smoke of battle on a summer day in 1916, he rarely shared when he came home. He grew up in a society inured to hardship.

He grew up in the West Midlands from Welsh stock on both sides of his family. His great grandfather William Edwards was a farm labourer born in 1785 at Chirk, a small community in North Wales with a coal mine and a medieval castle. William married a local girl, Elizabeth, and they had three children.

Edward, the youngest boy, born in 1820, married Martha Jones and they moved to the Midlands where the population was booming with large families and from immigration across the British Isles and Ireland. The furnace of the new industrial state offered good wages to men willing to work long hours in hazardous occupations. It was a landscape in the throes of transforming from quaint villages and market towns to an industrial hardscape of factories and mines connected by a new railway network. Appointed consul to Birmingham by President Abraham Lincoln, Elihu Burritt reported it was "black by day and red by night", and the area to the west became known as the "Black Country". The air choked with smoke, walls blackened in soot, and waterways were polluted by emissions from mines, brickworks, and a myriad of other industries driven by steam from burning coal. An old Yorkshire saying that "where there's muck there's brass (money)" was an admission that the spoils of capitalism were paid in grime and working-class toil.

Coal mining offered the best-paid jobs, and Edward was the first of three generations in his family to go underground. After a few years in Bilston, Staffordshire, he moved to Ibstock in Leicestershire where some of his direct descendants were still dwelling over a century later. The town colliery was typical of many. A plume of smoke from a tall chimney was a signature of the energy generated in its boilers to drive a winding engine for transferring miners in a lift cage underground and hauling the spoils of their labour to the surface. Hewers at the mine-face cut coal from seams three to seven feet thick with pickaxes, hammers, and even their bare hands by the light of naked oil lamps. The rippers behind them excavated stone above the seams for arching wooden scaffolds to support tunnel roofs. The black "ore" was lifted into tubs for pit ponies to wheel to the lift shaft. In the colliery yard, other men and boys washed and graded coal before loading it into railway wagons for transporting to factories and steelworks. It was brutal work with none of the modern safeguards against "fire-damp", although Ibstock never had a mining disaster in a century of service.

Edward and Martha had five children. The boys followed their father down the mine, and the unmarried girls went into service as maids and cooks for the local gentry. Emmanuel was their fourth son, born in 1860, and he had 15 children with Eliza Boobyer after they wedded in 1883, of whom at least two died in infancy. Samuel Edwards, born in 1896, was the ninth baby. He lived until 1964, an enviable span for a man who had a hard life.

His family lived at 94, Melbourne Road in Ibstock, a two up — two down rented house in the middle of a terraced row of red brick walls and black slate roofs punctured by multiple chimneys. The front door opened directly on the pavement of what is now a busy road. There were five rooms and from the kitchen Eliza could look down a narrow garden to a shed and coal cellar. Coal heated the house and provided energy for cooking and lighting from coal gas conveyed by pipes that snaked from the town gas works, a giant circular superstructure with steel ribs supporting a bell that slowly moved up and down like a monstrous lung expiring poisonous vapour. Coal was the engine of progress and source of prosperity before environmentalists derided it. No one was surprised when the new town two miles away was proudly named Coalville.

The Edwards boys went underground as soon as they reached school-leaving age, which rose to 12 in 1899. Samuel's first job was to lead and feed pit ponies, but as he grew older, he advanced towards the coalface where heavy labour was better rewarded. Among the best-paid workers in the land, colliers were proud of their occupation despite its dangers, regarded like millionaires where the most productive men brought home £5 a week. Stingy companies soon felt the gathering political power of miners roused by left-wing militants. When negotiations for a minimum national wage broke down in 1912, young Samuel came out on strike with miners across the country, forcing the Asquith government to concede. Their victory generated hope for a fairer and more progressive society until a shadow crossed Europe after an assassination in Sarajevo. The news sounded remote to an island nation, but the crisis escalated to a climax on 4 August 1914 when war was declared with Germany.

Just 19 years old, Samuel was eager to volunteer for military service alongside thousands of other young men. They enlisted in the Territorial Force or banded into battalions of "Pals" for General Kitchener's New Army. What a lark! What a lucky break from the pit! What a chance to see Paris and Berlin! They were eager to teach "Fritz" a lesson and wanted action quickly in case the show was over by Christmas.[7] They wanted to display patriotic fervour in uniform and avoid the shame of a white feather thrust in their hand by a woman in the street. It was the old lie: *Dulce et decorum est pro patria mori.*[8]

Samuel walked to Coalville to enlist on 24 September where an army medical officer examined him. No prize specimen at only 5'6" tall with a chest expansion of 2" and 130-lb on the scales, he was declared fit for combat and posted to the South Staffordshire regiment of line infantry. The army needed miners to tunnel under enemy lines for laying massive bombs.

By the time he arrived in France over a year later, the war was drawing into a long campaign and every day brought news of more casualties at the Front. Raw recruits filled the boots of troops not coming home. The romance of war had dissipated, and by 1916 Samuel had seen action and survived a gas attack. The "Pump and Tortoise" (nickname of the 1st Battalion) transferred to the front line north-east of Amiens in the Somme Valley where British and French forces were massing for a major offensive to break the stalemate of trench warfare. Generals Haig and Rawlinson assured their troops they would walk to victory after an immense artillery bombardment cut the wire and forced the enemy to skulk for miles along the line of trenches. But heavy rain delayed the "push", giving away the element of surprise, and Fritz brought in crack reinforcements and dug bunkers too deep for bombs to penetrate.

At 7.30 AM on the first day of July the Tommies lined up in the trenches, prepared to follow the heels of junior officers across no man's land. The opposite side was barely 300 metres away. Would it be like the Glorious Twelfth when upper class toffs in Britain went hunting grouse in the northern moors, or another futile exhibition of British courage? *Theirs not to reason why, Theirs but to do and die...*[9]

The men dashed through the mud across a crucible of craters, past the litter of shell cases and stench of rotting corpses towards the wire. They followed a creeping barrage of explosions from artillery behind them to keep defenders' heads down, but when they reached the coils of razor wire it was still uncut. Machine-gunners emerged out of bunkers to rake exposed troops with withering fire.

Twenty thousand British soldiers died or went missing, the greatest military disaster in British history for a single day, and the battle continued for weeks. Men of great promise were lost or scarred physically and mentally. A few survivors became household names, like Lt. J.R.R. Tolkien, Capt. A. A. Milne, and 2nd Lt. Wilfred Owen, who died on the last day of the war. The other side suffered great losses too, and Gefreiter Adolf Hitler was one of the casualties. Shrapnel bullets like ball-bearings hit Samuel in the right arm and shoulder. As an infantryman not born to fame and privilege, he registered no great significance among the casualties, but in surviving to raise children he would leave a mark on history.

At a field hospital he was triaged so the more seriously wounded soldiers were given priority to save their lives, which sometimes required amputation. Nurses with red crosses emblazoned on white bibs irrigated Samuel's wounds with antiseptic solution, covering them with bandages until a surgeon came. Over the next five months he had five operations to remove shrapnel and debride tissue, and his luck prevailed because he evaded infections before sulfa drugs and penicillin were available. Although his arm was saved, it remained stiff, painful, and scarred for the rest of his life. If there was any compensation for the suffering, it was news that his platoon had routed the enemy at Mametz and taken many prisoners. Now declared unfit for combat, Samuel was transferred to the reserves until he was demobilised at the end of 1918 with a small pension and two campaign service medals.

When he returned to Leicestershire, the colliery would not take back a veteran with a disabled arm and scarred lungs. He had fought for King and Country, laboured in an industry that fueled Britain's greatness, but returned an uncelebrated hero like thousands of other veterans. But luckier than many pals and comrades, he came home to a woman he met during the war, and if she made a promise before he left for the Front, she would keep it. She was that kind of person, a strong-willed woman who worked as a machinist in a Manchester cotton mill. It wasn't for sympathy of a wounded soldier or the want of marriageable candidates in that generation that she kept her word; in Samuel's modest frame she saw a decent man with a strong heart, and a willing breadwinner. He would only make a meagre living, but it would be enough to support a family.

Margaret was born in Manchester in 1893, three years his senior and third of five children of bricklayer Robert Street and his wife Rachel Clarke. Like other working-class girls, she left school as a young teenager without qualifications to work in a local mill. Her spool room roared from thousands of spinning wheels, pulleys, and spindles turning raw cotton bolls from the American South and British India into yarn for weavers in Lancashire and Yorkshire towns. Cotton was king and Manchester was its capital until foreign competition and automation encroached on the industry. As the first industrialised city in the world, Manchester chose the beehive to symbolise its populace. Margaret's community assumed hardships in the anticipation of progress as times were improving. It was a region that grew sturdy character and conscientious labour, where couch potatoes had no place. Margaret was a product of an environment that bred strong women, and she grew into a northern matriarch.

The army registered Samuel as an Anglican, but it was a default label for last rites. He never professed any religious conviction, and his children only attended Sunday school to observe a national custom. After marrying at a registry office in 1920, the couple moved close to his family in Ibstock where Sammy was born two years later.

Ibstock was foreign to Margaret and she was homesick for Manchester. Samuel needed a job to match his ability since he was no longer the able-bodied man of 1914. The best fit was railway tunnel mining, sometimes called "platelaying", a job most men would shrink from. It wasn't safer or healthier working along a railway line or in a tunnel than in a mine, and less well-paid, but it guaranteed steady employment. Working for a railway company required the family to move to Batley, a Yorkshire town near Leeds, from where Margaret could take a short train ride to visit her mother in the big city.

Batley is the birthplace of the shoddy trade which introduced a word to the English lexicon for anything cheap or second-hand. Scavengers colloquially known as rag-and-bone men used to scour the streets up and down the country for refuse and discarded property, taking the woollen goods to Batley for recycling. Yarn was rewoven into blankets, carpets, and uniforms that made Batley prosperous from shoddy goods.

The Edwards made their home at 30, Oakhill Road. It was a terrace like the one Samuel grew up in, but the locality was clean and attractive near Wilton Park and local shops. Their second son, Robert Geoffrey, whom we know as Bob, was born at the maternity home on 27 September 1925. A third son, Raymond Harry, arrived two years later to the day, and the two younger sons were close chums as they grew up. Margaret pushed their pram through the park past a copper beech where a memorial plaque now honours Bob as Batley's most famous son. But there were no auguries of distinction in those days, and the Edwards blended with other families whose fathers worked all day and mothers stayed at home with their children.

Samuel joined a gang of labourers for the ¾ mile long tunnel between Batley and Morley on the Yorkshire-Lancashire line. Their job was to secure railway lines in their shoes by keeping the fishplates tight and wooden keys in place. They spread ballast, replaced fallen bricks from roofs, and cleared embankments to avoid brush fires from passing trains. Working inside the tunnel was hazardous by lamplight without a radio or high visibility clothing; they only had a lookout to wave a flag at an approaching train and whistle to warn mates in the void. As a locomotive and rolling stock charged close by in the dark, they had to dash into tiny alcoves to press their backs against the wall. Samuel didn't complain. He had faced greater danger and was familiar with smoke and damp.

Margaret yearned to return to Manchester. In the late 1920s, she moved the family into her widowed mother's home until a new council house became available in the nearby district of Gorton. It was wonderful, and the rent was modest. They had a living room and kitchen, three bedrooms upstairs, a bathroom and a toilet, a great advance on older housing stock where residents had to go outside for the "necessary" or traipse to the municipal bathhouse. The back garden was 30 metres long, a generous space for children to play and Samuel to grow vegetables. It was a vast improvement on the cramped Victorian slums slowly cleared across the city. But Samuel had to commute to Batley, and when that job ended his next one was in the York-shire Dales where he stayed away all week. The household now revolved even more around Margaret. She was ambitious for her boys to benefit from the educational opportunities in the city and carried the most sway over their young lives. But Samuel's absences did not turn him into an irrelevant or careless father as he provided a gritty example of love and duty.

2

THE DALESMAN

The city Margaret knew was quite different to the gleaming, bustling place Manchester is today. A short bus ride from Piccadilly, the gothic town hall in Gorton's civic centre was familiar to her grandparents. But where cloned rows of terraced houses crouched beside mills and chimneys towering like minarets, there are now modern housing estates, high-rise flats, and offices. The remaining stock of old buildings has been sandblasted to uncover the original shades of ivory and parchment under a century of soot, offering a substrate for lichens to crust in cleaner air. Where workers swarmed on foot to factories, the pavements are now almost empty, and commuters pass in roaring engines.

Wildlife retreated as the city's population and industry expanded, leaving only railway property and around the reservoir as feral land for children to trespass and explore. Manchester did not have a Frederick Olmsted, the architect of Manhattan's lungs in Central Park, and the city fathers reserved few of the green spaces now acknowledged to be beneficial for mental and physical health. The Edwards only escaped the conurbation on annual holidays to Southend-on-Sea, courtesy of Samuel's rail pass, so the urban boys seldom saw farms or moorland in the hinterland.

A city so alien to nature was beautiful in Margaret's eyes, and she would stay the rest of her life. There was abundant civic pride from strides in public health and growing prosperity, albeit from a low level in her grandparents' generation. It was then a larger mirror of what Edward Edwards witnessed in Ibstock. The misery of the masses and child labour moved Charles Dickens to write *Hard Times*, and John Ruskin condemned Manchester as the home of pollution. Now there was sewage treatment and garbage collection, and piped water the envy of many rural folk. But a welfare system to care for the poor, disabled, and elderly was still a pipe dream.

Gorton was not a pretty place in the 1930s, but it had virtues. Without "helicopter parents" to hover, kids could roam the cobbled streets in relative safety and invent their own entertainment, anything from hopscotch on chalked pavements to exploring derelict houses. Local shopkeepers knew children by name and quickly informed parents if one was hurt or in trouble. Before television, families made their own entertainment or went to the cinema or the Belle Vue Zoo and a thrilling ride on the roller-coaster.

It was everything we mean by "community", and simple pleasures were satisfying in less materialistic times. Mothers chatted across dividing walls to neighbours while hanging out the washing; men met after work for a beer and darts at the local pub or British Legion. This was a strong society sown by industry and left-wing values that thrived until people were decanted from rows of decaying dwellings to alien housing estates and high-rise flats.

Manchester had a history of radicalism harking back to the Peterloo Massacre triggered by the Corn Laws and lack of suffrage. In a male-dominated society where they were denied the vote, women were not shy of expressing political opinions at home. Margaret had plenty to say. She was the generation after Emmeline Pankhurst who, coming from a family of political agitators in Moss Side, led the British suffragette movement and condemned the government for ignoring the huddled masses and workhouses.

Women like Margaret had an impact beyond hearth and home. They were needed in wartime for factory jobs, and afterwards this confidence boosted their struggle for the vote. Without a property qualification or much education, she lacked this right until the 1929 election of Ramsay MacDonald's Labour Party. The party had strongholds in northern cities and Gorton has returned a Labour representative to Parliament continuously since 1935. The Edwards were unwavering supporters, and overhearing their parents inclined the boys to the same principles and beliefs. Labour was the new idealistic party, offering hope in the economically distressed 1930s when 17% of Mancunian men were out of work. The party's progressive, egalitarian policies were bulwarks for international stability and against the oppression of rising fascism. Thus, Bob became an avowed socialist from an early age, and one day he would seek political office.

Most parents had no greater ambition for their children than to follow the path that gave them security. Margaret was different. She was determined her boys would have a better life than their father's. She was willing to pay a price for their success if it took them away from their roots, which was frowned on by previous generations who depended on grown-up children to care for them in old age and infirmity before there was National Insurance.

She created a loving home her sons would try to replicate when they married, but no one called her mellow. Her voice thundered above the din of rambunctious kids. She was a forceful and headstrong woman of a type like Ena Sharples, the battle-axe in the everlasting TV soap opera based in Manchester's

"Coronation Street".[10] Ena was a harridan in a hair net who stopped brash men in their tracks. Her backstory matched Margaret's life, for they were the same vintage, married wounded veterans, and each had three children. There were plenty of real-life characters up and down the county like them, a Lancashire hotpot of plain-speaking and stubborn views, never suffering fools but friendly and loyal, except to snobs.

If this is a fair summary of Margaret's character, it is also true of Bob, who worshipped her and respected women throughout his life. He took after his mother more than his siblings did, and assimilated his father's work ethic, friendliness, and sense of humour.

He noticed Samuel's tenacity, on full display as he tried to ripen tomatoes without a greenhouse in Manchester's overcast summers. The garden was Samuel's refuge from a boisterous household. He would pause to push back his flat cap after shovelling dirt to light up an unfiltered *Wild Woodbine*. Smoking was a habit acquired in army days when cigarettes were issued free with rations to steady troop nerves. Samuel said he still needed them to clear phlegm from his lungs weakened by the gas attack and aggravated by the sooty air. He was content to leave domestic decisions to his wife, rarely objecting to her ruling the roost. Like other men of his background, he avoided talking about the horrors of trench warfare or perils in mines and tunnels, although he couldn't hide a disabled arm and a hacking cough. At some point in his young life, Bob found a heart for people who are disadvantaged or endure kinds of suffering the rest of society hardly notice, and perhaps his father's life brought them to attention.

Bob was proud of Welsh ancestry from his dad's side, but he professed to be a "Tyke" (Yorkshireman) and never a "Manc" (Mancunian). Yorkshiremen and Lancastrians are historic rivals, although they can form alliances against the "common foe" in the soft underbelly of southern England. Urban dwellers in the two counties share many characteristics, although only Yorkshiremen boast their home is God's own country. They are regarded as more argumentative and pig-headed than the other side of the county line, and it is said you can always tell a Yorkshireman, but you can't tell him much. Bob celebrated the type, although he didn't have the Yorkshire brogue presented in the comic film *The Full Monty*, nor did he have a Mancunian accent like the animated character in *Wallace and Gromit* but had an educated northern voice that has no specific address. He never gave much credit to Manchester, the city that nursed his genius, and is more celebrated today in a small Yorkshire town than the city where entrepreneurs and scientists have flourished, including Ernest Rutherford and Alan Turing, both of whom had a Cambridge connection that Bob would eventually make his own.

Educational opportunities were improving for his generation, and Margaret was determined to see her sons in the best schools. They began at Old Hall Drive, a primary school of brick and terracotta blending with the neighbourhood architecture. As it was only a mile from home, the boys went on foot unaccompanied except on wintry days when smog blanketing the region turned midday to dusk and flaming torches were posted to guide traffic. It was as easy to lose your way as in the more famous London "peasoupers", and the 1931 smog caused hundreds of deaths from bronchitis and pneumonia.

When Sammy was bullied, his mother transferred him to a more distant school at Stanley Grove. His brothers had to follow. Harry grumbled about losing his friends, but Bob was more flexible, and the switch proved successful because all three passed the 11-plus examination. It was a ticket to the elite Manchester Central High School for Boys, later known as a grammar school, and a notable achievement for working-class parents with limited resources and no background to coach pupils. It helped to live in a city with a tradition of fine public libraries, and Bob was a voracious reader. He could talk the hind leg off a donkey on almost any subject from an early age. He enjoyed fiction, too, and the mystery writer Daphne du Maurier was a favourite in adult life. No boys are angels and Bob was a strong and husky lad who stood up for himself and gave as good as he got in the playground. School discipline imposed corporal punishment, even for peeping through the keyhole at the girl's school next door. "Piggy" Stewart, the German teacher in a crumpled tweed suit who brought his dog to classes, had unerring accuracy when he flung a blackboard rubber across the room at an inattentive boy.

The high school locally known as Whitworth Street was in the top tier of the public education system with superior facilities and a graduate staff to groom boys with academic ability. Children who failed the 11-plus went to schools with a less challenging curriculum that emphasised trade skills for blue-collar employ-ment. Bob advanced in a hierarchical system that conflicted with the egalitarianism his parents taught since it rewarded early success and offered children who developed more slowly few, if any, possibilities of recovering from their disadvantage.

At high school, many pupils aimed for a career in the professions or civil service, and the brightest tracked to coveted scholarships at Cambridge or Oxford University. Of the three brothers, Bob was notably curious and eager to learn, and a boy with his ability and social background might aspire to become a schoolteacher or engineer, but no higher.

Whitworth Street was more than an academic hothouse, having clubs for hobbies, a magazine for budding writers and poets, and a theatre for Shakespearean plays with the girls' school. It didn't excel so much in sports as scholarship, and that dismayed

Bob's competitive spirit. He was a keen rugby player, listened to cricket and soccer championships on the wireless, and supported Yorkshire cricket and Leeds United soccer, pitting him against classmates loyal to local teams. Clubbable when it suited, he was always his own man even as a youngster.

Margaret goaded the boys to aim ever higher. A college education was a lofty goal when fewer than 2% of their generation went to university, mostly males from middle class homes. Most pupils left school without qualifications, like their parents, and Margaret was furious when Sammy decided to leave at the minimum age. After taking odd jobs, he joined the *Manchester Evening News* as a delivery boy. Social scientists claim the oldest child tends to be more ambitious than equally intelligent siblings, who are more rebellious, but the Edwards family broke that hypothetical association. Sammy was successful on his own terms, rising to become a circulation manager at the firm and first to own a car and buy a house, but his mother's defeat made her more determined to control the younger pair. Margaret and Samuel called them Geoff and Raymond, but the boys changed in their teens to the names we know them by, and for unknown reasons. It was an atypical family.

They were still at school in 1939 when Europe was spinning in political turmoil. The children sensed the apprehension of older generations for whom memories of the last dreadful war were still raw. An alumnus published in the school magazine a story about gas masks that could make Samuel shudder, and a current pupil wrote a grim poem.

Lie, my precious, softly snoring!
Suck your thumb while guns are roaring.
Never mind that nasty Göring!
Baby's gasmask's on![11]

When war broke out with Germany on 3 September, the British government hastened to protect strategic facilities and the civilian population from bombing raids. As a manufacturing centre and inland port, officials expected Göring's Luftwaffe would drop high explosive and incendiary bombs on munitions factories and terrorise residential areas before a planned invasion of England. With U-boats blockading ports, domestic lawns and school playing fields were converted to "victory gardens" to grow vegetables for a country unable to feed itself. Back gardens were dug for air-raid shelters and A.R.P. wardens in bluette uniforms patrolled at night for breaches of the blackout. Years of peace were abruptly upended.

The first bombing raids came in August 1940, growing heavier until the Christmas Eve blitz that claimed 627 lives across the city, 161 in Trafford, 14 in Hyde, and 59 in nearby Oldham. Casualties were not confined to security personnel but affected civilians of all ages. Nazi propaganda declared the whole city was bombed to the ground. Bob remembered, "it was pretty scary". Air raids continued until the final shock of a V1 flying bomb falling in Oldham on Christmas Eve 1944 killed 41 people. Margaret's mother lived in a target zone, and Thomas and Harold Leah were two child victims a few blocks from the Edwards' home. Nowhere in the city was safe.

In 1940, headmaster E.F. Chaney struggled to recruit qualified men and women to replace a dozen teachers who joined the armed forces. Fearing an attack on his school he sent the boys away to the seaside town of Blackpool where they could attend a local school. They were dreadfully unhappy and preferred taking a chance with an air-raid in Manchester than the real menace of a landlady in Blackpool. They flowed back a few months later, except for a few who never turned up. The headmaster lamented, "it is feared that many of these (boys) have drifted into quite unsuitable, and, in many cases, temporary occupation".[12] He despatched inspectors to find the truants, including Bob and Harry. They were having a whale of a time with their mother's connivance at a haven close to Samuel's workplace.

Samuel's gang worked on the 80-mile railway line from Settle to Carlisle in the Yorkshire Dales, a remote section from half-way inside the Blea Tunnel to the middle of the Ribblehead Viaduct. It was a strategic corridor for moving goods and troops across the wild moorland. Local farmers and A.R.P. wardens patrolled with pickaxe handles and one antiquated shotgun as security against German saboteurs and stormtroopers. The location was as safe as anywhere in England, and the boys' father could keep an eye on them. The only bombs that fell in the dale killed two cows.

They boarded with farmhouse tenants Tom and Gertrude Bonnick for an entire year. It became a tipping point in Bob's life. The boys' father may have met Tom in the last war, or perhaps for the first time over a beer and Yorkshire pudding in the pub beside the viaduct, exchanging war stories as veterans do.

Tom was born further down the dale at Ingleton in 1891, becoming a manservant to a local gentleman. Like Samuel, he didn't wait until 1916 for conscription but volunteered immediately on hearing war declared, enlisting in a West Riding branch of the Duke of Wellington's infantry regiment. Wounded by shrapnel during a ground attack, he would have died except a returning Tommy noticed his body twitch and dragged him back to a field hospital. After a long convalescence, he was posted to the Labour Corps for men deemed unfit for combat but sufficiently able-bodied to repair roads and railways, buildings and phone lines. After the war, he returned to marry Gertrude Campbell in Ribbledale where they rented the hill farm, taking in paying guests to supplement a meagre income.

The dale resembles Bronté country 30 miles away. The heather-clad moors dissected by ancient drystone walls run up the grey-green "fells" (hills) with tops splashed here and there with white "scars" (cliffs). Hill-farming looks romantic to tourists, but life was tough where few crops could thrive and hardy Swaledale sheep barely tolerated the rain and snow driven by a west wind. Farmers and shepherds worked the year round, only taking off a rare day to visit relatives or see the Blackpool Lights.

The Bonnick home was Broadrake, a 17th century farmhouse of grey stone from a local quarry and white-washed like other farms in olden times. It sheltered beside a row of sycamores in an almost treeless landscape but had a magnificent view of the viaduct and benefitted from early morning sun at the foot of Whernside, one of the Three Peaks with Ingleborough and Pen-y-ghent that attract hillwalkers today.

The house was bone-cold most of the year, despite coal fires burning constantly, and lighting was by oil lamps until electricity arrived in 1956. A "beck" (stream) rising from a spring on the hillside filled a barrel with drinking water, which froze over in winter. Baths were taken infrequently in a tub drawn in front of a fire, and the toilet was outside with a pair of seats for companionable chitchat through a dividing wall. It was a foreign place for city boys. They would love it.

Samuel waited with Tom at the Ribblehead railway halt for his family to arrive. The locomotive stopped with a deep sigh, panting gusts of steam and smoke as if anxious to leave the wasteland. Margaret descended from the carriage with the boys and a trunk of warm clothes and books. The two brothers were wide-eyed at the landscape while their mother looked around anxiously for the man who would care for her sons. Tom had brought a horse and cart to convey them across the dale to his home. There were no tractors, and apart from a noisy red and yellow bus the only motorised traffic belonged to a local doctor or vet on call from Ingleton. Bumping along the dirt track in the cart, the boys' eyes flitted from farmhouse to fells. It was a new world that Bob recalled it "was wonderful — isolated, free as air and two of us together".[13]

When they came down for breakfast each morning, Tom was already working outside or sitting by the fire with a cigarette and an ear to the BBC. Gertrude could prepare a heartier breakfast than wartime rationing allowed in the city because they raised mutton and chickens, collected eggs, and milked cows by hand to churn into unpasteurised buttermilk. There was no enforcement of pasteurisation until 1946 when Victor Rothschild urged legislation at the House of Lords in his maiden speech. This was a lord with whom Bob would exchange blows one day, although their spat was over the definition of fertilisation, not spilled milk.

The Bonnicks had only a single child, Eleanor, because Tom said one is enough and Gertrude remembered the strains of growing up in a big family. Bob ignored this advice when he married, but his respect for the man was otherwise boundless. Tom was like an adopted uncle, and Bob was especially close to him because they were both chatterboxes who revelled in friendly banter. Nothing was too much trouble for him, even helping his wife with chores in the home, something unheard of then in Yorkshire but chimed with Bob's sense of fair dues. Bob thought he was the finest man in the dale.

The boys enjoyed rude health that year on a farmhouse diet in the bracing air. The high school in Ingleton was too far to attend and they wanted to be fully immersed in the farming life. Tom was happy to oblige, teaching them how to dip sheep and wash fleeces, scythe hay and whistle to border collies. They led dray horses dragging carts of stable muck to the fields where Land

Girls and prisoners-of-war planted oats, potatoes, and turnips in the reluctant soil. They wanted to learn how to repair drystone walls: two stones on one, then one on top, followed by a "through-stone". None of these lessons would be needed in their lives, except the art of teamwork.

Bob was built for physical labour, but he didn't leave his curiosity behind in the city. He noticed farm practices were primitive and encumbered by tradition; they were charming sights for visitors but a heavy burden on families who made their living from the land. Surely, science could improve the lives of his new friends with better equipment, fertilisers, and breeds of animals and plants. But what did a city boy know compared to rural wisdom handed down by generations? And, yet, when the nation's survival in war time depended on food production, it was too important to leave farming to sentiment. Dreams of what the life sciences could offer started to dazzle, but at this point he was only thinking about agriculture. The same year on the opposite side of the grey Atlantic, too remote for an English boy to imagine, there were Americans trying to fertilise human ova in a dish. He would embrace the same challenge one day.

At the end of a workday, the boys often wandered down to the tunnel to watch their father emerge from the gloom, waving his wet, sooty arms. From the bridge, they saw him plod to the platelayers' shed beside the track to deposit tools and dry by the fire with a cup of tea and cigarette. Meanwhile, Margaret was enduring the bombing campaign in Manchester, occasionally taking the train for a day visit when she brought sweets for all the children.

At the end of the year, when the boys' education could no longer be postponed, it was safe for them to return to Manchester. Their mother thought the dale was only a temporary sanctuary, but it was an overwhelming experience for Bob; it wasn't in the entrepreneurial city that he first dreamed of science but in the wilds of Yorkshire among rural folk. Margaret wouldn't understand his new passion for farming, and he wouldn't care if other people scoffed at his ambition because she gave him confidence to believe in himself.

He vowed to return as often as possible to Ribbledale, the most precious place on earth. Decades later, he brought his family for vacations and was remembered by local people as the chatty young farmhand. Even when he became a celebrity he never swaggered, but as a true Yorkshireman rolled up his sleeves to help a farmer friend repair stone walls, dip sheep, and plant trees. The shift from mental to physical exertion was spiritually rewarding, like the "blessed hours" Tolstoy's nobleman Konstantin Levin found scything hay with his serfs. It was a haven for quality time with his wife and children, where he could recharge energy drained by the pressures of work and publicity and remember when he roamed the hills.

3

GUNS & GRADUATION

When Bob and Harry returned to "old smoky" they had tales for their friends and got stares from their teachers. Although they lost a full year at school, their rural education counted more for them than what they missed. They prized the new knowledge—how to assist a difficult birth for a lamb, hand-milk a cow, build stone walls, and steer powerful horses—none which they could learn in the city and were the envy of their peers.

But a gap year was a hole in the academic curriculum, and more serious for Bob as he had only one year to catch up before taking public examinations at age 16. Harry had two more years to prepare. Students who failed left for the workforce or enrolled as apprentices in local industry whereas successful students continued for two more years of advanced study in the sixth form for the Higher School Certificate. He needed to pass both hurdles for a ticket to university and avoid disappointing his mother. That Bob never floundered was a sign of his ability, the blessing of an excellent memory, and a fierce determination to succeed.

The vision of a farming career was incomprehensible to city boys who looked down their noses at rural life. It was hard to understand why a bright and sociable lad would want to work in the fields, which didn't require any school qualification. At best, he could only aspire to be a manager, and would never afford a farm of his own. But he was always confident in his own judgment, and so, after passing his exams, he applied to the school of agriculture at the University College of North Wales (now Bangor University). It was a natural choice for someone of Welsh heritage, and wasn't far from home, but more importantly it had an excellent reputation in the life sciences. Harry's choice blended more with family history as he would study chemical engineering at the Manchester Institute of Technology. Their mother was ecstatic at the prospect of two sons with degrees, although their success came at the price of unravelling a close-knit family. Harry would emigrate to Canada and Bob never lived in Manchester again, although it fell to him to do most of the travelling for the sake of preserving family bonds.

But before Bob could go to college, his 18th birthday snagged him. It was still wartime and he was eligible for conscription to military service. That he regarded it as a setback was not a sign of less patriotic fervour than his father had in 1914, but a reflection of social fatigue with war as the Normandy Landings brought an end in sight to the hostilities. Bob's patriotism was the quiet sort, except for devotion to Yorkshire which was worn on his sleeve.

A delay until December 1944 for posting to the General Service Corps brought his parents relief. By the end of training it would be too late to be deployed to battlefields as the war would be won, and then Sammy would come home from air-sea rescue missions in the North Sea. After Christmas, Bob took the train to a boot camp outside Fort George in Scotland to train as a driver and mechanic. It was a fabulous assignment for a boy eager to drive. This was the start of a love affair with cars, although he never liked working under the bonnet, which was a pity since mechanical knowledge is handy for a man who owns a series of old "bangers".

Six weeks later he was transferred to the Royal Northumberland Fusiliers to work with tracked vehicles in Kent and Sussex. Most of the regiment had been caught up in the evacuation from Dunkirk and were reorganised for foreign campaigns, including Operation Overlord. As the embers of war contracted towards the Nazi heartland and VE Day approached, the likelihood he would ever see combat fizzled out.

The post-war months were uneventful until the spring of 1946 when he received news of a crisis at the Bonnick farm. Tom was ill with shingles and unable to work, a calamity in haymaking season. Bob applied for leave of absence without pay to help his friend and was surprised when it was granted. Army life was boring in peacetime; he preferred labouring in the fields and coming home to the reward of Gertrude's home-cooking and chinwagging with neighbours. They included the Bonnick's daughter Eleanor who was raising her family nearby at Bruntscar farmhouse where Bob would make a temporary second home 30 years later. He gave her a framed portrait as a memento of summer 1946 in the dale, but it was stolen by her cousin who had a crush on the handsome devil in uniform with a shock of dark hair.

After an absence of several weeks he returned reluctantly to his unit. For a man temperamentally inclined to question authority, the army was not Bob's natural home and he had no ambition for promotion, nor any intention of staying longer than necessary. But an intelligent and confident manner attracted the notice of his commanding officer, and after promotion from a private soldier to lance-corporal there was the offer of a commission as second lieutenant. Bob was astounded.

His promotion required a transfer to the Middlesex, another regiment with a list of battle honours, although that wasn't a reputation he cared for. The Middlesex counted George Washington among its officers in Braddock's War against French Canada, its encounter with Napoleon's troops earned it the nick-name of "Diehards", and the regiment suffered huge losses in both world wars. Bob would never serve in a famous battle, but the transfer meant he would no longer be "mucking about" with army vehicles in the English mud. He would leave in the summer of 1947 with the 2nd battalion for security duties in the Middle East. It was the final year of the disastrous British Mandate inaugurated by the Balfour Declaration in 1917 promising a Jewish homeland. The government naïvely expected a new nation would be united.[14] After the humanitarian crisis of the Holocaust, there was a tide of European and Russian Jewish migrants heading for Palestine, which the British authorities tried to thwart. It was dangerous territory for British soldiers cast between the struggle of militant Zionism and Arab resistance.

Bob sailed for the Middle East in July 1947 on the *Staffordshire*, a passenger-cum-cargo ship of some 10,000 tons with four masts and a tall funnel. His deployment would last five months. After briefly stopping at Gibraltar, the voyage continued across the Mediterranean Sea to Malta where it paused long enough for the men to enjoy swimming in a warm sea. It was Bob's introduction to foreign lands, and by the end of his life he would be acquainted with many countries. They docked at Port Said on the northern end of the Suez Canal from where the men had orders to travel down the coast where they saw signs of recent hostility: fresh graves, buildings turned to rubble, and a funnel poking above the Red Sea.

It was a spartan existence for his platoon under canvas. Each man had a tiny cupboard beside a padded bed for personal possessions and to prop a picture of a mother or sweetheart. To relieve boredom between parades and exercises, they played soccer in the sand in the cool evening hours, and afterwards in twos and fours they shuffled cards by lamplight until a bugle sent them to bed. His squad was a temporary family, and Paddy the battalion mascot like a family dog.

British soldiers were welcome in Egypt at peace and could make brief sorties to explore the country when on leave. It was sunset time of la belle epoque for a liberal and sophisticated society that had attracted English writers and artists for over a century, and there was plenty to see. Bob and his friend Tony visited the pyramids and sphinx, took excursions into the desert by camel, and rode a rickshaw in the city. They explored Cairo on foot. Men wore the Turkish fez, women the hijab, and European women sheltered from the sun under umbrellas. It was an extraordinary mixture: a cosmopolitan and multilingual city less polluted and less populated than today; poverty and glamour lived side by side; the haunt of spies in rabbit warrens of the medieval city and the grand hotel where Lawrence of Arabia stayed; a place to sip mint tea while watching engravers or wood-carvers and men delivering water in goat skins; where business-men made deals in coffee houses and belly dancers performed in nightclubs; with bazaar stalls offering a smorgasbord of exotic sweetmeats and fruit to English boys who grew up on fish and chips. Wandering the winding streets of the citadel where Arabic graffiti covered the walls, an urchin or beggar would hold out a hand pleading for "baksheesh", and vendors pleaded to make a bargain. And at salat times a muezzin perching like a bird in a minaret warbled a call to prayer without the aid of a loudspeaker. The city ravished the senses of alien visitors.

Bob was smitten and never forgot Cairo or its friendly citizens. He came back repeatedly and later in life the Egyptian authorities treated him as a celebrity. They asked him to help launch the Middle East Fertility Society four years after the Saudis fêted him with the prestigious King Faisal International Award for Medicine in 1989. The London gynaecologist and Egyptologist Eric Jauniaux sometimes accompanied him, answering endless questions about antiquities and Pharaonic medicine. Bob wanted to try everything, go everywhere from Alexandria to Luxor to Aswan, and had the rare privilege of entering the labyrinth of the Step Pyramid of Djoser, the first great stone building in the world. Never a warrior type, he felt bound to visit graves of his regiment at El-Alamein, where he surrendered a normally sunny demeanour to quiet contemplation.

Egypt had a massive impact on him, but it was only a brief waypoint for the battalion's tour of Syria, Iraq, and Jordan. When he came home, he was as reluctant as his father to talk about military service, except to murmur he had seen "terrible poverty and horrible things". Yet he couldn't resist telling an amusing story. Perched on a tank in Jordan, he had held up his hand to halt the entourage of King Abdullah, a tale you want to believe despite his reputation for wicked teasing.

Most of the time in Palestine he was on patrol in a small truck with a Vickers machine gun in the back that his father would have recognised. The men practised shooting at targets and setting off mortars. After terrorist attacks on public buildings, police stations, and railways, they searched for stockpiles of weapons and explosives, and anyone caught and convicted faced the death penalty. For their own safety, soldiers camped inside a double apron of barbed wire with armed guards.

The Irgun, an underground militia organised by future prime minister Menachem Begin, bombed the King David Hotel in Jerusalem, killing 91 people of several nationalities. And in July 1947 they abducted two British sergeants in the Intelligence Corps, regardless that one was Jewish and both sympathised with Zionism. Incarcerated in an underground bunker at Netanya, the pair was threatened with death if the British Army executed three captured Irgun terrorists. After the sentences were carried out, the sergeants were strung up in an olive grove and their bodies were booby-trapped. The "Sergeant's Affair" made British patrols more nervous, and there was public outrage at home and condemnation from British Jewish leaders. Long afterwards in 1989, an article in the *Jerusalem Post* celebrating Bob's presence at a scientific congress claimed he was hostile to Israeli nationalism because the sergeants were in his platoon. It is an unlikely story, although his experiences in Palestine cast a shadow that deepened after the Six-Day War.

He was an internationalist by inclination, although not yet groomed by experience of world travel, and he never let national politics spoil a personal relationship. Twenty years after the founding of the Jewish state, he was at a conference of the International Planned Parenthood Federation (IPPF) in Santiago, Chile, where he met the Israeli endocrinologist Bruno Lunenfeld. Although the agenda pressed for more public access to contraception, the two urged the meeting to embrace the rights of all women to have children. That common ground blossomed to a lasting friendship, and they even agreed on an international solution for the vexed issue of sovereignty of Jerusalem. The relationship didn't sour when Bruno admitted he may have confronted Bob's troops as a junior member of the Irgun.

At the end of the Middle East tour, Bob boarded the *Dunnottar Castle* at Port Said for the homeward voyage in time for Christmas. He looked forward to college later in the year, but the army wasn't a waste of time as it gave him experience of leadership a young civilian would not otherwise have. At the end of his life, he said, "When you've got a platoon to look after it makes you think a little harder". It made him a more mature freshman than students straight out of school. He had grown up in a comfortable zone of people of similar class and attitudes, so the army did the service of tossing him among men of diverse backgrounds that fostered a cosmopolitan outlook important later in his career. Moreover, as an ex-serviceman he had the benefits of subsidised tuition and a modest living allowance for college. These were not so much the gesture of a grateful nation as recognition that security and prosperity require human investment in science and technology.

He was never ashamed of his roots or abandoned his principles after upward social mobility and celebrity status. He was the same Bob who hated the snobbery and privilege of the officers' mess, a haven for reactionary Tories. He was a fan of Clement Attlee, the Labour prime minister from 1945 to 1951, a statesman of modest manner and sensitive conscience in turbulent times who became a friendly ally of Harry Truman, and even won respect from his political opponent, Winston Churchill. Attlee led a programme of national reconstruction that offered social progress with a Welfare State invested in public housing, education, and, above all, the revolutionary National Health Service (NHS). Loyalty to those ideals grounded Bob's future ambition to plant clinical work in a national hospital, if possible, and made him aspire to political office.

Servicemen had to wait for their number to be called before they were released to civilian life. When his came up, he left the army in February 1948, receiving two service medals and ribbons to match his father's. During the next six months until he moved to Bangor, he stayed at home enjoying his mother's cooking and working as a clerk in a Salford office of the new health service. The job was "totally boring", but the experience opened his eyes to the lives of others and taught him to look for something more stimulating. He still thought it would be agriculture.

Bangor is a small Welsh city on a hillside overlooking the Menai Straits and has not changed much since Bob first set foot there 70 years ago. He rented a bedsit near the city centre, but never stayed in one place for long. His flexible nature was always looking for something better, and never paused for long in his whole life.

The craggy backdrop of Snowdonia was white capped in winter and a plume of smoke often traced the mountain railway to its summit, over 1,000 metres above sea level. The gothic cathedral was not the most arresting sight of the city, squatting in a depression to escape notice from Viking raiders, but the square university tower made of local stone commanded attention. Students and professors streaming along the paths often spoke in the Welsh language, and voices in the refectory occasionally burst spontaneously into communal song. Wales is not called the "Land of Song" for nothing.

The freshmen in Bob's class were strangers to each other, coming from all corners of the UK. At the first lecture in agricultural chemistry he sat next to John Slee, who became his best and longest friend. Recently turned 23, Bob was five years his senior, a significant gulf at that age and there were differences in experience and social class. John came straight from a fee-paying school, albeit not an elite academy denigrated by inner city boys as a school for "toffs". Looking back on those times, John thought they were "unlikely friends", but when young strangers are thrown together in an unfamiliar environment differences can melt, as they did for Pip and Herbert Pocket in *Great Expectations*.

John's family wasn't wealthy, but his parents invested heavily in their only son. They evacuated during the war to North Wales where they rented half a farmhouse for three years, and it was there he fell in love with farming as a teenager, as Bob had. When he failed to get a place for veterinary studies at the "Dick Vet" in Edinburgh, he decided on farm management or agriculture research, mirroring Bob's ambition. John found his new friend hard to place. His rough edges smoothed by a friendly manner, he was ambitious, unusually confident in his own judgment, and nattered like a rattling mountain stream. Bob was unlike any boy he knew at school.

47

They rarely talked "shop", but often fell into conversation about politics and sport. As most people do, John passively absorbed the political convictions of his parents, who were staunch Tories, but Bob moulded him into a committed socialist in less than a week. Bob was persuasive even then, and relentlessly pressed his beliefs on anyone willing to lend an ear. He liked the quote, "for each according to his ability, to each according to his need", although Marxism was alien to him.

They both loved classical music and joined the college gramophone society. Sauntering back to their separate digs with music still ringing in their heads, they often sung or hummed in unison, an exhibition that would never draw stares on a Welsh street.

Sport was dear to them too, and they had uncommon talent and competitive spirits. Since John usually won at tennis and Bob at badminton, neither of them felt hurt for long. Still a keen rugby player, Bob joined the Welsh team for intervarsity competitions until he broke his ankle in an awkward fall. He played wing forward, like a mirror of his politics. Wanting to preserve the fitness he gained in army days, he resumed hill-walking for the first time since he lived under Whernside, before it was a fashionable pastime in Britain. He would race up Cadair Idris, one of the closest mountains, while someone timed his return to base with a stopwatch. With a twinkle in his eyes he told them tales of beating the train to the top. There was little spare time to have a serious girlfriend, and few opportunities in a class of only four girls out of twenty-four. Neither of them dated until they moved to Edinburgh, where they found their life partners.

The outdoors provided Bob with the oxygen denied by dreary lectures and laboratory classes. The agriculture course was meant for future farm managers who needed practical advice about the tonnage of manure, pounds of seed, and gallons of weed killer to spread on an acre of land. Teachers yielded slowly to the advance of science. There was pioneering research in Britain at the Rothamsted Experimental Station under the famed Ronald Fisher, but undergraduates in the 1950s were expected to absorb traditional wisdom like blotting paper and never question authority. The old-fashioned curriculum exasperated both young men.

John's professor advised him to switch to academic science, but he continued to graduation with honours in 1951. Bob didn't finish the agriculture course, abruptly quitting at the end of his second year and grinning that his professors were glad to see the back of him. It seemed a costly mistake. But he was more interested in how seeds germinate in the womb, why a calf fetus has multiple placentas, why sheep have a fixed breeding season, and so many other mysteries of biology and genetics.[15] Pressing these questions on his professors made them nervous because they had no answers, so he switched to the zoology course. He was willing to pay a price for cutting loose from agriculture, but it looked reckless since he could only afford to stay one more year at college, and that meant qualifying for only a pass degree without honours. It infuriated his mother, who called him foolish, and only in hindsight was it a wise move.

The head of the zoology department was a reproductive biologist, Francis W. Rogers Brambell, FRS. Born and educated in Dublin, his headmaster opined that the boy had no aptitude for any career except natural history, advising his parents to send him to farm in the colonies, which was not meant as a compliment. But they had faith in their son, and hope was vindicated when he won prizes in zoology at Trinity College Dublin. A research career took him to London where he studied reproduction in chickens and mice, and after collaborating with Alan Parkes, who would later become Bob's supervisor, his outstanding talent earned him a chair at Bangor at the fledgling age of 29.

A tall man with a bristling moustache and owlish stare behind horn-rimmed glasses, Brambell had a dignity and scholarly reputation that commanded respect, and yet he had a sense of humour too. Pomposity was entirely foreign to him. His biographer wrote he had a remarkable understanding of students and an ability to get the best out of them. Bob greatly admired his new professor, and this short chapter in his life became a rung on the ladder to his career.

When Brambell was a young professor, reproduction and embryology were coming out of the dark ages of descriptive science, hardly different to natural history. There were few men who shone light on this enigmatic and untrodden field or succeeded in stimulating student interest, but he succeeded with Bob. His curiosity roused from examining a specimen under a microscope, Bob asked, "Why does only one sperm enter an egg?" There was no slick answer, but it was the kind of question the professor savoured because mystery is the sauce of science.

Bob was his student when Professor Brambell was engaged in a project that crossed disciplines and would be his greatest legacy. He wanted to know why newborn animals with naïve immune systems don't succumb to infections after birth. The answer was in their mother's immunological history: antibodies generated to pathogenic bugs transferred across the placenta to fetuses, or after birth in the colostrum of the first milk of some species. It is a discovery that still resonates in the debate over breastfeeding versus formula milk for human infants. If Brambell shared his growing knowledge of a connection between immunology and reproduction, it helps to explain why Bob chose to combine those fields in his own research.

After the joy of zoology, Bob was crestfallen when he left Bangor in the summer of 1951 without an honours degree. It meant he didn't have the qualification for a career in science, except as an assistant to a professional scientist, and that would never satisfy a man with his ambition. It was not a lack of ability or effort that put him in these straits, but bloody-mindedness for kicking against the degree regulations and being without the financial means to repair his qualification. He had lately found a field that inspired him but felt like a crab drying on the beach when the tide goes out. But he wasn't gloomy for long and believed another wave would come along soon. One day he would learn that a mediocre record does not condemn a student forever, as Brambell, Francis "Tibby" Marshall, and Alan Parkes proved by becoming eminent. Bob would recover from his crash to follow them.

4

NORTHERN LIGHTS

When John Slee graduated at Bangor he never expected to see his friend again. He had accepted a job at the Animal Breeding Research Organisation in Edinburgh, but the offer was conditional on passing a diploma in genetics, which required a year of study at the King's Buildings campus of the University. As he was entering the gaunt Institute of Animal Genetics on the first day, he heard a familiar voice calling his name. When he turned around, Bob was coming up the steps behind him wearing a broad grin.

If John ever mentioned he was going to Edinburgh he had forgotten, and if Bob ever heard about the diploma he had over-looked or buried the knowledge because he wasn't qualified for admission. While casting around for ideas, he remembered how much he enjoyed genetics in the zoology course, and it may then have taunted him like a mischievous sprite. There was nothing to be lost by firing off an application, which he wrote by hand and dropped in the nearest red pillar box. Loath to sit waiting for a response, he tried to forget about it, busying himself with a temporary job in the Manchester docks, hauling combs of bananas out of ships until something better turned up.

When a letter with an Edinburgh postmark arrived a few weeks later he glumly assumed it announced a rejection, so it was a stunning reversal of fate to be offered a place for the diploma. He never knew why or how his luck turned. It may have helped that the course was new and possibly short of applicants, or perhaps good-old Brambell had written a glowing reference. Regardless, it gave him a chance to put a blighted record behind and climb another rung of the ladder.

Edinburgh offered more than the first tremulous step to a career in science: it was a city of gracious architecture steeped in culture, science, and history that was worthy of the name "Athens of the North". The city was compact enough to explore every nook of the Old Town and take a bumpy ride up and down cobbled streets to the Georgian New Town. The panorama could be enjoyed on a walk under Salisbury Crags in Holyrood Park. A distant lament from a bagpiper's drones on the castle walls reminded the young men they were in a foreign country, making their relocation feel more glamorous. There was an international arts festival in the summer and year-round concerts at the Usher Hall to nourish their musical souls, and appetites for thrills were sated at the speedway. Beyond the city limits, the Pentland Hills beckoned the hillwalker in Bob, while Portobello and North Berwick offered bracing seaside strolls against the North Sea breeze. The duo fell in love with the place.

Bob found a lodging in the Bruntsfield district, but a habit of changing lodgings soon surfaced while John quickly settled down. He had no plans beyond completing the diploma, although the optimism of Micawber preserved his poise. He was like a freshly fertilised egg with potential to grow but without the assurance of viability until he had a womb to nurture him as a scientist. He found it in Edinburgh.

The backstory of many outstanding scientists is the history of their mentors and predecessors, and Bob owed more to Conrad Hal Waddington than any others. "Wad" made the final decision for admission to the course as director of the institute, which was founded in 1911 largely at the behest of Francis Marshall before he moved to Cambridge.

Wad made the opposite journey after the war from Christ's College in Cambridge where Marshall was the Vice-Master. He was an embryologist who became a midwife to mammalian genetics when it was in the doldrums and mostly neglected in the medical curriculum. He gathered a world class faculty to create a mecca for young scientists in the same way that Cambridge became a centre for mammalian embryology in the following decades. The institute grew organically into a mosaic of research projects on a variety of species in a large animal house managed by friendly Scottish women. People said he could pull money out of a hat as funds poured in for central services for microscopy and filmmaking, graphic art and statistical advice. He could boast several Fellows of the Royal Society of London on his staff, and the institute would be the incubator of future Fellows, including Mary Lyon, Anne McLaren, Bruce Cattanach, and Bob.

But it was far from a battery house for boffins to peck at arcane subjects. The mix of projects reflected public concerns and national security, ranging from livestock production at a time of food rationing to the genetic impact of atmospheric fallout from atomic bomb tests. Wad's style of management was laissez-faire, and he encouraged staff to gather for morning coffee and afternoon tea as sacramental time for sharing ideas and forging collaborations across specialties. American visitors trained in a culture that didn't brook "wasted" time had to adapt to a more relaxed regime. In its heyday the institute was more than intellectually stimulating and scientifically productive: it was fun to work there. It was a time when scientists felt freer to explore novel leads, before they had to slavishly follow the blueprint of a grant. Wad believed a loose leash was the surest path for creativity. The diploma course was a source of new blood to nourish the vibrant organism he built, and senior researchers and eminent visitors were encouraged to talk to the class. A bright and ambitious student in this ferment could dream of joining them in the pantheon of science.

Wad was far more than an administrator. He was a renowned scholar and scientist who strode across the boundaries of paleontology, philosophy, geology, evolution, and embryology. Ignoring academic walls, he was proof that the reign of polymaths had not ended with Hermann von Helmholtz. In Cambridge, he wasn't daunted in debate with the philosopher Ludwig Wittgenstein, nor with the theologian Tom Torrance in Edinburgh. He called Henry Moore, Ben Nicholson, and a host of avant-garde architects and artists his friends. The door to his personal library was always open, and Bob sneaked in to browse the multifarious collection. But it is for embryology that we remember Wad, and particularly for introducing the word "epigenetics" to the lexicon, a subject now assuming enormous significance for explaining development and even cancer.[16]

Wad was the *éminence foncé*, seldom seen in laboratories or corridors. A strange, retiring man with a manner that intimidated students, he was perfectly likeable to anyone who had the privilege of deeper acquaintance. Bob's first encounter with him was in a corridor where he mistook a bald, scruffy man in a polo-neck sweater for the janitor. This was an era when senior faculty wore a jacket and tie. To a green student, Wad had awesome power. When John asked him how to fund a scholarship for a PhD after the diploma, Wad lay down his pipe to call Lord Rothschild in London and a minute later casually muttered that he was funded.

He was too busy for much contact with students, leaving their supervision to the staff. Few people expected more than a polite nod as he passed them, assuming he had forgotten their name, but after graduating with a doctorate he could leave them glowing after poking his head around a door to say, "Nice work, Dr ....". It was hard to fathom whether it was a smokescreen or if he had quietly followed their work all along.

Bob held him in boundless admiration and felt a political kinship. He often followed the director across town for seminars where Wad debated with experts in science, sociology, and theology, and the experience prompted him to explore city churches. To imagine Bob in a pew listening to a homily from the pulpit is as strange as Alice listening to the Walrus, but the pilgrimage was another sign of his hunger for knowledge and understanding. Alan Braden, a zealous Australian visitor, tried to persuade the two friends to join his church, but Bob shared Wad's rejection of numinous authority, believing man's destiny is in his own hands. Yet, he was never scornful of people of faith, even marrying in church and befriending clergymen who had the mettle to rally with him.

Wad was no stranger to controversy and conscience led him to take unpopular positions. His political brand and sympathy for détente in the Cold War era encouraged critics to attack him. They sniped at his apparently soft attitude to Lysenkoism, regarded outside the Soviet Union as a loathsome repudiation of Mendelian genetics. They conflated his concept of epigenetics with the Lamarckian heresy that claimed children inherit characteristics acquired in life by their parents. The stock example is a black-smith's son born with strong arms gotten from his father's heavy labour. He urged scientists to debate and explain their work to the public, which also went against the grain where many in his profession haughtily denied they owed that duty. But Bob took the lesson to heart and would pay a price.

He was sure of his field before completing the diploma. Reproduction was a supreme life science, immensely important for food production and society. Genetics was its natural partner, offering fresh understanding of how to preserve health and explain the causes of disease. He was determined not to flunk his chances again, especially after the director promised him a three-year scholarship for a PhD if he performed well, which of course he did.

Graduate students were asked to choose their project from a list of options. The hot topic was genetic damage to germ cells from radiation fallout, much more than a theoretical risk it turned out less dire than feared. John decided to study the *Ragged* mutation in mice, which causes skin and heart abnormalities. Bob cast his net wide before making a decision.

He found his subject during a lecture by R. Alan Beatty, a staff scientist who specialized in fertilisation and the process of parthenogenesis or "virgin birth". Alan suggested he make embryos with three or four sets of chromosomes (called triploids and tetraploids, respectively) instead of the normal diploid pair inherited from a mother's ovum and father's sperm. Such abnormalities occur too sporadically in nature to study them. The project was led more by curiosity than any obvious application to farming or public health, but the enigma and beauty of ova and embryos soon won Bob over and he never lost the fascination.

The extraordinary responsibility of eggs as a bridge between generations intrigues the scientific mind, but as the rarest cells in the body they are hard to study.[17] They were objects of curiosity for centuries as natural philosophers searched for the primal stages of life in the womb until the 19th-century aristocrat Karl Ernst von Baer of Königsberg discovered them hiding inside ovarian follicles. There were many blind alleys and false paths in the quest because, although they are relatively large cells, mammalian ova are too small to see except through a microscope. They are ovulated singly or in tiny numbers and never released outside the body in mammals, except for a few Australian species. Even the brilliant mind of William Harvey who deduced the circulation of the blood stumbled when he searched for them, though he understood their supreme role as the source of life (*omne vivum ex ovo*, all life starts from an egg). As William Blake saw a world in a grain of sand, a biologist might regard eggs as the latest editions in an unbroken chain reaching back in biological history to the first cell. And, now, a brash young man came along to crack some of their mysteries.

Bob's lifelong fascination began in Bangor where he peered at mouse ova and embryos. He became skilful at handling these tiny objects, pricking them out of bulging follicles with a needle or finding them freshly ovulated in fallopian tubes. They were transferred to dishes in a glass pipette that he fashioned in the flame of a Bunsen burner to perfectly fit their diameter. After depositing eggs in a drop of saline solution he examined them under a microscope by turning the focusing knob. A glistening pearl inside its transparent shell (zona pellucida) came into view, an awesome sight.

Nothing in the realm of cell biology has more perfect geometry than a naked ovum. It would have been extolled as a divine object by the Ancient Greeks if they had seen it or reminded astrologers of a fateful blue moon inside a corona. The elemental appearance of the humble sphere is deceptive, though, because the cytoplasm contains apparatus of profound complexity and a set of chromosomes delicately poised on an intracellular muscle waiting for a signal to contract at fertilisation.

When the first thrill of something marvelous changes to the dull routine of familiarity, a continuing absorption must be sustained by a belief in the object's significance and meaning. Bob never lost that enchantment, but the greater awe was ahead. The number of people in the world who had ever seen a living human egg was less than his fingers, and one day his hand would tremulously hold them in a pipette.

Relationships between graduate students and their supervisors, which were customarily formal in Britain, grew more affable in the 1950s. Bob narrowly lost his bet with John to be on first name terms with his boss. He saw little of Alan because he spent long hours in the mouse house at the rear of the building. It accommodated thousands of mice of different strains and mutations in racks of boxes five rows high. He liked to play tricks on new students by handing them a box of mutant dwarf mice, knowing they couldn't resist lifting the cover to peep inside. The diminutive animals seemed to be spring-loaded, and after the shock of jumping out of the box and darting across the room everyone chuckled as they gave chase on hands and knees.

After a day in the mouse house, white lab coats absorbed a fishy odor from mice said to resemble acetamide, an industrial plasticiser, and were sent to the laundry. Mouse antigens were a serious menace from breathing the air or handling animals or wood shavings in their cages. Up to a quarter of people regularly exposed to them become sensitised, making eyes and nose run and skin itch. For a whole decade, Bob bore a severe allergy until he switched to human subject research.

He needed thousands of mouse ova for his experiments, and limited numbers were his greatest handicap. Mice ovulate around ten ova every oestrous cycle, recurring every 4 or 5 days, but this happens in the middle of the night and they are stale by breakfast time. The biological clock required working the night shift. He could predict which animal would ovulate the following night by checking vaginal cells because they change appearance when oestrogen from follicles reaches a peak level, but it was a tiresome routine seven days a week.[18]

At the end of the day, when others headed home or to the pub, Bob was starting in the mouse house and blazing the lights until the small hours. His life was badger-like. If he was not so much in love with his work, he would have regretted sacrificing a social life and the chance to date girls. The only other nocturnal denizen was Mary Lyon. She was ahead of him after finishing her PhD in Cambridge with the cantankerous and brilliant Ronald Fisher, and moved north in 1948 to study radiation. A solemn scientist who made a famous discovery about the X-chromosome, she never married and would have been mortified if her landlady caught her alone with Bob in the mouse house after dark.

One day late in 1953 there was a new face knocking at the mouse house door. He was still wearing outdoor clothes and lugging heavy bags, but Bob was ready with a box of dwarf mice as a surprise. The fruitful collaboration that followed was predicted by the man's urgent need to see the research facilities before his lodging. He had arrived in town only an hour earlier on a train from Southampton after disembarking from Buenos Aires. He was Julio Sirlin, a tall, prematurely balding Argentinian with a dark beard and Spanish accent. Julio was a year younger than Bob but had already earned his doctorate and published papers on frog development. He wanted to switch to mammalian genetics and hoped to find a kindred spirit in Edinburgh to share scientific adventures. He did. Bob recalled, "Julio was the first man with whom I collaborated who was prepared to work at my pace". They were soon planning joint studies, leaving Bob even more sleep deprived without daytime naps. The pair became friends who shared a love of opera, tasty food, and eventually a flat in the Marchmont district.

Julio introduced the idea of using radioactive chemicals to trace cell movement and development. His favourite molecule was adenine, a constituent of nucleic acids, before the role of RNA in gene action was well understood. They compiled an ambitious list of experiments and published 12 papers together, in addition to Bob's solo studies and Julio's collaboration with Wad. Julio was a driven researcher and he goaded students to work harder. His good intentions provoked more resentment than appreciation, though never from Bob or John except when he criticised the assistant who became John's wife.

Julio befriended a Jamaican woman with tawny skin nick-named Lindo ("lovely" in Spanish). After they left Edinburgh and married, he joined the Cornell Medical School in Manhattan, but their story did not end happily. She had a reputation for making saucy remarks to men that made him jealous, but it was a terrible shock when she committed suicide at age 38. Julio's hard-hitting manner made him unpopular in New York, too, and his insistence that RNA played a role in learning was controversial and, there-fore, an obstacle to winning research grants. Without this funding, he had to find employment by routine testing of human sperm for a fertility clinic.

Bob juggled with more projects than is wise for one man, but the ball he dared not drop was the one Alan Beatty gave him. Alan was a pernickety man who taught students a strict scientific code, but he failed to rein in Bob's appetite. The wayward apprentice admitted, "I was a very pushy student because I always wanted to do the next thing before I finished the first one". But his super-visor was patient and gave his student lots of rope. Nor did he poach credit from any of his students by adding his name to a paper unless he made a material contribution to the work. Bob adopted the principle when he became a research supervisor. His first paper reported chromosome abnormalities he engineered in mouse ova, a solo publication in *Nature* in 1954. Competition for pages in prestigious journals is more intense now, but it was a notable achievement and sign of promise.

Reproductive technology was still a primitive art. There was artificial insemination for cattle and Margaret Jackson in Exeter adopted it, rather covertly, for couples to have children when the husband was sterile. Bob used it when male mice were reluctant or unable to mate, and that was the first time he controlled fertility in any species. He squirted sperm through the cervix of females to fertilise ova for testing the effects of drugs and radiation on chromosomes of gametes. He created embryos with abnormal sets of chromosomes ("ploidies") — one or three or even four sets instead of a normal pair. It was a kind of genetic engineering, if not in the modern sense of adding or deleting specific DNA sequences or entire genes.

He chose to study mice when the shallows of human genetics would soon be flooded with discoveries from advancing technology. He had the gift of perfect timing. Human fetuses with abnormal chromosome sets were identified and found to perish early in pregnancy, just as they had in his animals. Only those with a normal pair ("diploid") survived. But why were animals and humans more finicky about chromosomes than, say, commercial bananas that inherit three sets or potatoes that have four?

This progress kindled a new fascination, although extrapolation of his studies to human genetics could only go so far. The diploid set is larger in humans than mice (46 compared to 40 chromosomes), and chromosomes of common ancestors have been chopped and swapped around, so the genes strung along chromosome threads like pearls have gotten progressively different in sequence and position as species diverged from evolution. After the mouse house gave Bob a flying start, potential agricultural applications of his work were gradually crowded out by a new absorption in human development. But if Alexander Pope was right that the proper study of mankind is man, how would he make the migration as a young researcher without a medical qualification?

He submitted his dissertation for the PhD degree in 1955, entitled *The Experimental Induction of Heteroploidy in the Mouse*. It was a hefty tome of data and review of the background that sufficiently impressed his examiners they waived an oral examination. While not an unprecedented decision, it was a rare mark of distinction. As his work with Alan tailed off, he collaborated more with other colleagues, including a student who would become very close to him.

He was not burned out after the punishing workload and always eager to share news after browsing the latest journal. If a paper excited him, he might burst into an office or the coffee room to turn bewildered heads as he poured out the story, whether listeners were interested or not. There was plenty of news to satisfy his appetite. In 1956, Swedish researchers revised the correct number of chromosomes in normal human cells from 48 to 46. Two years later in Paris, Jérôme Lejeune reported a child with Down's syndrome had an extra chromosome-21. The following year, Charles Ford in Oxfordshire found a patient with Turner's syndrome had a missing X-chromosome.

The trickle of discoveries grew to a steady flow. There was no longer any doubt that unbalanced sets of chromosomes cause birth defects and, occasionally, sexual ambiguity. These abnormalities account for an astonishing third of all fetal deaths, and the full toll is even higher from earlier losses that go undetected and are now called biochemical pregnancies. Prenatal testing using amniocentesis and placental biopsy were on the way, but they failed to throw much light on the causes or suggest ways of preventing mistakes in chromosome number. Bob realised the knowledge gap was in his field and he had transferrable skills, although there was no opportunity to switch to human studies in his institute. He needed help from a gynaecologist as a gatekeeper to human specimens, but until then had to be content with animal subjects and his theories.

Chromosomes are like pairs of dancers who must remember their partner and place. "Strip the Willow", popular at Scottish ceilidhs, offers a vivid image of matched male and female partners facing each other in rows corresponding to paired chromosomes, but the analogy fails to illustrate the complexity. Before "dancing", chromosome partners swap bits of DNA to create genetic novelty, and separate twice, once before ovulation and again after fertilisation. Although the chromosome pairs normally separate perfectly, the cytoplasm containing them divides asymmetrically to create one big cell (the ovum) and a tiny bleb (a polar body), which quickly dies. This process is called "meiosis", meaning a "lessening" because it produces a single set of chromosomes ("haploid") in the ovum to match the single set in a sperm. Their union restores a normal balanced set of 46 in humans. Bingo!

Bob understood the fate of embryos is decided when chromosomes "dance" during these cell divisions. If partners failed to separate faithfully, ending up together in a cell, they produced "aneuploid" embryos that cause Down's syndrome when an extra chromosome-21 is retained in the ovum, or Turner's syndrome if the ovum loses an X-chromosome to the polar body. Unbalanced sets can arise in other ways too.

The main risk factor for Down's syndrome is the mother's age, which has been attributed to fertilisation of a stale ovum when intercourse is less frequent in older couples or from cumulative background radiation and toxic chemicals. Some years after he moved to Cambridge, Bob offered a more radical idea, called the "production line" hypothesis.[19] He gathered evidence that ova are ovulated according to a strict timetable, like a series of railway trains on the same track to a station with the last in line poorly engineered. It was reminiscent of the fable about faulty goods off the factory production line on Friday afternoons!

The ultimate cause of Down's syndrome remains unknown and is hard to study deep inside the pelvis. But when ova are ripened in a Petri dish their chromosomes are accessible for microscope studies, and thus he dreamt about developing IVF to study abnormalities. There was a practical reason, too, because ova fertilised and ripened in vitro could be applied for breeding farm animal stock, but he was focused on human biology and genetics, even flirting with the daring idea of treating infertility. Few people in the mid-1950s took him seriously. Human applications were repelled by the shadow of eugenics, although the risk of that abuse seemed as ridiculous to him as a scientist as it was abhorrent as an egalitarian. His ideas were still unformed but began to gel.

It would have been natural to ask Professor Waddington for advice, although no record exists of such a conversation. Wad was a futurist disposed to musing, and always ready to express his visions. When frogs were cloned in Oxford, he predicted mammalian cloning would happen, and two decades after his death sheep were cloned at an Edinburgh research farm. He anticipated technology for choosing the sex of babies, and that happened too. But his prescience about human IVF was chary.

In view of the difficulty of guaranteeing that an egg fertilised outside the body is going to develop normally, it may be 30 or 40 years before these methods are introduced into clinical practice.[20]

There was something that niggled him about IVF, and he had coined the word—epigenetics. If culture conditions didn't perfectly mimic fluid in the fallopian tubes, embryos might not switch genes on or off at the correct time, a concern shared by other eminent scientists. It would be his former student who would prove them wrong, though Wad would never know because he died three years before Louise Brown was born.

IVF was not Bob's brainchild, although he eventually earned the honour of being called the Father of IVF. Americans had tried it earlier, and the Viennese biologist Samuel Leopold Schenk aired the idea exactly a century before Louise Brown was born. The physicist and writer Freeman Dyson warned against narrowly heaping credit for discoveries on an individual because science is a project of bricolage; even Newton and Einstein acknowledged how success builds on success, and sometimes on failure.

There is no such thing as a unique scientific vision any more than there is a unique poetic vision.[21]

It takes more than one person to bring a novelty to application. A day-dreaming natural philosopher deserves recognition for sowing the seeds of ideas, but ideas are two-a-penny. It is the engineer who deserves more credit for making them into something new and valuable. To be frank, IVF did not require a great leap of inspiration, considering fertilisation outside the body has been the norm for most animals since the dawn of evolution. But turning vertebrate animals back to external fertilisation was never going to be easy.

Before we return to Bob's life, we need to review the backstory. It is circular as it begins in one Cambridge and ends in another. The Harvard biologist in Cambridge, Massachusetts, Gregory "Goody" Pincus took the last year of his fellowship to study in Europe where he spent most of 1930 in Cambridge. Bob arrived a generation later as Goody's alter ego and met the older man briefly in the last year of his life. They both had charisma, chutzpah, and flourishing thatches of hair. They both migrated careers from genetics to reproduction and, above all, had enormous appetites for work and dogged determination to succeed. According to Dyson, great scientists are rebels against the tyranny of conventional belief. Goody and Bob are examples of supreme disruptors.

Pincus worked with John Hammond (later Sir John) at the School of Agriculture and at the Strangeways Laboratory in Cambridge, already famous for cell and organ culture. After a few months of experimenting, he succeeded in keeping rabbit embryos alive in culture fluid, and even tried IVF. It was a notable achievement when culture technology was still a primitive art lacking the antibiotics needed to avoid infections, so Francis Marshall sponsored his paper for publication by the prestigious Royal Society.

Returning to the other Cambridge, he hired Miriam Menkin as an assistant to continue the project with human ova. Ovarian biopsies were supplied by the gynaecologist John Rock at the Free Hospital for Women across town in Boston. As his research began to attract notice, Pincus was bound for a permanent position on Harvard's faculty until he made the mistake of pursuing a pet belief. It was spurred by an observation he made in England that unfertilised ova can divide to look like normal embryos. Could they make fatherless offspring?

He knew parthenogenesis occurs naturally in some insects, and at the Rockefeller Institute in New York it was reported that pricking unfertilised frog ova with a needle made them develop into larvae, and even adults. Somehow, they managed to acquire a normal paired set of chromosomes without a sperm. The parthenotes were all males, but he knew sex in mammals is determined strictly by sperm and, hence, the absence of a male contribution meant their offspring would only be female. He returned in 1937 for more experiments in Cambridge, England, where he undoubtedly met the young Waddington trying to culture embryos at postimplantation stages. Returning to the USA confident in his results, he claimed that parthenogenesis happened under special conditions in vitro or in the cooled fallopian tubes of unmated doe rabbits, producing female offspring as expected. He doubted it ever happens in nature or only rarely.

The American press went wild. The *New York Times* announced *"Rabbits Born in Glass"*, and journalists speculated that "Pincogenesis" would make men superfluous for making babies. But Harvard faculty scowled at the embarrassing publicity, which Pincus never courted but could not avoid. They denied him tenure, said to be for "political reasons", which was perhaps a cover for anti-Semitism.

An experiment never repeated was no longer openly scoffed at after his towering achievement of the first contraceptive pill in the 1950s. Nevertheless, parthenogenesis is still held by experts to be impossible in mammals, except by engineering key genes. Alan Beatty could not see flaws in the Pincus study, whereas Bob was skeptical when he reviewed the claim.

...accidental fertilisation (from an imperfectly vasectomised buck rabbit) could not be excluded as a distinct possibility.[22]

After the wounding episode, Pincus found himself out of work and penniless until he moved to Clark University to join another entrepreneurial scientist. The two subsequently founded the Worcester Foundation for Experimental Biology in Shrewsbury where he dropped embryology and succeeded famously with reproductive endocrinology.

Miriam Menkin was left adrift when Pincus left Harvard and could not afford the fees to finish her PhD, but she was the perfect pick for John Rock who took over the IVF project. He wrote in an anonymous editorial in 1937 that it was "a boon" for barren women with blocked tubes. She ripened ova in vitro and mixed them with sperm to see what would happen. She was fastidious in the lab and a tireless persuader of patients to donate tissue.

Over four years of effort up to 1944, she collected 800 ova for testing in different culture conditions, but hardly any were penetrated by sperm. The proudest result was a 2-cell and a 3-cell "embryo". On hearing the news, the eminent head of embryology George Streeter at the Carnegie Institution of Washington declared they were the "real thing", that is fertilised eggs.

The project was wound up after four more years when IVF seemed hopeless for patients. Rock gave Menkin the honour of being first author of their final paper, which was no less than she deserved but unusual for an assistant. It is impossible to know if the objects they photographed were real embryos or merely the products of parthenogenesis or degeneration. They deserved credit for carrying the torch, although Bob and his contemporaries mostly ignored them, and as far as we know he never discussed the subject with Rock, who lived until 1984. But Rock and Menkin left an important legacy. By flushing embryos from tubes removed during routine surgery they were able to pin-point their precise age after fertilisation because the women volunteered to keep records of their periods and unprotected intercourse. The embryos were transferred to the pathologist Arthur Hertig who prepared them for a library of permanent specimens at the Carnegie Institution. As a timetable of early human development, it was a key reference for embryologists to compare with embryos grown in vitro.

There was surprisingly little outcry about their work, which was supported by the National Research Council and hospital administrators. Many of Rock's patients were Boston Catholics like himself and may have dated pregnancy from when they felt a "quickening", as the first time they were aware of conception. He understood official church policy about contraception, which was illegal even for married couples in Massachusetts, but craftily taught it to medical students. He had seen too many mothers burdened with more children than they could cope with. After closing the IVF project, he accepted an invitation from Pincus to take the clinical lead for trials of a new contraceptive pill, believing that because Pope Pius XII permitted the rhythm method the Pill could be regarded as an extension of the safe period in the menstrual cycle. A later pope, Paul VI, took a harder stand against any unnatural interference with fertility in the papal bull *Humanae Vitae* published in 1968, ten years to the day before Louise Brown was born and never revoked. For his achievements with fertility control, Pincus was nominated for the Nobel Prize but died in 1967 at age 64, and because he could not be honoured neither could Rock or their collaborator, a Chinese immigrant who became a scientific star.

Min-Chueh Chang was a gracious and modest man from Shanxi province who graduated in Peking.[23] He won a scholarship to Edinburgh in the late 1930s to study agriculture, and when John Hammond noticed his talent, he offered a place in Cambridge, which was happily accepted to escape the Scottish climate and diet. After war broke out, a policeman appeared at his door to tell him sheepishly the bicycle he rode, a ubiquitous vehicle in Cambridge, would be confiscated because as a foreigner it was a threat to national security! Chang never lost his fondness for English eccentricity. A commendation for his doctorate by Francis Marshall enabled him to extend his stay as the war with

Japan encroached deep into China, but in the austerity of Britain in 1945 and the continuing troubles in his homeland, he applied to join the Pincus lab in America.

Chang's reputation is forever linked with his work on the Pill, but hormonal studies were distractions from his first love of embryology, just as Bob would wait for a propitious time to return to eggs and embryos after years of contraception research. One of his early discoveries was recognition that sperm must be conditioned, or "capacitated", for several hours in the female body before they can fertilise ova (simultaneously discovered by Bunny Austin in Australia). It was a revelation that scotched his new boss's claim to have achieved IVF in the 1930s. By 1959 he produced the unequivocal evidence of healthy offspring born to surrogate mother rabbits after transferring eggs fertilised in vitro. If Chang had been interested in human IVF, and Rock had been available as a clinical partner, the first human IVF baby might have been born earlier, and in America. But his contributions helped to inspire an Englishman.

5

RUTH

On the first day of a statistics class, Bob introduced himself to a young woman with chestnut hair sitting beside him. That was Ruth Fowler. They didn't remember feeling any special chemistry at that first encounter but became friendly and played doubles at tennis with John Slee and his partner.

Ruth lived in a four-storey tenement block with three other girls, including Ann Silver, a family friend who remembered Ruth as a high-flying intellectual. While her flatmates feverishly prepared for examinations, Ruth would flop on a sofa with her head in a book chosen for curiosity's sake instead of the curriculum but, nevertheless, always had good grades. Edinburgh students chose a specialty subject in their fourth year for their honours degree. Ruth wanted to study physiology in the medical school and took Ann along to discuss the programme, but she didn't take to the director. While Ann enrolled, Ruth switched to genetics, graduating with a first-class degree in 1953, then registered for a PhD at the Institute of Animal Genetics.

The following year, when better acquainted and both were working towards their doctorates, Bob decided to skip a Friday night at the mouse house to invite Ruth to a concert at the Usher Hall. They searched for a coffee house afterwards because Edinburgh closed early in those days. He sucked on an empty pipe while telling her the story of growing up in Manchester with a mother who goaded him to college, and how he hoped for a life in science.

When young men declare their greatest heroes, listeners expect the names of famous sportsmen and musicians, but Bob chose four scientists, impressing on her the seriousness of his career choice. He may have regretted it when she lightly blew him away, replying offhandedly that she was related to two of them. The physicist Ernest Rutherford was her grandfather and the meteorologist Luke Howard was a more distant relative. Bob knew she came from Cambridge, but a family connection with patrician scientists came as a shock. A revelation she rendered so modestly affected him, and the knowledge of her top degree compared to his mere pass dented his pride. As they wandered across the Meadows to separate lodgings, he resolved not to ask her out again. This sudden diffidence in a self-assured man reflected a sensibility still felt across social classes. Ruth did not come from a wealthy or aristocratic background, but the distinction of her family created a gulf.

Rutherford came to Cambridge from New Zealand in 1895 at 24 years old. The great discoveries he would make were not only products of prodigious talent but an immense capacity for work; genius is dormant without intense exercise and never flowers from casual effort. Three years later at McGill University his research on the disintegration of uranium and formulation of nuclear theory won him the Nobel Prize in chemistry in 1908. His biographer, James Chadwick, another nobelist and an old boy from Bob's high school, eulogised: "The change he introduced into atomic theories was not a reformation but a revolution".

Rutherford moved to Manchester, and after the Armistice in 1918 became director of the Cavendish Laboratory in Cambridge, remaining there until his death in 1937. He was interred in

Westminster Abbey among such luminaries as Newton and Darwin.

Ruth's mother, Eileen, was the Rutherfords' only child and she would marry one of her father's colleagues, the mathematician Ralph Fowler. The Fowlers had enviable lives — professional distinction, comfortable home, flourishing family — but there were shadows from tragedy. A brilliant scholar and sportsman, Ralph was badly wounded in the Gallipoli campaign and lost a dear brother at the Somme along with school friends in other battles. Ralph and Eileen settled in the imposing Victorian villa Cromwell House on Trumpington high street, which had four acres of lawns and garden, a stable and orchard. They had a cook, housemaid, two gardeners, and a nanny. Soon after Eileen delivered her fourth baby in 1930, she developed an infection from which she soon died. The child who survived was Ruth Eileen.

Ralph's expertise was in demand and he was often called out of town. Appointment to the Plummer chair of theoretical physics at Cambridge and the offer of directorship of the National Physical Laboratory were extraordinary tributes for a pure mathematician. It was a dilemma to balance work with the care of four young children, and even the most loyal servants cannot replace a mother. The Fowlers were already friends of the Cook family in Cambridge, and after Eileen died, he invited them to move into Cromwell House, knowing their children received the attention he wanted for his own. Phyllida and Derek Cook, another wounded veteran, had an older daughter Lesley, twin girls Joanna and Alison, and a daughter who died in infancy. The family merger was an immense success, and Ralph came home as often as possible, but it wasn't a perfect arrangement. Ruth was an unhappy child.

Her father was engaged for calculating the ballistics of spinning shells and torpedo trajectories in the Great War. He was recalled in 1939 and for this service the King awarded him a knighthood. In 1940 he was sent to collaborate with North American allies and took along his two young daughters to avoid the anticipated Nazi invasion of England. It was a hard decision to split up a family and cross the Atlantic Ocean in wartime, yet parents who sent their children out of the country received taunts for cowardice and disloyalty. There were hugs and kisses on the platform at King's Cross in London as Ruth and her sister Elizabeth and the Cook twins climbed into the railway carriage and gave a final wave when the engine pulled out of the station yard belching smoke.

They sailed from the Liverpool docks on the *Duchess of Atholl*, a large Canadian steamship with twin funnels. It joined a small armada of vessels escorted by a cruiser until they were far out in the ocean, continuing alone on a zigzag course towards the haven of the St. Lawrence River. It was a terrifying voyage scanning for suspicious ripples on the grey waves that might announce a predatory U-boat. Out of the same port a fortnight earlier the *City of Benares* sank with the loss of around 100 lives, many of them children evacuating to Canada. The *Duchess* went down later from an attack near Ascension Island.

The children stayed in Toronto while Ralph took a train for engagements in Washington DC and at Princeton. His two girls boarded with a professor, enrolling at a private school to reflect their social station, but all the children agreed the Cook girls had the happier experience in a more modest home. Elizabeth returned to England two years later to enter the Perse School in Cambridge and proceeded to university in the city before training as a physician in London. The other three children came home in

1944, the year Ralph died of a heart attack at age 55, said to be from overwork.

Ruth loved to be back near the countryside with her pets and horses, although sentimental feelings didn't get in the way of selling rabbits for the local market when rationing made meat scarce. She followed her sister to the Perse where her teachers reported she was a clever and conscientious pupil. Phyllida was an international hockey umpire who encouraged her ward's interest in sport, although Ruth paid a price later as the exertion weakened her hips.

She was a stoical young woman and never shrank from expressing opinions about matters she felt strongly about, even after she married a strong-willed husband. She resisted pressure to follow the family tradition to Cambridge University until she changed her mind at the last moment, but too late to win a scholarship in 1949 she went to Edinburgh instead.

After graduating in genetics, Ruth chose Douglas Falconer to supervise her doctoral research because he was closest to her original interest in physiology. Douglas used selective breeding to produce giant and dwarf strains of mice, which he hoped would reveal the genetic basis of differences in body size. He handed this ambitious project to Ruth. She measured body size and carcass composition but could only dream of measuring growth hormones that might explain differences since methods were not available then.

Douglas was the doyen of quantitative genetics, which requires the narrative to pause for explanation (or readers to skip over). Classical Mendelian genetics made great strides when the subject was new because it focused on genes with pronounced effects entirely their own. Douglas specialised in the harder goal of identifying genes for complex traits that are common. To take an elementary case comparable to Mendel's pea plants, a single copy mutation of the dominant gene *FGFR3* causes dwarfism in humans and has a simple pattern of inheritance. If both a man and woman carry one mutant and one normal copy of the gene, their children have a three in four chance of being short in stature like themselves, while the fourth child is expected on average to be of normal size. But instead of clear-cut differences, most heritable traits vary across a spectrum that require special statistical methods. For instance, many genes affect the amount of meat in beef carcasses and milk from dairy cows, each contributing a fraction of the total effect. Quantitative genetics has huge implications for human health, too, including fecundity, a field Bob would make his own, and most degenerative diseases are genetically complex, not least the diabetes which Douglas suffered from.

Waddington put Douglas in charge of the mouse house because he needed the largest colony of animals. It took diplomacy to balance the demands of pushy young men and women who vie for animal accommodation. Mary Lyon's colony grew so much she moved to Harwell for more space, and Bob's murine empire was an expanding hegemony. He soon had more cages than his supervisor, even pressing to double his allocation for over a thousand animals. He needed them for multiple projects, including a new one he launched with Ruth. His ambition made seasoned scientists shake their heads, but after five years he succeeded in picking the dangling fruit of most projects, although it took several more years to write them all for publication. The final tally was almost 40 papers.

The slow fuse of friendship with Ruth burned hotter one day in the mouse house as they chatted over the top of racks while they worked with animals. After a couple of years of the night shift, Bob wanted to liberate time for some social life, which meant time with Ruth. It led to collaboration as well as romance.

A wild idea shared with Ruth came into his head after over-hearing his supervisor discuss an experiment with an American visitor. Allen Gates was a courteous, clean-cut Yankee who trained at the Jackson Laboratory in Maine, regarded as "mouse heaven" by animal geneticists. Allen had brought a supply of a hormone extracted from pregnant mare's blood (PMSG), which has the proprietary name *Pregnyl*. It sounded like a potion concocted by the three weird sisters in *Macbeth*, but Allen assured Alan Beatty it stimulated follicle growth in mouse ovaries. It was the only hormone possessing that property apart from its natural counterpart in the pituitary gland, follicle-stimulating hormone (FSH), and that was rarer than gold dust. At the Jackson, he found a shot of PMSG followed two days later with the pregnancy hormone, human chorionic gonadotrophin (HCG), advanced the age of puberty in mice, and they ovulated dozens of ova at once.

These striking results were seeds for human fertility treat-ment, though recognised as such only with hindsight. The aphro-disiac treatment mimicked the natural sequence of gonadotrophic hormones, FSH to stimulate follicles to grow and LH (luteinizing hormone) to make them ovulate and attract hot males. Allen went to Edinburgh to acquire techniques for testing ova from superov-ulation as no one was sure if they were fertile. He knew that if juvenile mice mated to generate fertilised eggs the uterus was still too immature to allow implantation. He needed Alan Beatty to help transfer them to adult animals as a test of pregnancy potential.

When Bob asked if superovulation worked in adult animals the other two shook their heads. Everyone knew that PMSG inter-fered with natural hormones, but Bob was not a man who easily took no for an answer. He cajoled Ruth to help him test Allen's hormones on their fully-grown mice. There was more than scientific curiosity at stake for her too. Her giant mice were lazy lovers and the dwarfs (Bob dubbed them "Peter Pan mice") never became fully mature. If they were superovulated and mated she could make more of their kind, but if the embryos failed to implant there was the option of transferring their embryos to surrogate mothers. For Bob, there was a potential double pay-out: he would harvest more ova and control his timetable by choosing when to inject animals.

They gave each animal three units of PMSG and the same of HCG two days apart. By breakfast time the next morning they would know if ovulation happened. After warnings by higher authority that they were wasting their time there could only be timid hopes, and so it was with enormous triumph and great satisfaction that Bob burst into Beatty's office to proclaim it worked perfectly! The tubes in all their animals were bursting with ova. Instead of 10, there were 20, 30, or even more. It was a notable breakthrough and although they did not count their chickens from a pilot experiment, the news buzzed around the institute. They found the experiment worked every time, which was remarkable because fertility is a fickle thing. Ruth bred more animals, and Bob stopped haunting the mouse house at night.

They published their discovery in the *Journal of Endocrinology* in 1957, with Ruth as the first author. It was the first of a series of joint papers describing methods that were quickly adopted worldwide and still used today. Next, they asked the question that brought Allen to Edinburgh. Were superovulated ova healthy? Another batch of mice was given the dual treatment and paired with males to see if they became pregnant. The first signs were encouraging, but their delight changed to alarm when mice became so gross they dragged their bellies across the cage floor. Superovulation generated a superpregnancy. Caesarean sections were needed to deliver pups early because it was unkind to let mothers go to full-term. The forked uterus of every pregnant animal was so overcrowded with fetuses they looked like pairs of pink and brown sausages, pushing organs aside, pressing on the diaphragm, and straining for enough blood to nourish the load. The experiment foreshadowed a negative aspect of human fertility treatment with ovarian stimulation, and now recalls the ill-famed case of a woman dubbed "Octomom" by the media because she delivered octuplets after excessive doses of fertility hormones.[24]

The natural quota of ovulations in a species has evolved to match the optimal number of fetuses that can be accommodated in the uterus: from one in humans to ten in mice. Even twin pregnancies are riskier than singletons in our species. Of course, animals like frogs and sea urchins with external fertilisation must superovulate willy-nilly to maximise their chances of leaving descendants in an unprotected environment. Ruth and Bob had forced their mice to behave like elephant shrews and relatives of chinchillas which ovulate large numbers of ova before natural wastage eliminates the excess for safely delivering a small litter.

Unlike some hormones, fertility hormones are not highly specific, even acting across a gulf as wide as from amphibians to mammals. That is why PMSG from horses works in humans, and HCG from humans became a mainstay in animal production technology, but it was preferable to use hormones from the same species. Antibody formation in women blunted the effects of PMSG, so where would human FSH be found?

Carl Gemzell in Uppsala was extracting growth hormone from the pituitary glands of human cadavers. He had little interest in the small fraction with gonadotrophic potency because treating children of small stature was the priority. It was stored at the back of his freezer and forgotten.

Egon Diczfalusy, a gynaecologist at the Karolinska Hospital famed for discovering the source of oestrogen in pregnancy, asked Gemzell if he had enough FSH to test in patients. He wondered if women with healthy ovaries who never had a period in their lives could be stimulated to ovulate. A few days after injecting the hormone, oestrogen levels were higher in urine to confirm that follicles were growing for the first time, and a subsequent shot of HCG triggered their ovulation. It was a striking parallel with the Edwards' studies in mice on the other side of the North Sea, but Bob didn't know a supply of human FSH existed until he moved to America in 1958.

Diczfalusy was a member of the G-Club, named for specialists interested in the gonadotrophins and cofounded in 1953 by Bruno Lunenfeld, then training in Switzerland to be a doctor after retiring from the Irgun. It was a ginger group to improve fertility treatment. A meagre supply of FSH from Sweden only enabled about 100 pregnancies across several European countries by the mid-1960s. Parenthood brought immense joy after years of trying for a baby, although a few patients tragically developed Creutzfeldt-Jakob syndrome, a progressive form of dementia caused by prion proteins in post-mortem tissue. It foreshadowed similar symptoms reported 40 years later from mad cow disease. There would soon be happier news from a safe and abundant source of FSH — urine!

The pituitary gland, ovaries, and placenta are endocrine organs that "talk" to each other via hormones to coordinate the progression of menstrual cycles to pregnancy to birth. Rising levels of oestrogen and progesterone "talk down" gonadotrophins from the pituitary gland to stop follicle growth and ovulation in pregnancy. It is a phenomenon mimicked by the contraceptive pill. But when the follicle store is empty after the menopause, ovarian hormone levels crash, and the pituitary behaves like a gland frustrated by a lack of hormonal chitchat. It pours more FSH and LH into the bloodstream as if in a fit of shouting to get a reply from the ovaries that never comes. Levels of FSH rise ten-fold in urine, which is a far easier medium to extract hormones than either blood or gland tissue.

The Italian chemist Piero Donini at a drug company later called Serono understood this physiology in the 1940s. When America halted drug exports to Europe during the war, he extracted insulin from beef pancreas to treat diabetes. After the peace he turned to FSH, drawing on his earlier experience of purifying HCG from human pregnancy urine.

Laboratory chemicals were in limited supply in 1947, so he rummaged in the boiler room for sacks of *Permutit* (zeolite) used to soften water. After loading the granules in a chromatography column, he poured a pot of urine from menopausal women in the top, hoping for drips of concentrated hormones out the bottom. The column clogged. Next time he mixed the urine with kaolin, and after further treatment passed it through the column. This time persistence paid off with a potent product. "Eureka!" After further refinements, he published the method in a company journal, casually mentioning that the semi-purified FSH might be useful for patients. It is almost identical to the hormone in younger women, but he gave it a new name, human menopausal gonadotrophin (abbreviated HMG), later known as *Pergonal*. The drug would eventually become standard treatment around the globe, including the clinic created by Bob and his associates, but for several years Donini's paper gathered dust in a Rome library.

HMG didn't get attention until the G-Club met in that city in 1957. Diczfalusy was astounded to hear an active preparation existed nearby at Serono's HQ. He told Bruno who was engaged in his own struggle for FSH, said to be motivated by a quest to help infertile Jewish people after the war. As a young, idealistic man, Bruno was sure he could convince company directors to produce HMG on a commercial scale, but they courteously turned him down, for where would they find enough menopausal urine?

His optimism was vindicated when board member Guilio Pacelli petitioned his uncle Eugenio Pacelli, better known as Pope Pius XII. Reigning from 1939 to 1958, this pontiff had a more progressive attitude to medicine, science, and family-building than his predecessor, although his reputation suffered from failing to condemn Nazi atrocities. Perhaps that is why he chose to help a young Jewish doctor, although the Vatican had another motive as it owned a majority of Serono shares. In one of the most bizarre episodes in the annals of the pharmaceutical industry, company operatives collected urine from hundreds of retired nuns across Italy, transporting the liquor in tankers to Rome where Donini had a production plant to extract HMG.

There is a splendid irony here. Hormones from women who took vows for lifelong chastity and were past childbearing age helped younger women to have babies. Treatment with a natural drug was deemed compatible with Catholic doctrine provided it aimed to overcome a failure of ovulation, but it was never approved for use with IVF patients after 1980. HMG from nuns carried little risk of contamination or pregnancy hormones that could jeopardise treatment, but it took 25 nun-days of urine collection to make enough HMG for a full cycle.

Bruno's superior at an Israeli hospital insisted he test the safety of HMG on himself before starting a trial on patients. An injection in his buttocks left him sore, but otherwise there was surprisingly little reaction from a product only 2% pure. His first patient, who hadn't had a period for six years, conceived immediately after sequential treatment with HMG and HCG. She delivered a healthy girl in 1962. Religious conservatives accused him of cheating Providence, an early warning shot of opposition to come with IVF, but the news was widely celebrated. When the Italian authorities approved general sales, demand for the drug soared because physicians had nothing to offer patients. These were the first ripples of a tide seeking treatment. More companies entered the field and more purified forms of the drug were manufactured, but they struggled to collect thousands of litres of urine needed to meet international orders, so they turned to the emerging technology of recombinant DNA technology. Molecular medicine promised almost unlimited quantities of FSH, and so pure that patients could inject themselves, like insulin for diabetes.

While HMG was still growing frost in a Serono freezer, Bob was focused on animal biology. After submitting his dissertation, Wad awarded him a fellowship for two more years in Edinburgh, which enabled the collaboration with Ruth and for her to finish doctoral work. Perhaps it was teamwork that brought them together as a couple, and there was something more than intelligence he respected about her. Reluctant to use make-up and never a follower of fashion, she was exactly as she seemed, and that was part of her beauty. On a rare break for a fortnight in the Lake District of England, they hiked in the hills together, and the conversation veered away from mouse gynaecology to something else. Bob had a modest salary and could not offer her security, but Ruth had a practical mind and prevailed over his caution. She urged realistic goals for wedded life together and suggested they start with a honeymoon in Italy. He thought it was too extravagant but finally agreed on a savings target of £125 (£3,000 at current value).

They chose a wedding date in the summer of 1956, but first she had to introduce him to her family, which included not only her brothers and sister but Phyllida and her family too. Derek

Cook had died. For all the years as her ward, Ruth could never call her "Mum", but she felt deep respect and affection for the woman. She groomed her man from Manchester for the interview, crossing fingers the family would not think he was brash and hoped he would warm to the broad conversation that animated their home.

She travelled ahead to the Cotswolds where the wedding would be held in the summer. After the two families grew up together in Cambridge, they went separate ways at the end of the 1940s. One of the Cooks became a farmer and Phyllida settled nearby in the village of Shipton-under-Wychwood where she named her new home Cromwell House after the beloved one in Trumpington.

When apart, the now engaged couple frequently exchanged letters in which they mixed domestic and scientific news. In one, he reported their latest joint paper was ready for submission to *Endocrinology*, but his supervisor made critical comments that were "not good". In another, he swore he would never ask her to iron his shirts because he had purchased nylon ones. He had good intentions denying he would lay domestic burdens on her because she had a career of her own, although she would indeed carry them when they had a family. He often addressed her as "Rufus", although it is a man's name and she wasn't a redhead. Her baptised name Ruth was a much better fit for a loyal and patient wife, mother, and collaborator, and fulfilled the meaning of that name—she was his friend too.

They rendezvoused at the Cheltenham railway station from where she drove to the village. Her family remembered him as a courteous, well-dressed young man. He soon got into a good-humoured conversation, although the twins muttered that he rushed words too quickly with a northern accent to catch their meaning. The interview was an ordeal, and it was a relief to get back to Edinburgh where there was a letter waiting from Phyllida.

I am so very glad that you enjoyed your weekend with us. It would have been quite an ordeal, especially (I hope!) in anticipation. For our part we were very happy to welcome you as one of the family, and any apprehensions ... have been cast aside in the most auspicious manner.[25]

Soon afterwards, Bob attended John's marriage at a Scottish kirk, a doubly proud moment after both graduated with PhDs in Edinburgh. Bob's father shared his son's sly sense of humour, saying he had a medical appointment with a "real doctor", and complimented his son's good fortune for not footing the bill as best man at John's wedding. Someone had told Samuel an apocryphal story about a Scottish convention.

The Slees settled permanently in the Edinburgh region where John pursued a scientific career, at one time studying how sheep acclimatise to the Scottish climate. The Edwards would make several moves after their marriage before they settled in Cambridge. Family members from Manchester and colleagues from Edinburgh, including John as best man, came down to the ceremony in the medieval parish church at Shipton-under-Wychwood.

After the honeymoon, Bob and Ruth returned to their Edinburgh flat for a final year before spreading their wings. But where would they fly? In the New Year of 1957, she was finishing her dissertation and their future looked precarious as they would both be unemployed in the autumn. Bob was on the lookout for jobs and cornered Alan Parkes after a lecture at the institute, urging the distinguished guest to invest in genetics research. Parkes was impressed with his credentials and ebullient enthusiasm, offering him a junior staff position at his London laboratory, but not until later the next year. But what would the couple do in the gap year?

Research posts in reproduction were never plentiful, and fishing for bridging positions didn't draw bites in the UK. It is a perennial problem for academics to find jobs in the same location, compounded when they are at the same level in the same specialty. Ruth was unsuccessful at an interview and called Bob to express disappointment before he left Edinburgh for a few days. He left a tender message on the mantelshelf for her to read when she came back, acknowledging the freedom she surrendered when she became his wife.

... I am sorry you are married, for that is your greatest handicap. However, your husband loves you very much and he will make up for disappointments ...[26]

His message was seasoned with news of family and science, grumbling that 23 mice failed to mate the night before. He assumed she needed that information and was lucky to have a partner who would always understand.

He was waiting to hear back about an application to an American laboratory. A trans-Atlantic journey was a rite of passage for many British and European scientists, and time spent at a prestigious university or institute put a final gloss coat on a curriculum vitae before stepping on the academic ladder at home. The obvious destinations were in Massachusetts with Gregory Pincus or at the Jackson Laboratory where Allen Gates trained, but Bob reached further afield to the more exotic location of the California Institute of Technology in Pasadena.

There was great relief when a letter arrived from Albert Tyler, an expert in fertilisation and immunology, offering him a year at Caltech. Bob would later dismiss the episode as "a bit of a holiday". It was a change in the direction of research, from which he would backtrack later, disappointed it didn't produce another bumper crop of papers. For him, California was diastole to Edinburgh's systole, but he underestimated its significance. When weighed with new connections and fresh ideas the year shaped his future course, moving him another rung up the ladder.

6

BLUE SKY

Bob and Ruth sailed from Southampton in August 1957 on what was a pleasure trip compared to Ruth's voyage 16 years earlier. She could enjoy a peaceful week at sea while Bob read about a New World he would visit repeatedly.

They boarded a train at Penn Station in Manhattan bound for Detroit where they bought a second-hand Plymouth automobile for a leisurely journey across country. Bob was mostly in the driver's seat, steering along straight highways and twisting country roads through vast acreages of fields and over mountain passes that challenged the lumbering gas guzzler to speeds that could catch the notice of the Highway Patrol. Mirages simmered over asphalt, and in the heat of day without air conditioning they rolled down windows to catch the breeze.

Road journeys were much slower before the arterial system of interstate highways and bypasses, and more adventurous. It was the first time he had met Americans on their home ground after encounters in the army. Their openness and optimism chimed with his own character, and that a man's attire or accent did not advertise social status or wealth matched his ideals. And, yet, he had ambiguous feelings, admiring the supremacy in science and technology, but loathing unfettered capitalism that left millions of citizens behind.

Towards evening, they watched for mom and pop motels to spend the night and reflect on what they had seen. Everything, except the language, was different. There was the sheer size of the country, little towns of white clapboard houses and churches floating in oceans of corn, a landscape that changed from plains to mountains to high deserts quite unlike those Bob had seen in the Middle East. When they spotted the first saguaro cactus with its "hands up" they knew they had arrived in cowboy country and were closing in on California. What would people in Gorton say if they saw him now, those who thought a trip to the Blackpool Lights was the highlight of a year?

Pasadena was no less contrasting. Its wide boulevards were lined with palm trees and gracious homes with porches set back from pavements, and sprinklers played on manicured lawns. There was not a speck of soot.

Caltech nestles in one of its neighbourhoods, a compact and elegant campus of white stucco buildings with rows of evergreen oaks and olive trees. Its appearance owes nothing to Gothic architecture and much to a Spanish style fit for the climate. There would be no fall leaves that year, and cheerful blue skies and warm nights replaced the dreary weather in Britain.

They rented a furnished apartment on the corner of San Pasqual Street, a two-minute walk from the Division of Biology. Shopping was still a humbling experience in England that only recently emerged from post-war rationing, so they were amazed at the range of fresh foods and consumer goods, and how far Bob's stipend stretched. When they heard English voices next-door, they introduced themselves to Huw and Maggie Pritchard. He was a computational chemist from Manchester on sabbatical leave in Linus Pauling's department. They were neighbours for a year and made an enduring friendship after the Pritchards settled in Canada and the Edwards returned home.

At first sight, his decision to join the Tyler lab was an odd choice, for it wasn't the lure of surf, sand, and sunshine that brought them to California. Albert studied marine worms and sea urchins whereas Bob was a mammalian embryologist with a growing ambition for human biology. But his new mentor had a tremendous breadth, ranging from developmental biology to physiology and ecology, which is hard to emulate today. There was also the chance to meet other heavyweight professors and visitors like Lord Rothschild, a Cambridge zoologist who wrote a monograph on fertilisation that year at Caltech.[27] Most of all, the lab offered him the chance to learn immunology and its boundless possibilities, something that was missing in his training. Albert had conjugated immunology with reproduction to create "immunoreproduction", which faintly echoed Brambell's hybrid in Bangor.

A native of New York, Albert moved to Caltech in 1928 with his mentor, Thomas Hunt Morgan, winner of a Nobel Prize for the chromosome theory of inheritance. Morgan was famous for studying fruit flies but had a deep interest in marine biology too. He often drove down the coast to the Corona del Mar to collect specimens with his protégé and their friend Linus Pauling.

It is tempting to wonder if Pauling had an influence on Bob. Although they worked in different departments the greater informality of senior American scientists compared to British kingpins surely enabled the two men to brush shoulders in the campus or at parties. Bob was never too shy to introduce himself. Pauling was one of the most celebrated scientists in the world after his Nobel Prize for the chemical bond, and he was a pioneering molecular biologist who, had he not stumbled in the race, would have beaten Watson and Crick to DNA. He won a second Prize later, that time for Peace. As much as his eminence in science, Bob would have respected his principled stand in the peace movement and the suffering he endured from harassment in the McCarthy years. He was a brilliant example of a public intellectual for a young man who would have his own battles with the Establishment when he returned to England.

The Population Council in New York funded Bob's fellowship and Albert's team. Reproductive biology lacked the deep pockets of the common killer diseases, but paranoia about world population growth brought it some golden years. The growth of human numbers had never stopped since Antiquity, notwithstanding plagues, pandemics, and world wars. The first person to raise a warning was Thomas Malthus, who predicted populations would outgrow their ability to feed themselves. If that prospect struck alarm in early 19th century England, it rang a doomsday bell in the 1950s when our teeming numbers passed 2.5 billion. Malthus was a numerate Anglican priest whose mathematical rationale was easy to grasp.

Population when unchecked, increases in geometrical ratio. Subsistence increases only in an arithmetical ratio. A slight acquaintance with numbers will show the immensity of the first power in comparison of the second.[28]

This rumble from the past grew to a roar when Paul Ehrlich prophesied an apocalypse from his scientific pulpit at Stanford. Earlier in the century there were indictments the "wrong" kinds of people were being born, but after the repudiation of eugenics from World War 2 a new fear emerged: there were too many of us. A taxi ride through the crowded slums of Delhi turned Ehrlich into an evangelist for fertility control which he fused with an intellectual understanding of population dynamics. His best-selling book predicted violent conflict, pollution, and starvation would collapse our civilisation.[29] The stork had passed the plough.

Malthus had a moral solution—abstinence—evidently observed more in theory than practice during his era because families increased to record sizes. Not until the next century did efficient contraception and safe sterilisation become widely available and accepted, largely owing to the advocacy of Margaret Sanger in the USA and Marie Stopes in the UK. In the late 1950s, they paraded the revolutionary new Pill engineered by Pincus and Rock.

The United Nations and numerous governmental and non-profit organisations endorsed efforts to avoid unplanned pregnancies, said to be 40% of the total, and sponsored contraceptive services in countries that had high birth rates. The Ford Foundation in New York offered grants for reproduction research, funding Bob for two decades in London and Cambridge. The Population Council rolled out a similar portfolio, founded in 1952 by John D. Rockefeller III at a meeting in Williamsburg, Virginia, where his father sponsored restoration of the colonial city.

Albert's commitment to human population science was no contradiction for a beachcombing biologist. With his brother Edward, a physician-scientist affiliated to UCLA, they belonged to an international network with collaborators in New York, Amsterdam, and Bombay. They tested for antibodies in semen and blood for binding sperm into clumps ("agglutination"), which would imply interference with fertilisation. Some men and women were positive, especially prostitutes, and some of those were infertile, nourishing the idea of a contraceptive vaccine. Vaccination was a familiar and accepted practice to avoid infection all over the world; if it could eradicate polio, why not knock out sperm? That was the challenge Albert offered Bob.

It was not an original idea. There was a connection between Albert's studies of sea urchins and an older history that went back to the early days of immunology. In 1912, Frank Lillie in Chicago noticed that water from tanks containing sea urchin eggs caused sperm to agglutinate into immotile clots and lose fertility. Under a microscope he watched the process: freshly dispersed sperm gradually coalesced in "egg-water" like cumulus clouds to finally resemble cumulonimbus as more sperm were caught up. These cloud names coined by Ruth's ancestor Luke Howard perfectly fitted the phenomenon.

Lillie called the unknown substance "fertilizin", and the molecule it locked on the sperm surface "antifertilizin". When Albert entered the field, he found fertilizin originated in the jelly coat around eggs and the molecules had at least two binding sites held out like hands to grab sperm which formed into bunches and chains. It was a paradox if eggs produced a substance to block fertilisation, but he knew there must be a rationale, perhaps as a protective device against too many sperm by analogy with his Gila monsters that needed ways to avoid poisoning by their own venom. More than that, it reminded him of antibodies that cause blood clotting in people transfused with an unmatched blood group. Although analogies are never perfect, the controlled production of antibodies to knockout sperm was a compelling idea.

At the turn of the century, the European grandee who discovered phagocytes, Élie Metchnikoff, and another who first described human ABO blood groups, Karl Landsteiner, injected bull semen into guinea-pigs to generate anti-sperm antibodies. The possibility of developing a contraceptive vaccine was captivating, but immunisation of women against sperm in South America failed and a US patent for the process came to nothing in the 1930s. Albert had a thick file of reports in animals and humans from the previous 60 years, but no study was convincing.

Bob embraced the project with typical enthusiasm for here was a chance to make a breakthrough for human good with novel technology. Among its attractions, a vaccine would not interrupt menstrual cycles, and few people would balk about blocking fertility *before* fertilisation. The Population Council network had evidence that people with antibodies remained in otherwise good health, except for extremely rare cases of anaphylactic shock after exposure to sperm during intercourse. There was potential for a contraceptive vaccine in men as well as women, but what looked like a winning situation had drawbacks. Would it be reversible, for if not it was another form of sterilisation? Could it neutralise the horde of sperm? The immune system can be boosted with adjuvants, but they were too toxic for human use.

Bob's commission was basic research, and any promising discoveries arising would be transferred for others to take forward in clinical trials. He already had experience from vaccinating animals in Edinburgh where he tried to control the sex ratio of offspring. This was a bold attempt after news of a unique male antigen, called H-Y. He thought by making antibodies to H-Y he could exclusively block fertilisation by male sperm, so that only female pups would be born, which could be a boon to the poultry and dairy industries. The project was abandoned, although the pipedream of controlling the sex ratio came true in other ways.

In his first experiments at Caltech, he vaccinated female mice with sperm and gave saline injections to a control group which should be unaffected. He hoped to find the test group would fail to conceive after mating and continue in good health with uninterrupted oestrous cycles. After several weeks, he sighed for he had 50 "happily pregnant mice" in the vaccinated group, the same number as controls. The antibodies were too weak to hamper sperm. It was a bitter disappointment after a bigger investment of effort than this summary describes. He filed the data away, wondering what to do with them, if anything.

He did not know that Anne McLaren had taken the same path independently after moving from London to his former institute in Edinburgh. They had parallel careers, and both leaned to the left-wing of politics, although their backgrounds were poles apart (she was the daughter of the 2nd Baron Aberconway) and he was impulsive compared to her cautious and systematic nature.

Anne had more success than he had. Antibodies generated in her mice impaired fertility, giving encouragement for a new kind of contraceptive. Bob was gobsmacked when her paper came out in 1962. He never understood how similar methods could produce different results. When he moved to London, he brushed the dust off his American notebooks to publish his data and was lucky because editors tend to snub negative results. Their papers puzzled readers who wondered which carried the greater authority, because they appeared in the same journal (*Nature*) and were funded by the same organisation (Ford) with opposite conclusions. Bob's interpretation was prudent for we are still without a contraceptive vaccine against sperm, nor indeed for any other target in reproduction.

Apart from that short report, he had little on paper to show for his time at Caltech. It wasn't for lack of trying, or the temptation of Santa Monica beach, but because other experiments turned out negative too. Every scientist confronts this problem, and Bob confounded historians by leaving no lab notebooks from that era to pore over. With eyes fixed on the horizon, he seldom looked back. If he ever jotted bright ideas on a fabled napkin or back of an envelope it was never curated for a museum display but swept like autumn leaves into the trash for landfills.

However, not all his negative results disappeared, thanks to the care of others. Albert gave him freedom for the blue-sky research he loved and reported some of the missing data at his prestigious Oliver Bird lecture after Bob moved to London. The study built on unfinished work in Edinburgh to control the sex-ratio with a new strategy to capture different targets to H-Y using antibodies raised in female mice against sperm. In Albert's words, published after the lecture:

He ingeniously tried to "stack the cards" by repeatedly backcrossing males of one inbred strain of mice to females of another so that he would obtain individuals in which the Y chromosome of one strain (A) ... was associated with a background of autosomal genes that were largely from the other strain (B) ... then used the spermatozoa of these males actively to immunize the females of Strain B.[30]

Back-crossing is a clever strategy requiring several generations of mating of hybrid animals back to the parental type to transfer genes from one strain to another. It was a well-conceived plan and a huge endeavour, but it, too, ended with a 50:50 ratio of male to female pups in immunised females. Bob sat in the audience as Albert praised his endeavour, but behind a glowing smile he was frustrated by another failure with sperm and resolved to stick to eggs.

Another forgotten study that was rediscovered only recently among Tyler's papers in the college archives was Ruth's project. They record an extraordinary effort as an unpaid researcher collaborating with Albert and his technician; it had hallmarks of her husband's dabbling too, who was supposed to be fully occupied with vaccines but could never stay away from an exciting new project.

She wanted to fertilise mouse ova in vitro, but that was too much to expect within the year, so she started with embryos already fertilised (i.e., in vivo). It was a bold hope only a year after an Australian report in which 32-cell embryos (called morulas because they look like mulberries) doubled in size in a dish to become hollow balls, called blastocysts. This is the stage before implantation. The result was more convincing than Gregory Pincus's claim over 20 years earlier and was a milestone in embryology. For technology that is now routine it is hard to imagine the struggle in the 1950s, and it took a decade of effort before the entire span from fertilisation to blastocyst was achieved in vitro.

The records at Caltech reveal that Ruth set up experiments seven days a week, only pausing for Christmas and New Year's Day. They were directed more by trial and error than a systematic comparison of culture conditions, foreshadowing the way Bob would develop human IVF. Mouse embryos were cultured in almost every conceivable way: in glass dishes, plastic boxes, hanging droplets, even salt cellars (*sic*). They tried different supplements in the culture fluid: amniotic fluid, ascites fluid, blood serum from varied species, pyruvate as a simple carbohydrate for embryos to digest. They used HeLa cells, the immortal cell line derived from Henrietta Lacks' cancer, hoping they would feed embryos in place of the fallopian tubes. They tried culturing embryos in Puck's medium, not a fanciful label but named for a doyen of cell culture who created the cells now used in bioreactors for synthesising gonadotrophins. After discouraging results, Ruth shipped embryos by air to Dr Puck in Denver, Colorado, to see if he could get better results. He did not. The effort was exhausting and after six months there was little more to show than Bob had with his vaccines.

Every time freshly fertilised eggs were placed in culture they refused to develop beyond the 2-cell stage, an obstacle that soon stymied other researchers entering the field. There was the rare reward of an embryo making it to the morula or even blastocyst stage, but the culture medium was often infected with bugs. They didn't know if embryos were harmed by their short stay in an artificial medium, a critical issue in future for human IVF, so Bob checked the chromosomes. They were always normal diploid. A more definitive answer came later that year in Edinburgh where Allen Gates showed Anne McLaren how to transfer embryos from culture to surrogate mothers. She found they implanted in the uterus and delivered healthy pups two weeks later. This was encouraging evidence that IVF would be safe too. Bob read her paper in September as he prepared to sail home with Ruth, probably wishing they had done the experiment.

Another observation Ruth made is more significant in hindsight. When some blastocysts hatched out of their shells, a necessary step before implantation, she wondered what the naked embryos would do in a glass dish without a juicy uterus to bury themselves. Most of them died, but one had outgrowths sticking to the dish, and every day spread further until there were countless thousands of cells four months later. They no longer looked embryonic, more like fibroblasts, but there were no other differentiated cells. In a more enigmatic entry, she recorded a mass of small cells growing for ten days without changing appearance but paid little attention as they looked nondescript. Was this a patch of embryo stem cells for, if so, it would be a world first? She would not have been the first to miss a sublime object for in the 1820s two Swiss scientists searching for mammalian ova noticed tiny spheres in ovarian follicles and threw away the very objects they longed to find.[31] Her observations never appeared in print, but they may have lingered at the back of Bob's mind as three years later he started another blue-sky project to isolate the now renowned embryo stem cells.

If published pages are counted as an index of productivity, Bob's time in America was a letdown, but some benefits cannot be weighed so easily. It was in California where he first witnessed a productive collaboration between a scientist, Albert Tyler, and his brother Edward, a gynaecologist committed to research. Edward was a federal consultant for the first oral contraceptive and ran a clinical trial for clomiphene citrate, the anti-oestrogenic drug that Bob's team would use one day as a substitute for HMG. Gynaecology is a peculiar field that faces opposite directions at once, like the head and tail of a coin, helping to restrain fertility in some people and promoting it for others. Edward Tyler campaigned for fertility control and was an advocate for infertile patients. In his 1950 address to the American Medical Association at San Francisco, he called infertility a field of deep neglect and ignorance, and no field was more difficult to evaluate and treat. He was the kind of clinician Bob would need as a partner one day.

It would be false to depict the Edwards duo as feverishly bent on science to the exclusion of all else. They had an enviable gift of switching off to take an interest in their surroundings. In April 1958, they took a short vacation to Borrego Springs before the desert heated up in summer. Bob pulled his sleeping bag out of the tent to watch the stars where there was no light pollution, like dark nights he knew in the dales. He mused that his fellowship could be extended for another year, and maybe lead to a permanent job in California. There were vast opportunities in America, but he would miss the becks and fells back home, and old friends. Ruth was reluctant to live so far away from her family, and a few weeks later she announced she was pregnant with their first child, expected in January. Yes, they would go home.

They planned another trip to see national parks with the Pritchards where they set up camp in Yosemite Valley. He was first up the next morning in khaki shorts, rolling up sleeves to cook breakfast. In the chill-air of the evenings, they lit a campfire to chinwag about almost anything except science. There was only one exception, a throw-away remark before setting out that stuck in Maggie's mind. They arranged to rendezvous at the campus before jumping in cars, but Bob did not turn up at the appointed time. Ruth led their friends to track him down, finding him still in the mouse house. When they opened the door, he was scurrying to finish work and examining a mouse by holding it by the base of its tail. Maggie asked what he was doing.

"Margaret", he said, "one day because of this mouse a woman who cannot now have a baby will be able to have one." Those words came back forcefully 20 years later when she read headlines in Toronto's *The Globe and Mail* reporting the birth of Louise Brown.

7

BLASTOCYSTS

There were personal and professional reasons for the Edwards to return home in 1958, but it came with a jolt as well as with joy. They were back among family and friends in familiar places, but had exchanged blissful California for grey clouds, cold bedrooms, and the native diet. Had Ruth been more willing, Bob might have stayed in the USA, but then history would have been different.

He had a five-year contract with Alan Parkes as a research officer at the National Institute for Medical Research (NIMR), a hothouse of medical science at Mill Hill in north-west London, the British equivalent of the National Institutes of Health (NIH).[32] On a modest salary of £1,250, inner London house prices were out of reach, but further afield in the village of Elstree, Hertfordshire, they found a pleasant row of 3- and 4-bedroom houses on Deacons Hill Road. One of them for sale was affordable at £4,850 with a mortgage and a down payment from American savings. There was enough left to buy an old Morris 8 for Bob to drive five miles to work.

Although Ruth became a homemaker, she filled her spare time by writing and editing papers with her husband. She was not going to drop out of science and kept abreast of research as best she could. Their first daughter Caroline arrived soon after moving in, and Jennifer was born the year after. Apart from weekend trips to Kew Gardens and Hampton Court, they made few excursions.

West End theatres and city dining were expensive and, anyway, London was rather staid, and the dynamism we now know was some years off.

At the NIMR, Bob had boundless opportunities and the freedom to exercise his scientific imagination. There were outstanding people on the staff from every branch of biomedicine, and the institute's state-of-the-art equipment and medical library were the envy of universities. Without students to teach, he could plunge into research without interruptions and attend seminars by staff and visitors to broaden his knowledge of medicine as well as science.

Alan Parkes (later Sir Alan) was head of Bob's division and became his boss again in Cambridge.[33] He was Britain's foremost expert in reproduction and, despite a headmasterly manner with a crop of silver hair, he had a wicked sense of humour entirely lacking in his intimidating wife and collaborator, Ruth Deanesly. Alan grew up an undistinguished scholar at Oldham Grammar School in Lancashire, earning a place to study agriculture at Cambridge more as a reward for service in the First World War than on academic merit. Assignment to a college was a lottery, so it was fortuitous that he went to Christ's where Francis Marshall was a fellow and author of the standard textbook. He stimulated Alan's inquiring mind to specialise in reproductive biology and steered him towards a PhD at Manchester to study the sex ratio in animals. Alan had a knack for predicting fruitful avenues. After studying sex hormones in the golden decade of discovery from 1925 to 1935, he switched to cell freezing and pheromones at the NIMR.

Bob was a good catch and his experience at Caltech fitted a research portfolio for developing novel contraceptives funded by the Ford Foundation. Alan did not suspect the new man would switch from contraception to proception, which Bob called his "real work". He recruited talented women as well as men to his team. Easily recognised by her dogs that accompanied her everywhere, Audrey Smith was a pioneer of cell freezing ("cryopreservation") with her student, Chris Polge, and the inventor and biophysicist James Lovelock, popularly known for the Gaia hypothesis. Hilda Bruce, originally a nutritionist, is known for the eponymously named "Bruce effect" in which a pheromone in male urine inhibits pregnancy in mice of different strains. Alan brought in experts from famous perfume houses to sniff human urine for potent molecules that might have contraceptive properties, but the madcap idea died. Bob's closest colleague was the Australian Bunny Austin, nicknamed after a British tennis player and a renowned co-discoverer of sperm capacitation with Chang. Bob landed again in a talented and colourful team under an eminent leader, an example that ambitious students can emulate today.

The NIMR had a menagerie for research, but which species would Bob choose? Reproduction stands out from other systems for its amazing diversity. Some animals breed seasonally compared to others that are fertile the year round; many have short oestrous cycles whereas a few have menstrual cycles and still more only ovulate after mating; most animals are fertile into old age whereas women and whales stop cycling in mid-life; very few mammals lay eggs, the rest incubate babies in their bodies through a variety of placentas. Evolution played wild cards with reproduction. Medical researchers naturally prefer to study species that best mimic human biology, although choice is limited in practice by budget and availability.

Bob chose mice for their familiarity and exceptional advantages with immunology and genetics. Alan wanted him to continue the vaccination programme, but his heart wasn't in it and had to hide his doubts. A vaccine should be almost 100%

effective to compete with the Pill. It must be safe and free of risks from cross-reaction with non-targeted proteins that could cause blood clotting or destroy cells by setting off a "molecular mine" from part of the innate immune system called complement. Since contraception is for young women in peak health, he worried about unknown side-effects of vaccination, and Alan eventually came around to agree.

The dream of immunocontraception has not perished, nor has it produced a clinical product after decades of research on tantalising targets. There have been trials with antibodies to HCG and the zona pellucida shell around the ovum, but neither panned out. The latest candidate, a target found on mouse sperm called Izumo, is still under investigation. Bob's misgivings were prescient, but he could not abandon the field immediately, even becoming a founder of an international society for immunoreproduction while slowly drifting away. But he acknowledged the experience helped his future work.

In the same way as Waddington's library had a lasting effect on me ... immunology and other subjects proved immensely valuable as the human work on in vitro fertilisation came to fruition some years later.[34]

He was hungry to have embryos under his microscope again. And wanting to switch from mice to avoid his allergy, he chose rabbits as prime subjects as Pincus and Marshall did many years earlier. A reputation for exuberant fertility recommended them, although that is true of many prey species, and rabbits are poor models in some respects. Little was known about their genetics, and instead of oestrous cycles like other animals, ovulation is triggered by mating. There is, however, the compensation of larger ova that grow quickly to become blastocysts, even visible to the unaided eye. Blastocysts were elemental and beautiful to his eyes.

He needed them for two grand projects that revealed his progression from pure curiosity to clinical application. He was stepping on another rung, and in putting his back to agriculture and contraception was turning biology that originally inspired him towards IVF and genetic testing. He never explained his reason and it was probably down to intuition. He had found his field at last, joining knowledge and skills he learned and loved to something that might reduce human suffering. It was medicine. He had lived a charmed life but had observed blighted lives and seen tragedy in military service. Society prizes above most other endeavours the conquest of disease and trauma, whether physical or mental. Perhaps for the first time he regretted he did not train for the medical profession, so he could convey new knowledge directly to patients.

In the absence of surviving notebooks or diaries we don't know what triggered his next initiative, although it could have been a faint memory of experiments at Caltech. It was the Edwards luck again that he chose rabbit embryos because they were amenable to culture and large enough to manipulate with the relatively clumsy apparatus of those days.

Discovery is never completely blind, always guided by prior knowledge. He knew somewhere inside each blastocyst there must be a small patch of cells with a universal role. While the flattened outer layer serves to implant embryos in the uterus to form a placenta, some of the inner cells are responsible for building the whole body of the future baby. That patch was called the embryonic disc, now the inner cell mass. No one before had tried to isolate it for study. When Ruth observed mouse blastocysts they often hatched spontaneously from their shell, but this doesn't happen in the rabbit, so he had to release them from their prison with enzymes to watch what the cells would do.

He had not progressed very far when there was an unexpected phone call one day from Glasgow. It was John Paul, the leading British expert in cell culture technology. He heard through the grapevine that Bob was working on the same project to his own, and instead of regarding him as a competitor and racing to finish ahead, Paul invited a collaboration, which included the biochemist Robin Cole. Bob could contribute expertise they lacked in embryology while they were expert at keeping cells happy in culture. This was 1962 and he had one more year of funding in London. He felt insecure and isolated after Bunny left for America. Alan had moved to the Marshall chair at Cambridge and invited Bob to follow him there, but the opportunity had to wait a year, like his first offer of 1957.

The chance to learn from the Scottish specialists was irresistible. He could apply what he learned to other projects, including IVF, but there was a dilemma. The Edwards family had grown to five since their third daughter Sarah arrived, and Ruth did not want to uproot them for a year before moving to Cambridge. She seldom objected to Bob's plans and understood the benefit of this one, so she proposed a compromise: he could commute to Scotland and come home for weekends while she would manage during the week with babysitters. She drove him to Heathrow Airport every Monday for an early morning flight to Glasgow where he rented a lodging close to the university. What began as a whimsical project and took only a year to complete became one of his signature achievements.

The men shared a lab working to a background of sport commentary on the radio. After a long working day, they retired to a pub or restaurant to chew over experimental data with a pint of ale. Bob found it was tricky handling embryonic cells after releasing them from their shells and they sometimes stuck inside his pipette, although this property helped them to attach to the Petri dish, which was his goal. On contact, blastocysts deflated to spread across the surface as a thin sheet, like a broken hen's egg in a hot frying pan. If the white represents the outer cells that normally form rudiments of a placenta, the yolk is the knot of inner cells of interest. They were unlike cells ever seen before in Glasgow, and it was tricky to find a cocktail of medium in which they could thrive.

The "yolk" never spread beyond the "white" but grew into a chaotic mass containing all three germ layers of embryos that are ancestral to the 200 or more cell types in the body: nerve, muscle, blood, et cetera. They never saw miniature organs growing like kidneys or hearts but were ecstatic they made so much progress and quickly. They dreamed of steering cells to make bespoke tissues, opening a path to regenerative medicine for repairing hearts, spinal cords, and other organs.

That goal would require lots of cells, perhaps billions. Wanting to push growth as far as possible, Bob scooped out the inner cell mass of some blastocysts with a needle under a microscope to place them in dishes coated with collagen fibres or a "lawn" of feeder cells. Such methods later became standard. The cells loved the association, dividing quickly to make clones from which he took samples to repeat the process. When he avoided infection, cycles of re-cloning were repeated for months to generate vast numbers of cells. Some fractions of them stored in the freezer obligingly resumed growth after thawing.

The cells seemed immortal, a property usually associated with cancer where the genetic makeup of cells goes haywire, but the embryo stem cells retained their normal set of chromosomes (44 in rabbits). Results defied the dogma advanced by the Philadelphia biologist Leonard Hayflick that normal diploid cells have a programmed lifespan in vitro, which he found was limited to about 50 divisions for fibroblasts from human fetuses.

The trio published their findings in two papers with names listed alphabetically to conceal their relative contributions. They had taken technology to the limits, and since they identified cell types from appearances their critics could contradict claims they had nerve, heart, and other cell types in their dishes. The papers attracted little notice at the time, and when Martin Evans and Matt Kaufman in Cambridge reported the isolation of mouse embryo stem cells to great acclaim in 1981, they gave terse acknowledgment to their predecessors. Looking back in 2001, Bob was frustrated that the original discovery was overlooked because it was so far ahead of its time. He corrected the historical record in a short article for *Nature*.

On the verge of clinical application, stem cells offer a startlingly fundamental approach to alleviating severe incurable human maladies. Fondly believed to be a recent development, they have in fact been part and parcel of human in vitro fertilisation (IVF) from as long ago as 1962.[35]

The immense potential for growth and differentiation of cells in the inner cell mass was demonstrated a few years later in Cambridge. Bob's graduate student, Richard Gardner, injected one or two cells into mouse blastocysts, a procedure of extreme delicacy. After transfer to surrogate mothers, the cells were found to populate everywhere from nose to tail when pups were born. Isolated in vitro, these stem cells can be genetically manipulated to make transgenic mice as models of human genetic diseases, and for this achievement Martin Evans was a co-winner of the Nobel Prize in 2007.

Bob left that field for fertility research but never lost interest. Around 1980, after a decade of experience from generating human blastocysts in vitro, he drew attention to the enormous promise of stem cells for research and clinical treatment. But blastocysts were rarely available for research since patients needed them for treatment. In 1983, a couple of blastocysts became available for a study with Simon Fishel. After hatching out of its shell in vitro, one of them released HCG into the medium, mimicking an action that occurs shortly before implantation in the uterus, stimulating hormones so the embryo does not die in menstruation but continues in pregnancy. They hoped this evidence of normality increased the chances of finding stem cells in the dish, but they only saw cells like fibroblasts. The project was not pursued after embryo freezing became available later that year because Bob felt compelled to preserve every healthy embryo for patients.

The first human embryo stem cell line was not generated until 1998, and then in Madison, Wisconsin. It was hugely controversial. Three years later, President George W. Bush banned federal funds for research on new cell lines, leaving the hot topic to the private sector, but the story then took an unexpected turn. In Kyoto in 2006, Shinya Yamanaka realised that if the unique character of those cells was due to transcription factors, nuclear proteins that control genes like microprocessors, artificial molecules might mimic their actions to turn any somatic cell back to a ground state. Thus emerged "induced pluripotent stem cells" (IPS cells), for which he earned a Nobel Prize. It was a discovery to give hope of engineering custom-made cells for transplantation, just as Bob and his team predicted, but without sacrificing human embryos.

When Bob read the news in his eighties, he had already cast aside cherished ideas for new opportunities. He was fascinated with the regenerative ability of salamanders, something we mammals have almost entirely lost since our lineage split from amphibians over 200 million years ago. He suspected the capacity is still hidden in our genome and might be unlocked if the molecular keys could be found. It was too late for him to enter the field, but other biologists were studying regeneration, how injury prompts differentiated cells to turn into a knot of stem-like cells called a "blastema" to regrow limbs, tails, and organs. Bob had endless curiosity and no permanent commitment to a theory or technology, for he knew a better one would come along shortly.

He had new uses for rabbit blastocysts after the project in Glasgow. Previous attempts to control the sex ratio in animals had fallen flat, and now he wanted to try again, this time for a medical application. Choosing the sex of children for personal preference was bound to raise hackles, but he was thinking of something else that didn't reinforce the old male gender bias. Now based in Cambridge, he had bright graduate students to join his team who could be thrown an old chestnut that he had no time to pursue. He threw one to Richard Gardner, who caught it deftly.

Richard had technical prowess from injecting mouse embryos to make chimaeric mice, so Bob thought the much larger rabbit blastocysts would be a pushover. His goal was to biopsy the outer layer to identify their sex, which would, of course, predict the same for the inner cell mass that makes the baby.

They had to securely hold each blastocyst in turn on the tip of a pipette for the delicate operation under the microscope. A mechanical micromanipulator was needed to advance a miniature pair of iridectomy scissors used by ophthalmic surgeons, each turn of a knob moving the tool by only a few microns. Every step of the operation was extremely precise. The first involved cutting a tiny slit in the shell-like zona without damaging the cells that press against it from underneath. When a small loop of cells herniated through the hole, he snipped it off with the scissors for staining on a glass slide.

Each nucleus in female cells contains a "Barr body", which stains darkly with a DNA dye compared to pale male nuclei. The Barr body represents one member of a pair of X-chromosomes which became contracted to a dense, almost genetically inactive mass to compensate for the double dose of genes and match the single active copy of the chromosome in XY males. The process of X-inactivation was the most important discovery made by Mary Lyon, the geneticist who paced the Edinburgh mouse house at night with Bob. After staining the biopsy, they scored the results with complete concordance, which is uncommon when something is judged subjectively by independent observers. Meanwhile, the blastocysts were kept warm in an incubator. Some of them deflated like a burst tire but slowly recovered from injury by the time they were diagnosed and ready for transfer to host mothers.

Richard marshalled the embryos in small groups of either males or females for transfer. Bob took charge of anaesthesia and surgery, making a neat incision to squirt them from a pipette into each fork of the uterus ("bifid", as occasionally found in women). When he looked up abruptly he had a mischievous grin. There were six pearly embryos glistening on his white lab coat! Richard left the room speechless. Bob was skilful with a pipette but not always the most adroit experimenter when in a hurry or thinking about the next thing. After Richard recovered his composure, the rest of the experiment went well. There followed three anxious weeks until the end of pregnancy when they could check if their diagnoses were correct.

Although not every embryo implanted, there were six fully-grown female fetuses and twelve males all matching the predicted sex. It was a perfect result and controlling the sex-ratio was a great

115

achievement, with one niggling concern. One of the babies had a deformed head. They wondered if it was an adventitious problem that could be dismissed, and it probably was since thousands of biopsies of animal and human embryos have been carried out safely.

Bob sent their paper to *Nature*, his favourite journal. It got attention from a journalist at the *New Scientist* magazine who called him for an interview that did not go to plan. Bob stressed how embryo selection could be used to choose girls in families with histories of inherited diseases, like haemophilia from a recessive gene on the X-chromosome. A familiar example is Queen Victoria's family where the "royal disease" carried a much higher risk for males who had only one X- compared to their sisters' pair. Bob predicted the sex of human embryos would be checked as soon as IVF was available, so affected embryos were not transferred. Very few people shared his optimism, and the journalist ignored the medical benefit to publish an inflammatory story about trivial reasons for choosing sex. It caused a public rumpus. This was Bob's introduction to the press, and he would be more cautious at his next interview.

It would be over ten years until IVF became routine practice and he could return to the subject, but his efforts then were thwarted. The equipment used before was in mothballs and now inoperable, while his budget was too tight to replace it. Next, there was the disappointment that the Barr body was absent in human blastocysts, so another method was needed for preimplantation embryo testing, or PGT as it is now generally known.[36] The final triumph was enjoyed elsewhere.

There was news from California of an extremely sensitive and accurate way of amplifying DNA sequences anywhere in the genome. It was the polymerase chain reaction (PCR) that would become a tremendous boon in biology, forensic science, palaeontology, and medical genetics. Embryologists had been stumped for a technology to diagnose the sex of embryos until Alan Handyside working with Robert Winston at the Hammersmith Hospital in London announced a breakthrough in 1990. They tested biopsies from two families with histories of terrible diseases, and by selecting female embryos for transfer two sets of healthy twin girls were born.

Bob heartily congratulated Alan, who had received training in embryology in his Cambridge laboratory. IVF was still a small world in those days. Most practitioners exchanged news ahead of publication and welcomed observers to their laboratories. It was like a family firm where the joy of success was shared, and Bob was saluted as the godfather.

It might seem inevitable that his biggest achievement would be in Cambridge, the home of embryology, but IVF was a quirky story and he didn't anticipate how far it would fly. To follow that path, we must turn back to when he moved to the city in 1963 after a sojourn in Scotland.

8

CAMELOT IN CAMBRIDGE

When the Edwards moved from the London area in 1963, they made Cambridge their home for good. For Ruth, it was a beautiful city she grew up in and loved; for Bob, it was an alien place of privilege and snobbery in the flat fenland.

On an earlier visit to attend a conference, he was struck by the grandeur of ancient buildings and dazzling chapel vaults nestled beside a river that meandered north to the Great Ouse. But more than the architecture, he was engrossed by the plaques, portraits, and sculptures of great scholars (mostly men) who had dwelt there: Newton and Milton, Tennyson and Darwin, John Maynard Keynes and, not least, Ruth's grandfather, Ernest Rutherford. It was an intimidating place for a miner's son who came with an ambition to leave his mark.

It would take time before he felt at home there. Of the 25 colleges only two were for women, and none of them mixed. He thought the town-gown divide was anachronistic: university dons were treated like gentlemen while porters and "bedders" were called college servants. It was déjà-vu from army days when an unlikely commission plucked him from the ranks of mostly working-class soldiers to share the privileges of the officers' mess. His northern twang contrasted with the clipped accents of men from elite schools, not that they made him feel unwelcome, but the voices of privilege rankled his egalitarian heart. From the beginning, he refused to address students by their surnames after first acquaintance, contrary to the general habit. His affability cultivated new friendships and his unflappability gave him patience when he was addressed as "Mr Edwards" by the old guard who was making the point that from time immemorial the university only recognised doctoral degrees from Oxford, Cambridge, and Trinity College Dublin. And, yet, despite British fondness for tradition, there was change in the air in the 1960s. Society was becoming restless, America faced a divisive war, and the Beatles and Bob Dylan were heard playing on LPs in college dorms. It was a lucky time for a rebel to arrive in Cambridge where Bob would soon engineer his own revolution.

The family moved into a modern, detached house on Gough Way in the academic enclave of Newnham. Cycling was immensely popular with commuters, but too slow for him, he drove five minutes to work. With four bedrooms and a garden, their home was sufficiently spacious for an expanding family with pet rabbits, goldfish, and Butch the Airedale terrier they adopted from a shelter. Ruth needed more help with the children and housework because Bob was never going to be a 9-to-5 guy, but their budget could not stretch to a nanny, so they hired au-pairs instead.

She was pregnant again. If they privately wished for a boy, the birth of another daughter would not matter because she would be loved the same, but the statistical odds were getting more favourable. The midwife announced at the birth, "you have a girl", and quickly reassured Ruth there was another baby on the way. A few minutes later another beautiful daughter arrived to make twins Anna and Katherine (known as Meg). Five daughters born to two fertility experts was sauce for speculation, especially since Bob had studied how to control the sex-ratio. But the parents took the news in their scientific stride, knowing that five girls in a row is expected by chance three times out of every hundred. The next generation in the Edwards family produced a mixture of boys and girls to prove there were no quirky genetics.

Bob left behind in London the best equipped centre in the country in exchange for a suite of seven small rooms partly occupied by the Parkes group. It was accessed by stairs at the top of the five-storey Physiological Laboratory, a forbidding Victorian block on the Downing science site. Not originally intended for experimental work, the rooms were so poorly equipped there was only one chemical fume cupboard and hot water was unavailable in some rooms.

Alan had moved there feeling obliged to return to his alma mater because the professorial chair was endowed in the name of his dear old mentor, Francis Marshall, and the suite was named after him. Spartan facilities were tolerable because he was busy with committee work and editing a journal, and occasionally away on field trips in Africa. An old interest in reproduction of wild animals harking back to his days with Brambell returned, and he pursued it with students and a menagerie of chinchillas, coypus, and muskrats. To lend the Marshall Lab greater dignity he mounted the corridor walls with portraits of eminent scientists from the past, but none drew much notice except the bald man in the picture because of the enigmatic caption, "Knaus of the Unsafe Period". When he explained, students were amazed to hear that until the 1930s it was widely believed that women were most fertile during menstruation when they were actually at least risk of conceiving. The ghastly confusion was caused by a false parallel between menstrual bleeding in women and seepage of vaginal blood when dogs are in heat.

However, Bob did not move there in ignorance and put on a brave face. Visiting scientists from swanky American universities unintentionally hurt his pride when they said how hard it must be to do excellent work, but Britons of his generation were more stoical. Bob retorted that facilities and equipment were never mainsprings of original ideas, echoing Ruth's grandfather who declared that when they have no money scientists must think. But that was easier for a physicist to say in 1920 than half a century later when biologists needed a lot of paraphernalia for experiments.

Parkes had not lured Bob into academic poverty for there was money in the coffers from a Ford Foundation grant. It paid Bob's salary and covered the costs of an assistant and lab expenses but was "soft money" and his fellowship was untenured, nor did it allow a cross-appointment as a college tutor that most faculty enjoyed. Perhaps the funding agency hoped investments in reproduction research at centres it supported would create a "Ford pill", although the Marshall Lab was mostly focused on basic embryology. Without the godsend of American support it would never have grown to be a premier centre, and if graduate students understood they owed their careers to it they might have swapped customary expletives when experiments failed, to cry, "O, Ford!" or "For Ford's sake!", like citizens in *Brave New World* who knew the secular deity that protected them.

The campus and outlying centres offered huge compensations for deficiencies in the lab through access to outstanding scientists and government-funded labs. Beside the new Addenbrooke's Hospital, the Medical Research Council (MRC) stationed its Laboratory for Molecular Biology where staff have won a dozen Nobel Prizes up to 2018. On the opposite side of the city, the Agricultural Research Council had a research station close to Bob's original interests with a mission to improve livestock production.

Resuming studies of immunology, he tested the antigenicity of human sperm with Robin Coombs of the famous Coombs test for blood transfusion. This was to check if a vaccine to sperm might cause adverse reactions, one of the grant's objectives. But Alan was familiar with Bob's tendency to wander back to eggs and embryos, and a less subtle man may not have been so tolerant. Like Bob's former boss in Edinburgh, Alan shared the spirit of adventure and believed that freedom to explore is a surer path to breakthroughs than force feeding a research diet on a scientist. He knew that going down a rabbit hole sometimes leads to something unexpected that is no less interesting. Besides, discoveries in reproduction can offer complementary benefits. To illustrate the irony, a molecule specifically needed for fertilisation is potentially a contraceptive target and a tool to diagnose infertility. What is good for the goose is good for the gander. Alan put his faith in Bob's ability to make interesting discoveries, but he growled against research on infertility because "in an overcrowded world, it is hardly logical that time and money should be spent on the treatment of infertility".[37]

Bob's progression from contraception to proception was steady but never hasty. There was no family history to explain why he would hoist this banner, and his assault on infertility did not become a passion until 1968 when he met Patrick Steptoe. Regarded by most physicians at the time as a cluster of intractable problems, infertility was benighted by ignorance, more often suffered than declared, and so remained a largely hidden problem. In the absence of any professional training in reproductive medicine or contact with patients, his sources of information were sporadic lectures and skimming journals and textbooks.

Sometimes a flash of understanding at a propitious moment leaves a long afterglow. When married friends visited his home, he noticed they were dewy-eyed playing with his daughters. He didn't know why they never had children and didn't dare to ask, but it set him thinking. History and myth are full of stories about people privately grieving for the children they are denied, like Rachel pleading to God and Aegeus begging Medea for help. They were not just archaic stories: infertility was a blight that affected people he knew but seldom admitted.

He was tasked with teaching reproductive physiology to mixed classes of medical and science students. There was no training course for university teachers then, nor did students grade them, so lectures ranged from boring rambles to highly articulate deliveries. According to a dearly held ideal in academia, research and teaching mutually fortify each other, but in practice they are uneasy bedfellows. Research and scholarship are the primary drivers of professional advancement because of the prestige a university gains from publication and winning grants, so star researchers are tempted to dump teaching "loads" on their colleagues. There never was a more unjust maxim than when George Bernard Shaw wrote, "He who can, does; he who cannot, teaches", because undergraduate teaching is the lifeblood of universities.

There were members of Bob's department who were not only brilliant scholars but also had engrossing styles of teaching, none more memorable than the neurologist Giles Brindley. He stood on his head at the front of the class sucking a litre of cold tea through a tube to prove oesophageal peristalsis defies gravity. Demonstration offered a powerful reinforcement of the dry facts. Dr Brindley's most celebrated lecture was reserved for the American Urological Association where he prepared in his hotel room by injecting his penis with phenoxybenzamine to make an erection bulge in his trousers. Not merely an act of showmanship, he had a serious intent because there were few options for treating erectile dysfunction in men, none of them rosy before Viagra.

Alan had none of that panache and brazenness, but his subject was broad and colourful, so it was disappointing when he gave dreary lectures about the sexual endocrinology of every species except the one that interested the class. Although the British nation was casting off prim Victorian attitudes, he was raised in more prudish times and told a story of being reproached by his landlady when he asked to keep caponised cockerels for research in the backyard. She said, "I won't have that sort of thing here. I have two unmarried daughters." Perhaps that is why he stealthily avoided saying much about human fertility, never broaching the words "penis" or "vagina" as if they were irrelevant, despite half of his listeners enrolled for medicine.

He was happy to transfer lectures, practical classes, and student examinations to Bob when he arrived and Bunny Austin when he was available. It was not a large quota, but Bob threw himself into teaching with typical passion. It was his gregarious nature to enjoy the company of inquisitive young minds, and then he realised what he had missed at the NIMR in London. Bob cared about student welfare too, even contacting students who failed to turn up or finish an examination, but that diligence did not extend to timely arrival for lectures.

The hubbub from about a hundred waiting students in tiered rows hushed at the sound of his hasty footsteps on the stairs outside before he burst through the swing doors looking frazzled. He often carried a bundle of papers for them under his arm. They were densely mimeographed with graphs and tables for reference during the lecture and for study afterwards. If pages fell on the floor, he stooped to gather them, but in too great a swirl to notice his shirt tail had ejected from his trousers. He liked to chalk on the backboard to show how hormones communicate between organs and drew stick diagrams to depict how chromosomes dancing in meiosis can lead to birth defects. He got their attention, marching back and forth at the front, pointing at the board with a long stick like a jousting knight. His words gushing in an uninterrupted stream for 50 minutes were unrehearsed, but that didn't matter in a charismatic delivery.

Inquisitive students hung around afterwards. They wanted to know more about bypassing blocked tubes with IVF and his latest theory to explain Down's syndrome. These were fresh ideas, and so astounded some listeners they asked tutors if they were true or clamoured outside his office with questions. He never turned them away. Others paid a price for this boundless absorption with research and teaching, and most often it was Ruth waiting outside with a van full of girls for a prearranged rendezvous at the end of the day until she sent one to winkle him out.

A few students were invited upstairs by the artful communicator to peer at live specimens under his microscope. The encounter even changed lives and led to distinguished careers. Richard Gardner switched from neuroscience to study embryology with Bob. Martin Johnson switched from training as a doctor for a science career with him. Barry Bavister chose Bunny as his mentor when Bob had a full quota of students but was soon caught up by the same gravity field. The team grew faster after 1970 and people came from Europe, America, and as far away as New Zealand until every corner of the lab was occupied.

The laboratory became better-equipped with a manager who tried to keep it ship-shape against the entropy of students, but he had no authority over Bob's office, a study of creative chaos. Besides two phones, sometimes used simultaneously, there were three trays on his desk: one labelled "urgent" was several inches deep in papers, another unlabelled tray was twice as high, and a third appeared when he became an editor. Before the age of desktop computers, he used scissors and a roll of tape to cut and paste sections of manuscripts for editing.[38] He had a unique filing system that even mystified his secretary Barbara. It overflowed on the floor like paper icebergs for visitors to negotiate to reach a chair. But when he needed a vital page he unerringly knew where to find it and nimbly pulled the sheaf out like a conjuror, except when it caused a pile to avalanche or he rummaged on his knees for something misplaced in the trash bin. At a safe distance in another room, Barbara tapped on a Remington typewriter from notes dictated to shorthand before he had a Dictaphone. She was told to keep his windows permanently closed to avoid a breeze disturbing his papers and posted a notice on the door to forbid cleaners from entering. She could never relax even when he was out of town and experience prepared her for urgent calls from foreign conferences and airports to change his flights or help when he lost his passport or luggage.

Was that him? That gale-force wind
That rushed down the stair.
Hello, Goodbye, Hello, Goodbye …
He leaves us in mid-air.

The briefcase clutched
The papers grabbed
The breathless enthusiasm
That frantic last selection
Of the slides of cytoplasm.

But just before he passed us
Descending down the stair
The scene above was one of such
To leave us in despair.

"Ring up the station to make sure
They have the trains connected –

Then ring the Roy Soc, the Times, the Pope,
And make sure I'm expected."[39]

The Marshall Lab was a go-to place for embryology, and the fifth-floor suite overflowed into satellite accommodation in another building. There were projects on fertilisation and parthenogenesis, cell lineage tracing and immunoreproduction, embryo freezing and a theory of Down's syndrome, but none involved patients or human tissues. They were reserved for Bob's private quest in the north of England.

Denis New transferred to the lab in 1967 from the Strangeways Laboratory where Pincus and Waddington once worked. His office was notable for obsessive tidiness, contrasting with Bob's. He grew rat fetuses in vitro to study the effects of drugs like thalidomide, their pink bodies in bubble chambers sometimes attracting the gaze of visitors passing in the corridor. His methods pointed to ectogenesis, the cultivation of babies in bottles, although he knew it was impossible except in marsupials with a short pregnancy and a simple placenta. The press could have mischievously distorted his aims, but they hurried past, hoping for zanier stories in Bob's office.

When Alan retired in 1966 and the vacant professorship was advertised, Bob was still a research fellow, not even faculty yet, but he nevertheless applied for the job, counting on an impressive list of publications and glowing reputation. The university turned him down and appointed the director of the animal research station, who didn't want to move to the inferior facilities. After migration of the professorship across town, a vacant chair was transferred from Zoology to the Marshall Lab and filled by Bunny Austin. The decision never chafed for he knew academic committees like to sail "steady as you go" with a safe candidate and a following breeze instead of tacking into a headwind with someone like him. Besides, Bunny was his abiding supporter when he needed allies and persuaded the Ford Foundation to promote him to a readership, half-way to a full professorship, and that suited him.

The Young Turks on the fifth floor were members of the large and venerable Physiological Laboratory in which every storey behaved like a Balkan state, defending as much turf as possible. Unlike corporate offices where CEOs perch on the top floor, academic pageantry was turned on its head by planting Nobel Prize winners and "Sirs" in the basement. The prestigious subjects were nerve, muscle, and membrane physiology. Hormones were given a rank if they were from, or acted on, the brain, but reproduction was never part of the departmental tradition. Marshall himself had worked in the School of Agriculture, and the eponymously named lab was a cuckoo in the nest. Bob was regarded by the old guard as a disruptor, especially after press invasions beginning in 1969 which disturbed the serene lives of dons, many of whom thought the public did not need to know, and could not understand, the particulars of science.

Bob's critics admitted he was a jolly nice fellow and a creative scientist, but privately thought he was wasting time and talent on IVF; it was a delusional goal bound to have a messy end. They prized pure science and took students aside to warn them not to jeopardise their careers with him, which showed they cared but did not understand. Perhaps they didn't know about the fundamental research on embryology that went on quietly in the lab and was becoming a hot topic internationally. The voices of authority did, however, weigh heavily on youngsters. Could Bob be wiser than the bigwigs downstairs? He heard his critics but only took advice he wanted to hear and politely ignored the rest if it contradicted his convictions. His students were confused because IVF only worked in rodents and rabbits and imagined huge technical and ethical challenges facing clinical application. They never saw the IVF programme after it was established in Oldham with Patrick Steptoe, nor were they ever invited. Perhaps it was to protect them from the taint of controversy, or maybe in the cramped facility they would get in the way. The times were, nevertheless, propitious as most went on to fulfilling careers, and when IVF was vindicated it had an enormous impact on their field, as well as some private lives of Bob's former students.

It was felt this purely technical challenge was not something an original and creative individual should devote his time to. Little did I guess that my wife and I should be direct beneficiaries of this endeavour with a son.[40]

Had he come out of a distinguished academic stable he might have had an easier ride in a competitive and sometimes backbiting profession, but he had allies besides Bunny. A few of the younger dons feared the department's glory years were over and fresh blood was needed, but no one anticipated the triumph ahead when Bob would be celebrated with a plaque fixed on the outside wall.

It would be unfair to claim the clan in the Marshall Lab was friendlier than the fiefdoms below, because those doors were closed to observation. Each kept its own society and the reproductive group gathered in an equipment room for coffee and conversation. Bunny's gentle nature and Bob's egalitarianism fostered a harmonious environment of cooperation where crowded rooms and shared facilities might otherwise have caused friction. This chemistry lasted for over a decade but could not survive forever. By the end of the 1970s, Bob's attention was divided between numerous responsibilities, and Bunny had retired to Australia.

The founding group of students was fortunate. When they came for interview they were warned about a sink-or-swim policy in which they would be left like orphan ducklings to learn how to swim on their own. It was a widespread policy in the university that matched Bob's own experience as a student. It would horrify academic administrators today, who would accuse supervisors of being lazy or careless of student welfare and insist on a strict calendar of meetings to set goals and deadlines. The cost of that safety net is a loss of freedom for young minds.

Bob was far from careless. He encouraged students to formulate theories and plan experiments for themselves, making them feel almost an equal of their supervisor, and gave them long lists of journal references jotted on scraps of paper from the top of his head. He never looked over shoulders in the lab and left them to decide when to ask for help. The policy succeeded brilliantly for confident students, and they didn't flounder when he was away because there were lifebuoys close by, gifted young scientists happy to advise them.

As the lab began to buzz from the late 1960s, star scientists trooped in to see what was happening and asked to spend some time there. This was a huge bonus for trainees because it introduced them to people who might review their papers and grant applications in future, or even offer them a job. When Bob hosted a conference for the IPPF in Cambridge, it afforded an opportunity to watch him in action with world authorities. He gave a lecture explaining how fetuses evade rejection as foreign "transplants" by their mother's immune system and scotched a suggestion that intercourse might occasionally trigger ovulation in women, like rabbits. The most heated debate was about how hormones control the menstrual cycle. The American experts defended the standard story of the ovulatory spike of hormones, but Bob took a contrarian view that left them speechless and

131

students flummoxed. He didn't want an alternative theory ignored just because it looked crazy, although it was wrong!

As a fine writer with an encyclopaedic knowledge, Bob was Alan's natural choice as editor of *Research in Reproduction*, a quarterly sheaf of four pages publishing science news for the IPPF between 1969 and 1990. He wrote most articles, but if his protégés mentioned an interesting paper he asked them to write the review. Although the request could be irksome, it was a valuable opportunity to learn how to reach non-specialists.

Beloved by people close to him and immensely loyal, Bob had not changed since he chased rugby balls carried by chums to the touchline, when he would bawl, "Go for it, Jackson!" Credit for winning a game was shared by the team, not owned by the captain or coach, and it was the same in science. He lacked the narcissism that sometimes comes wrapped inside a driven and competitive skin, and never stole acclaim earned by his staff and students. But this generosity did not necessarily extend to rival teams, and he could make biting remarks in private about practices and theories he thought were ridiculous.

If this account seems to depict his students as fawning squires of a knight at Camelot, it must be recorded that he was stubborn and could be maddening. An exciting plan for an experiment agreed one day might be overturned the next morning with a "better one", and he was hard to budge once he decided on a course of action. Ideas poured out of him like newsprint off a press, so he was hard to keep up with. Nor was he always right, of course, not even most of the time, as even the most brilliant minds are fallible. But while plodders turn one stone at a time, a genius picks many and knows the difference between a 24-karat nugget and fool's gold.

Those who didn't know him well were baffled when he argued opposite views at the same time or defended an unpopular position. When an American doctor was accused of sensational malpractice, he came to the man's defence on a principle of justice because the case was *lis pendens*. He was a socialist who admired Margaret Thatcher, the Tory prime minister who bashed the mining industry, and praised the braggart Cassius Clay before he became the acclaimed boxer Muhammad Ali. He teased companions for his own entertainment and played the devil's advocate, for boredom was loathsome to him. He had a bias for obscure explanations over simple ones, an idiosyncrasy that alienated some people, but his associates never harboured ill feelings because they knew after he had his fun the baiting would end with a cheeky grin. His company could be tiring, so they were glad to see the back of him when he drove off to work in a northern hospital and had the satisfaction of imagining doctors and nurses sighing when they heard the mouse gynaecologist was on his way.

The trips that took him away from Cambridge began after an encounter with the gynaecologist Patrick Steptoe, but until 1968 it seemed likely he would spend the rest of his career studying fertilisation in animals. He had a surging interest in medical applications, and we must backtrack to his London days to begin the tortuous path to human ova.

9

OVUM HUNTER

The 1960s hailed new sensibilities about civil and human rights. It was a time when public attitudes to fertility and sex were liberalising and paranoia about world population growth fostered reproduction research. Infertility was regarded as a private matter and an orphan science. This was the background to Bob's early career, but he did not want to yoke his research to contraception, and certainly not to a doubtful vaccine. He continued a pet interest in embryology after-hours and at weekends if necessary, confident he was hitting the subject at the right time.

First among questions attracting his curiosity was the variable character of fertility and infertility. If his mice and rabbits generally fell pregnant at the first mating, why didn't humans too? A lusty young couple wanting to start a family must wait on average four months, and they are told to be patient for 12 months before consulting a doctor. Infertility is one of the most common blights of human health, along with heart disease and cancer. Bob suspected the quality of eggs was a key factor because they are rare cells vulnerable to ageing. Birth defects were only the tip of an iceberg of errors occurring around the time of conception that end in miscarriages or are lost so early they go unnoticed. Infertility is a peculiar characteristic of our species, like bipedal gait and naked skin. The mystery is sometimes framed as questions of whether we are in an evolutionary downspin or pollution is causing sperm counts to crash, but Bob's chief concern was not so much the ultimate causes but the proximate effects and whether they could be stopped.

His head was spinning with ideas, but where to start, and how? Mouse gynaecology could only take him so far, but he had to start there and had wonderful resources at the NIMR in London. Chromosome abnormalities were the top of his list as these errors mostly occur shortly before ovulation or during fertilisation. Research was snagged by processes happening at a hidden place in the body where they are almost impossible to study. He needed methods to monitor chromosomes when they are "dancing" (i.e., during the divisions of meiosis).

Many of the chromosomal anomalies in man and animals arise through non-disjunction or lagging chromosomes during meiosis in the oocyte. Investigation of the origin and primary incidence of such anomalies would be greatly facilitated if meiotic stages etc., were easily available.[41]

Culturing embryos at Caltech with Ruth gave him confidence to study critical stages of egg development in vitro, and their work at Edinburgh meant he would never be short of ova. He could inject female mice with PMSG to stimulate ovaries, but instead of a second injection of HCG for ovulation the immature ova would be pricked out of follicles to ripen them in vitro. It sounded like a doddle, but he knew cells are finicky about conditions and did not count on early success.

He was, therefore, amazed when he peered through a microscope on the first morning after culturing ova to find they had all ripened. The pale nucleus seen the day before in each ovum had vanished into granular cytoplasm, implying they had resumed the process of meiosis. Each cell had divided to shed the surplus set of chromosoma[pairs in a polar body, looking like a tiny moon beside the planet-like ovum. Even more wonderfully, the process was completed in 12 hours, the same as in the body. Even the arch-optimist was surprised.

But was a thrilling result simply beginner's luck or an artefact of culture? He had added HCG to the culture medium, believing it was necessary for development, so the next time he left it out as a control experiment. He reasoned that if ova failed to develop without hormonal stimulation the experiment would confirm the cells were behaving normally, but they were all ripe the next morning. Assuming he was careless with culture media, he repeated the experiment, but it always turned out the same. He was forced to conclude the act of removing ova from follicles mimics the action of hormones by kick-starting development.

It was a dream experiment, and he was exultant because it was going to be easy ripening ova in vitro. When he confirmed the results in rats and hamsters, he guessed he had stumbled on a universal process that takes 12 hours to complete. When monkeys were scheduled for autopsy in another lab, he begged for their ovaries. This time, however, he had dismal results and fewer than 20% of monkey ova were mature by 18 hours. He hoped for better outcomes with human ovaries.

Writing to gynaecologists across London, he asked for slivers of ovarian tissue from young women undergoing surgery. The say-so of a surgeon was enough as patients didn't have to sign consent forms in those days for something that would not harm them. He imagined doctors lining up to help a project that promised to uncover the cause of common birth defects, and casually mentioned he might fertilise some ova for deeper knowledge. He was shocked when a chain of replies was negative, some surgeons politely softening the blow: "This sounds terribly interesting, Dr Edwards, but …". The rare occasion he was offered help it was followed by a late call announcing the operation was cancelled, or the doctor was away. Rumours spread through the medical community there was a crackpot scientist in town wanting to make babies in test-tubes.

He confided his frustration in John Humphreys, a medical immunologist at the NIMR who knew Ruth's father at school (Winchester) and Cambridge (Trinity College). Bob admired the man as a fellow spirit in politics and science, noticing his arms were scarred from self-inoculation after testing vaccines. Humphreys was sympathetic and recommended Molly Rose. She was a gynaecologist at the Edgware General Hospital who understood the grief of infertility from running a clinic and, quite coincidentally, had cared for Ruth during her first two pregnancies. She was the first doctor willing to supply him with ovarian tissue, although declined his offer to be a co-author of his papers.

Thus began his introduction to human surgery and hours of waiting outside operating theatres for a call to collect specimens.[42] He found the seriousness, discipline, and authority of surgeons a contrast to the more lackadaisical attitude he was familiar with in research labs. The first sights of operations left him in awe of the scene in which the surgeon leaned over her supine patient covered by drapes, except for a gaping incision held by shiny retractors and illuminated by brilliant overhead lights. After removing organs for a hysterectomy, Molly neatly carved slices of ovary with a scalpel to drop in Bob's specimen bottle. He ran out with the precious hoard, tearing off a cap, mask, and gown to race back to the lab.

Sometimes a specimen had a smooth surface, which meant it was unproductive; he wanted to see bulging follicles from which he could suck out ova with a syringe. Ova were transferred to a Petri dish and warmed in an incubator overnight. It was a huge investment of time for a few cells, but he was grateful to harvest even one or two. No matter what he was engaged in, if a call came from Edgware or a second source at the Hammersmith Hospital he stopped to grab his bottle and fly out the room to collect a specimen. After two years he had only collected 60 ova, of which only three ripened by the next morning. What was wrong? He had hoped human and monkey ova would crown his studies with rodents so he could write a paper for a journal.

He buried himself for hours in the library to browse the current journals and afterwards descend to the archives for more clues. One day he opened a journal from the 1930s that would have saved him two years of effort had he seen it before. It made him ashen faced to realise he was scooped by Gregory Pincus 30 years earlier.

It was a name he knew and saw currently in the news as the driving force behind the contraceptive pill.[43] Holding Pincus in the greatest respect for immense contributions to women's reproductive health, Bob was loath to doubt the claim that human ova reached maturity in 12 hours, the same as small animals. Never dejected for long, he came around to thinking the report was good news because it brought the prospect of fertilisation in vitro closer. He assumed the failure was his imperfect technique, so he changed culture conditions for the next batches of ova. But they too remained stubbornly immature, as did those collected after an elaborate effort to mimic natural conditions by perfusing a whole ovary. He was stumped.

When Molly Rose called for what would be the last biopsy for a while, he recovered four ova after a long search. Perhaps never before had so few cells received so much individual attention. The first was still immature after 18 hours in vitro, as was the second two hours later. The nucleus of the third had disappeared by 24 hours, but without a polar body he couldn't say it was mature. He drove home to dinner and returned six hours later.

When I did examine the final oocyte, I felt as much excitement as I had ever experienced in all my life ...[44]

The ovum had lost its nucleus but gained a polar body in its place. This was the first time we can be sure a human ovum ripened in vitro, an unforgettable moment and a turning point in his research. He had to share the news with someone immediately and would wait to tell Ruth.

In Audrey Smith's lab, the graduate student Mike Ashwood Smith was trying to freeze bone marrow for transplantation to leukaemia patients when Bob burst in with news. Mike offered to help him examine the ovum under a fluorescence microscope, a state-of-the-art instrument and one of the first in the country. He promised to make the chromosomes glow green by staining the cell with a special dye and sandwich it between a coverslip and glass slide on the microscope stage.

They drew the curtains around the microscope, which glowed with an eerie light from an ultra-violet lamp at the back. Their memories of the next few minutes blurred when they recalled the event later, but they certainly saw apple-green chromosomes, resembling a clump of bacilli at one pole where a sperm would have entered the cell if it was fertilised. Until a few hours earlier when they started to "dance", the chromosomes had been in suspended animation since the ovum was formed when the patient was only a fetus. It was a breathtaking thought. Bob imagined a glossy image published on the front cover of *Nature*.

"Let's get a colour photo at high power," he said.

Mike racked down a longer lens with a magnification of x1,000 and fiddled with the focus to make a sharp image. He then fell silent. Bob breathed deeply in the darkness and could not see Mike looking glum. After a pause, Mike apologised for losing the cell, which was either squished under the lens or had rolled out of sight. Bob took over to search the slide for an hour, but at that magnification it was like looking for a transparent golf ball in an Olympic swimming pool. It was a huge disappointment to lose an historic cell, but the mistake didn't ruin their relationship, and Mike helped to manage the embryo freezing programme at Bourn Hall years later.

Aside from the loss of photographic evidence, it was a day to celebrate. The ovum had taken over 30 hours instead of 12 to reach maturity. Bob was gleeful that old Pincus probably recorded ova in an unhealthy state he called "pseudomaturation", and he would point the error out when they met at a conference in Venice in 1967. The other man didn't take kindly to being corrected by a young buck and they engaged in a verbal boxing match, but unlike the recent tournament at Wembley where Ali (then Cassius Clay) fought Henry Cooper, this time the American was beaten by the Brit. Bob admired the fighting spirit of his opponent, and paid him the ultimate compliment, saying Pincus would make a fine Yorkshireman.

He followed the older man's lead by transitioning from animals to human biology, spending even more time poring over medical papers and attending lectures by doctors. He began to air ideas about IVF with close colleagues, but the only one who was clinically qualified was Audrey Smith and she said IVF was wrong. When he asked why, she retorted, "Because it is". There were many more clashes with experts to come.

Alan Parkes left for Cambridge in 1962, and when Bunny Austin moved to the USA Bob was bereft of his closest colleagues. His supply of human ova dried up too, and he was toiling with immunology, only finding solace from rabbit embryos in his culture dishes. There was a bright spot when *Nature* accepted his paper on ovum maturation, but with Alan gone he felt the stare of the institute director, Sir Charles Harrington, a rather stuffy man who made a reputation from thyroid research. It may only have been Bob's impression, but he believed Harrington was opposed to any study of human eggs on his watch. The director was close to retirement age and would soon be replaced by the more sympathetic Peter Medawar, a celebrated immunologist whose wife ranked in the Family Planning Association. But John Paul's invitation to Glasgow settled his plans, and when he returned to the NIMR in 1963 his contract was ending and there was a job with Alan waiting for him in Cambridge.

Embryology flourished around the city, but the region was a desert for human tissue biopsies. Without a medical school there were few clinician-scientists he could beg for specimens, and local doctors were too busy to help. He had occasional calls from London, but it was a four-hour round trip in his "new" Vauxhall. The precious few ova available tempted him to try fertilisation, but he was not surprised by failure. He believed sperm must be exposed to a subtle essence in the female tubes to "capacitate", a mysterious process in which sperm become more energetic before releasing enzymes to fertilise eggs. Bob had no notion of how to achieve it in vitro.

To keep momentum and his skills sharp, he tested other species he thought might be better models than mice. He visited the city slaughterhouse to collect ovaries from cows, sheep, and pigs. It was a wretched business hearing the crack of the slaughter man's bolt before a heavy slump in the stall and waiting for the carcass to be gutted. This was not the romantic side of farming. He slashed the ovaries out of the gore with a scalpel and hurried back with them in a bucket to the lab. He never had such an abundance of material from hospitals, and it yielded much information. Ova from all three species took longer to mature in vitro than rabbits and rodents, and at around 36 hours pig ova were good models for humans.

With data from a wide range of animals plus a few human ova, he was ready to send another paper which he decided should reach clinical readers in the prestigious *Lancet*. The editor rejected it. Stubborn by nature, he wrote back to defend the significance of his work, winning the argument at the price of agreeing to shorten it. This became one of his landmark papers.[45] The concise article is a remarkable vision of research on genetics and clinical medicine that would be fulfilled in the next two decades. The topics included hormonal priming to harvest more ova; fertilisation in vitro; avoiding inherited diseases by selecting healthy embryos; transferring embryos via the cervix to bypass blocked fallopian tubes, only one at a time to avoid multiple births. Finally, he explained how embryology could help to explain Down's syndrome from ageing eggs.

This hugely ambitious agenda caught the attention of the press when it was published in November 1965, around the time the nation celebrated the immolation of Guy Fawkes. Published in the *Sunday Times* alongside news of Rhodesia's expected unilateral declaration of independence, there was a headline prediction more perceptive than the author knew: "Births may be by Proxy." Bob squirmed at allusions to a brave new world. It was the first time he had much public attention but was only a minor skirmish. A TV researcher called for an interview about human fertilisation, but Sir Alan overhearing the conversation shook his head, handing Bob a note: "Don't allow yourself to be interviewed by telephone". It was wise advice and the smoke of bonfire night dissipated.

Having hoisted his colours, Bob was obliged to set sail, for who else would take the voyage? The shortage of human ova was constantly on his mind, and when he asked for Ruth's advice, she reminded him of a meeting with Victor McKusick, an eminent Canadian geneticist and chief of medical genetics at the Johns Hopkins hospital in Baltimore. "Why don't you ask Victor?" she said casually. Bob thought it was worth a try.

Victor conveyed the enquiry to his friend Howard Jones Jr that a British mouse geneticist wanted to fertilise human ova but was unable to obtain them in his own country. Could he help? Howard was a renowned surgeon who switched to gynaecology early in his career to work with his wife Georgeanna, a pioneer of reproductive endocrinology with whom he shared a partner desk at Hopkins. When patients came to her with Stein-Leventhal syndrome (later called polycystic ovarian disease) she transferred them for Howard to treat with surgery. The standard treatment then for reviving menstrual cycles was to remove a wedge of ovarian tissue, although no one understood why it worked. Victor guessed Howard would take on the visitor as he was not afraid of controversy and was engaged in gender reassignment operations. Howard loved a fresh challenge, and there was no institutional review board yet to delay the project, so Bob was soon flying to Baltimore for a six-week visit from July 1965.

The McKusicks invited him to meet the Joneses at a local restaurant, hoping they wouldn't think he was a hair-brained scientist. If they had any doubts before, they were quickly swept aside by Bob's deep knowledge of embryology and bubbling personality. The next day they took him to a seafood restaurant where they taught him the art of extracting meat from steamed Maryland crab while he explained the intricacies of meiosis and prattled on about capacitation.

With limited time for a heady goal, they got to work immediately. The Joneses assembled a team of two clinical fellows and their medical student daughter to supply him with one or two biopsies each week. Occasionally he had the bonus of a whole ovary from a hysterectomy. Since polycystic ovaries are bloated with growing follicles under a sclerotic capsule, each wedge yielded 8 to 10 ova. Bob was overjoyed. He collected nearly 200 ova during his stay, more than he could get in five years at home, and there was another bonus. The collaboration led to a lasting friendship, and the link would help the Joneses to open the first successful American IVF clinic after they "retired" to Norfolk, Virginia.

Bob cultured the ova for 36 hours and to those that ripened he added a dilute suspension of sperm prepared by a method still used today to enrich motile cells, called "swim-up". Out of the first 56 ova, he discarded 17 still immature and a further 9 degenerated, leaving only 26 mature of which none had been penetrated, although he thought he saw a pair of pronuclei in four of them. If they did indeed correspond to the genetic contributions of egg and sperm, the eggs were perhaps fertilised after all. Howard was delayed in the operating room and when he eventually arrived, he admitted he hadn't looked down a microscope for 30 years and couldn't see anything. The pronuclei had vanished by that time, so they could not count the day a success. Besides, they ought to be wary of being carried away by enthusiasm considering fertilisation should not happen with fresh (i.e., uncapacitated) sperm.

For the next experiment, one of Howard's patients undergoing a fertility test consented to a biopsy of her cervical mucus. It should still contain live capacitated sperm as she had intercourse with her husband the night before. Bob saw the sperm swimming out of threads of mucus into the medium of the dish and transferred a fraction to seven mature ova. Twenty-four hours later none of them were fertilised.

They wondered if capacitation occurs only in the upper reaches of the fallopian tubes, and strictly at the fertile time of the menstrual cycle. No one knew, of course. The next time a hysterectomy specimen was available at that time of the cycle, Howard detached the tubes for conditioning the medium with them before 17 ova were added. In two of them Bob saw objects like pronuclei, but he could not be sure, so that attempt lengthened their list of failures.

The team gathered to discuss what to do next as time was running out, as were their options. If the substance(s) responsible for capacitating sperm was universal it didn't matter which species was used and they could widen their net to animal tissues. Human sperm were transferred to the uterus of a rabbit shortly before ovulation, hoping they would be capacitated, but when the organ was flushed some hours later, they couldn't find a single sperm!

Bob and Howard were not easily discouraged and kept dreaming up new experiments. They injected a combination of human ova and sperm into the fallopian tubes of a rabbit, a procedure anticipating the future GIFT procedure for patients.[46] When fertilisation failed, they tried the operation again, this time in monkeys. These experiments now seem outlandish acts of desperation, but thankfully there was no risk of chimaeric babies because human sperm cannot penetrate monkey ova. They were familiar with failure now, so another felt less of a setback.

Bob's visit seemed to be another waste of time. They had only seen a few ova they could call "interesting", but were they enough to publish in a journal? Bob had strained through the microscope for sperm tails, but human sperm are smaller and ova larger than in rodents, so it was like looking for a needle in a haystack. Chang insisted on seeing tails as vital evidence to exclude the possibility of pronuclei and polar bodies being mere products of parthenogenetic activation without penetration. Shrugging their shoulders, the two men admitted they were beaten, and could only claim a preliminary attempt at IVF in the paper they wrote. Bob wasn't downcast when he returned home, regarding his time in Baltimore as a triumph because he never had so many eggs to play with.

He continued racking his brain in Cambridge and asked at the animal research station for advice.[47] He watched veterinarians working with embryos of livestock, enjoying bovine placidity in a farm environment as a happy break from the intensity of hospitals and classrooms. They were collecting multiple embryos from the fallopian tubes of animals of high genetic value for transfer in a catheter to surrogate animals.[48] The preferred route to the uterus was via the narrow passage through the cervix, and although only a quarter of the animals became pregnant it was chosen for being painless. The alternative operation required anaesthesia for injecting embryos through the thick muscular wall. He kept it in mind for when embryos would be transferred to women. On another day, he saw a diffusion chamber inserted in a cow's uterus via the cervix to capacitate sperm. This was a technique worth trying in patients.

The year after his trip to Baltimore, Bob took his family to UNC Chapel Hill in North Carolina to work with the gynaecologist Luther Talbot. He brought a homemade chamber ingeniously modelled on an intra-uterine device. The surgeon would pass it through the cervix of a patient to the uterus from where it could be withdrawn by pulling on a thread. A nylon tube plugged at both ends, it had porous windows to expose sperm inside to uterine fluid, and volunteers were assured none of their husband's sperm would escape the tiny prisons. It was a brave effort by everyone, but when the sperm were retrieved, they could not penetrate ova. In hindsight, Bob realised it wasn't such a bright idea as the device might act like a real IUD to suppress fertility. Yet another idea was eliminated from his list, but the connection with Bob was worthwhile for Luther Talbot in preparing him as one of the first doctors to open an IVF clinic in America.

Years later when they were chewing over the fat, Bob and Howard agreed that although they didn't crack the problem of capacitation, they had done decent work together. Howard thought their interpretation of results was too cautious because capacitation was no longer the obstacle it was regarded in 1965. Chang and his talented student Ryuzo Yanagimachi found the process was brief almost to the point of non-existence in hamsters. Since human IVF was established, the swim-up technique is enough to rouse human sperm, and embryologists no longer check for sperm tails to decide fertilisation, accepting two pronuclei. Bob had seen pronuclei in some of their cells in Baltimore, but stubbornly wanted more evidence and was uneasy when Howard mounted a plaque at Hopkins proclaiming the first human eggs were fertilised there. That might be correct, but sterner critics would not be satisfied until the first child was born.

Capacitation was one of many obstacles to IVF that would daunt a less dogged optimist. The ova ripened in vitro looked normal under the microscope, but were they really? When he saw a polar body beside its ovum, he assumed the double set of chromosomes had split, but was it normal and did the cytoplasm undergo the changes necessary for an egg to develop into a viable embryo?

He heeded Chang's warning that ova ripened artificially would fail to generate pregnancies.[49] But where could he find them mature under natural conditions? Surely, it was a fool's errand. Even the boldest doctors would recoil from trying to pluck an ovum from its follicle before it ovulates. It was impractical, not to say unethical. He knew, of course, the timing of collection could be controlled with hormones, and stimulation increased the chances of finding ova. This is indeed how IVF has evolved, but it was assumed to require a laparotomy to gain access to the ovaries, a major abdominal operation. Bob had witnessed the ghastly gash in patients under Molly Rose's knife; he knew the risks and that the operation required days in hospital to recuperate. It would never be accepted by research volunteers or their surgeons. He had reached a roadblock, but he wasn't a man for turning. He needed a medically qualified team to complete the journey, plus another slice of Edwards' luck.

10

DREAM TEAM

When a scientific problem gnawed at him, Bob often took it to the peace of the physiology library where a portrait of Charles Darwin gazed out of a gilded frame. Bob would flip through the list of papers in the latest journals until a subject caught his eye and then pause for close reading.

The moment when Patrick Steptoe's name flashed to attention is uncertain, although it probably happened when he opened a November issue of the *BMJ* in 1967.[50] He saw nothing of interest until he turned to the back to read an appreciative review of a new and lavishly illustrated monograph about gynaecological laparoscopy.[51] The reviewer explained it is minimally invasive surgery using a special telescope that offers similar diagnostic details to laparotomy; it is adaptable for tubal sterilization, clearing pelvic adhesions, even draining ovarian cysts. He was trying to persuade gynaecologists to take a closer look, as if some readers were skeptical. To Bob it was a revelation.

Who was the author of the book? Bob had never heard of Patrick Steptoe, a consultant gynaecologist in a district general hospital in Oldham, only a bus ride from where Bob grew up. No medical prophet ever came out of Oldham! Doctors who write books and bring medical innovations work in academic teaching hospitals.

His curiosity stirred, Bob called Steptoe to repeat his patter about IVF, expecting to be brushed off again. He asked the surgeon if gametes could be placed together in the fallopian tube for sperm to capacitate and fertilise ova, like the attempt he made with Howard Jones in monkeys (the GIFT procedure). In a modulated voice reminiscent of actors, Patrick replied it was possible. He ventured to ask if the ovaries were clearly visible through the laparoscope for collecting ova. The answer was positive again—the Swede Raoul Palmer harvested an ovum with cruder instruments back in 1961. Bob's heart may have missed a beat: he was getting somewhere at last.

This was the breakthrough he was waiting for, but he hesitated to follow up Patrick's invitation for a meeting. His medical friends warned that Steptoe's craze for laparoscopy endangered women. And it was true that in the early days a hot bulb needed careful navigation inside the pelvis to avoid burning the gut, although Harold Hopkins at Reading had now developed flexible glass fibres for a safer and much brighter view of the viscera in cool light. Bob let the offer lapse, worrying that long distance collaboration would steal too much time from other commitments.

Three months later in March 1968 there was a symposium at the Royal Society of Medicine in London. Bunny gave the first lecture on capacitation and Bob followed with a talk about immunology. The programme lasted all day, but before Sir Alan gave a closing summary Bob scooted over to the next room where clinicians were holding parallel sessions. There was a slim chance he would learn something useful, but when a speaker derided laparoscopy, claiming he had tried it and saw nothing, his ears pricked up. He was still assimilating this opinion when there was disturbance at the back of the room as someone got to their feet. Heads turned when a man yelled, "Nonsense". The astonished chairman scanned the audience to locate the outspoken voice. A man replied, "I'm Steptoe. I have slides in my pocket and insist on showing them". Suspecting his technique would be criticised, Patrick had come down to London prepared for battle.

He marched to the podium in front of a screen on which colour photographs taken through a laparoscope were projected. Bob could see everything he dreamt of—ovaries with bulging follicles, a rouge corpus luteum from a recently ovulated follicle, the fallopian tubes and uterus. According to Patrick, the technique never harmed one of thousands of cases. Bob was mesmerised. Laparoscopy was the answer, and so he hurried outside after the session to catch Steptoe who was leaving alone. It was an historic meeting although never acknowledged as such until later.[52]

Patrick was 12 years senior to Bob. He looked like an old-fashioned medical consultant in a tailored suit and dark-framed glasses, his hair turning grey, but otherwise the two had similarities, both husky with a determined mien. "You never rang me back," Patrick accused him. Bob admitted mea culpa.

They had a rapport exchanging ideas. Bob had an expansive vision of what laparoscopy could do; more than collecting capacitated sperm it could help explain why conception often goes awry. The other man responded with nods. He asked about treating blocked tubes, which received a cautious reply because Patrick had often tried surgical repair without success. He had a list of couples who were desperate for children and adoption was harder after the abortion law. He cherished the hope of opening an infertility clinic and urged Bob to set aside the quest for Down's syndrome to develop IVF for infertility. It was not a fresh idea but came more forcefully from a doctor. The mission of medicine was the relief of suffering and preservation of life, but here was Steptoe advocating help to create new life, something Bob seldom heard from the profession, although the grief of infertility was exploited by quacks and charlatans for centuries.

His mind still racing when he got home, he was bursting to ask Ruth if she would hate a collaboration with a doctor 180 miles away. There was no email, texting, or Skype then, and it was a longer journey before the M1 and M62 motorways opened. He knew it was hard for her to grow up with a father who was mostly absent and didn't want to repeat history with their daughters. On the other hand, he would never find a better partner in medicine. They weighed the benefits for science against the sacrifice of family time. He assured her his visits would be short in the first year while setting up a new lab for pilot experiments, and as the project evolved, they would transfer ova fertilised in vitro. That meant a longer stay each time, perhaps a week, but they would have their first baby in a couple of years, three at most. In fact, it took over a decade and a quarter of a million miles of driving for more than 100 round trips.

Ruth wanted to know more about the man for whom she was sacrificing her husband's time. The Steptoes owned half of a divided Victorian mansion in Rochdale, Lancashire, where Patrick and his wife Sheena raised their two children. Before moving north, they had no connection with the region. Patrick grew up in the small town of Witney outside Oxford, the son of the town clerk and one of eleven children, with two dying in infancy. He was an outstanding scholar who became a youthful church organist, although he was not otherwise religious. He had enough talent for a musical career but chose medicine instead, qualifying at St. George's Hospital in London. Patrick saw plenty of suffering as a naval surgeon during World War 2 in the Mediterranean Fleet on *H.M.S. Hereward*. In May 1941, the destroyer was attacked by dive bombers and quickly sank off the coast of Crete. Half the crew drowned. The survivors were taken to an Italian prison camp where he provided medical care for them and was respected by the guards for his knowledge of wines.

Repatriated two years later in a prisoner exchange, he was appointed to the Admiralty and met Sheena Kennedy soon afterwards in London. A tall, elegant woman, she was an actress on the London stage who worked with the BBC and toured with a repertory company. As the daughter of a general practitioner, she understood the cost of being a doctor's wife and her husband's commitment to patients.

Although trained in general surgery, his superior encouraged an interest in obstetrics and gynaecology when it was a new specialty. That introduced Patrick to infertility, which he learned could become an obsessive pursuit that disrupts lives and even breaks happy marriages. Some women were so desperate for a child they became prey to false cures and succumbed to superstition; some men feared sterility so greatly it made them impotent. The fertility of husbands was seldom checked, and the medical repertoire for their wives did not extend much beyond tubal surgery, dilation and curettage of the uterus, counselling about the fertile time of the cycle, and a few hormone treatments. It wasn't a glamorous field for a specialist but could attract a compassionate doctor.

Patrick aspired to join an elite practice in London, but there was stiff competition and candidates waited for dead men's shoes. He was bitterly disappointed, which some said was owing to his forthright manner, and he never got over the offence. He took a consultant post at the Oldham & District General Hospital in 1951, where he exchanged the title "Dr" for the dignity of "Mr", according to the British custom for senior surgeons.[53]

A greater contrast than Oldham to London was hard to find. It still flourished as an industrial town with the smoky chimneys of cotton mills before foreign competition drained the economy.

It was an alien environment to the Steptoes, but local people were unfailingly friendly, and Patrick's dedication made him a minor celebrity. It certainly wasn't a destination for a doctor aching with ambition but offered a lofty challenge when the NHS was new. His catchment area of 300,000 people had a backlog of cases of fibroids, prolapsed wombs, and other problems postponed from the past when treatment had to be paid for.

He enjoyed the mixed duties of physician and surgeon that his specialty offered. After growing up in a large family and seeing poor women with more children than they could manage made him an advocate for woman's choice. He encouraged family planning services and welcomed the *Abortion Act* in 1967 but was frustrated he could do little to help people who could not have children. He had a busy week with nine half-day NHS sessions with the rest of his time spent with private patients at his consulting rooms in Oldham and Manchester or checking hospital inpatients on Sundays. Sheena had her own interests and didn't complain about her workaholic husband who came home late to relax at the piano keyboard.

It was concern about the burden of laparotomy, its risks and demands on staff time, that led him to Raoul Palmer, the master of laparoscopy in Paris, and then to Hans Frangenheim and Kurt Semm in Germany. He observed how operations started by insufflating the pelvic cavity with gas for the viscera fall back to make working space for a slim telescope inserted near the navel. Other instruments not much thicker than knitting needles passed through side ports moved organs into view.

Patrick came home after a conversion experience to convince the hospital management committee to buy the best optical equipment available from Germany. After practising with his new laparoscope on 30 cadavers, his first case was a nurse suffering from pelvic pain. His technique failed at the first attempt, but he was successful when he tried again and never looked back. Laparoscopy offered a diagnosis in 10 minutes or only slightly longer if it involved some surgery, and never required patients to stay in hospital overnight. By 1964, he had managed over 100 cases with the team of nurses he trained, and the number gradually rose to thousands. His reputation bloomed more overseas than at home, and he had far more experience with tubal sterilisation than counterparts in Catholic countries, performing 3,500 operations by the end of his career. A British establishment wedded to tradition made him more determined to persuade doctors of the surgical benefits of the French invention. Patrick's little book became a classic in its field, attracting so many requests to observe the technique that it made Oldham an unlikely place of medical pilgrimage.

A few weeks after their famous meeting in London, Bob visited the Steptoe home on a spring day when cheerful daffodils nodded in the garden. Settling down in a room dominated by a grand piano, Bob outlined a grand vision for IVF and embryo transfer. Patrick asked if it was safe, a question that would chase them for years. Bob pointed out that reproduction is a "forgiving" system that eliminates most mistakes. It was not known then that eggs are unusual in lacking the checkpoints that safeguard health in other cells, but most abnormal embryos fail to thrive, even disappearing before they implant and rarely lingering past the first trimester. He had seen the all-or-nothing effects of chemical mutagens and radiation on animal embryos in Edinburgh: they either died or progressed to healthy pups. If extreme treatment did not cause birth defects, why would a few days in culture hurt them? Another reason for confidence was that the critical period in development occurred after implantation and corroborated by the thalidomide tragedy. The greatest problems he anticipated were ethical—not biological—such practices as egg donation, genetic testing of embryos, and surrogate pregnancies. Instead of being fazed by gaps in their knowledge Patrick was eager to start. He said there was no shortage of willing patients and he had a small room for a laboratory near the operating theatre.

The pair was a perfect match of scientific and medical expertise, although the partnership did not blossom into a natural friendship. They needed each other but never shared family vacations or dined together, except on business, and any personal differences were hidden to present a united front to the world. Bob inclined to the left of politics, preferred an open collar, and tolerated unruly hair: Patrick was more conservative, sounded upper crust and looked perfectly tailored and groomed out of hospital scrubs. Bob was not a fan of "churchy music" and loyal to Yorkshire sport: Patrick played Bach at the piano and organ and supported Lancashire teams. Bob was chalk to Patrick's cheese.

Without this exceptional partnership IVF would have developed later and elsewhere, but they could not achieve their goal alone. A group of remarkable women formed the backbone of the team, which was apt since the burden of treatment falls on female patients. Steptoe had a team of nurses to manage the theatre, supervised by Muriel Harris. Bob hired Jean Purdy as a laboratory assistant, while his wife Ruth provided untold encouragement in the background. Her advice and warnings were conveyed privately over meals or across the pillow at night, so we will never know how much impact she really had. But it is surely true that she kept Bob grounded while balancing everything that was precious in his life for which he didn't have time. Without her he might have been a spinning top.

Neither Muriel nor Jean had any idea what they were in for when they accepted jobs with Patrick and Bob. Muriel originally joined the nursing profession when war broke out in 1939 after a science degree at Manchester University. She moved to London during the Blitz as a patriotic act to help casualties and returning north afterwards she was rewarded with promotion for dedication. She never married. Training a loyal group of nurses in the ropes of laparoscopy, she cared for them like a mother hen, and provided the flexible service Patrick needed for operations at unsocial hours.

Bob was lucky when he posted an ad for a research assistant in the *Cambridge Evening News* in August 1968. It attracted several qualified candidates, but the one with the least experience stood above the rest. Recently trained as a nurse, her application came with a warm reference from the matron at the Southampton Chest Hospital where she worked for a year. He thought someone with clinical experience would be valuable for the collaboration with Patrick. The woman was Jean Purdy, 23 years old with an old-fashioned English look and toothy smile, fair skin and long brown hair wound up on her head. She was sociable without being flamboyant, a team player yet content to work on her own. She joined the Marshall Lab in September, working with him until her death 17 years later. Like Muriel, she never married.

Jeannie was a local girl raised with an older brother by George and Gladys Purdy in a semi-detached house in Langham Road. Her father was a laboratory assistant at the university, and her mother a cashier in the co-op store before she was a stay-at-home mum. She had a happy childhood and was a bright girl who played on the hockey team and the violin in the school orchestra. A flair for music was matched in calligraphy, which demanded the sharp eye and steady hand she would need in the lab. She was an all-rounder with many friends and a staunch member of an Anglican church fellowship. On leaving school at age 18 in 1963, her class mistress wrote, "Jean's pleasant personality and ability to get on with other people make her very suitable for the profession which she has chosen to follow".

She enrolled as a nurse cadet for two years at Addenbrooke's Hospital, a short cycle ride across town where there was still nostalgia for Florence Nightingale in a profession that didn't yet offer degrees or have nurse practitioners. Training was mostly in the wards and classes in human biology and pharmacology were hardly more advanced than at school. The matron made the final decision to qualify cadets as registered nurses after an examination. Jean's first job was an unhappy experience for unknown reasons, and she wanted to be closer to home.

Never pretending to be a scientist, she brought a nurse's care for detail, and that was a vital foil to her boss's haste. Meticulous in preparing experiments, she became a pillar of the Marshall Lab and filled her gaps in embryology by reading in spare time. People said nothing was too much trouble for her. She was happy to help students and gently scolded them for being untidy or careless with equipment, saying, "That's horribold". She loved word play and the mangled expressions of the comic "Professor" Stanley Unwin.[54] But under a quiet and gentle manner there was another spirit that occasionally surfaced, as happened in an argument one day with someone defending apartheid during a boycott of South African cricket. She aligned with Bob's defence of underdogs, and he saw in her the mettle an assistant needed for the years ahead.

She became the go-between for two strong male personalities, and without that glue the IVF enterprise might have fallen apart in tough times. She had switched from hospital wards to a quieter life in a laboratory close to home but working with Bob would throw her back into the world of patients and take her away from a beloved family for long periods. She expected routine work, but it would be much more, starting after one of Bob's momentous experiments.

11

MAGIC FLUID

It was a year of smoke and fire. 1968. American students protested the Vietnam War on their campuses, and in France rioters brought out trade unions on a general strike. Cambridge students had more muted reactions to international events until a fracas at the Garden House Hotel prompted by the situation in Greece, and they tried to antagonise Enoch Powell when he came to speak at the Cambridge Union. The MP was opposed to the *British Nationality Act* that gave imperial subjects the right of entry to the UK and had recently been sacked from the Tory party's shadow cabinet after his infamous "Rivers of Blood" speech in Birmingham. The visit passed off without violence by smuggling him in and out of the building.

Bob and Patrick would get to know him when legislation for IVF was presented to Parliament 20 years later. As a member of the Labour Party, and a proud internationalist, Bob had a native hostility to Powell's polemics. But too busy to join the picket line, he was stirring up his own storm, looking more like a rebel and letting his hair down. It would be a triumphal year for him in science and a crowning celebration when his team, Leeds United, won the soccer championship. Earlier in the year, he published a method for choosing the sex of embryos, and now he hoped to fertilise human ova. He was brimming with optimism despite the unsolved problem of sperm capacitation and the continuing handicap of few eggs.

Albert Tyler at Caltech never had those problems. Sea urchins released clouds of ova into the water within minutes of an injection of a potassium salt, and sperm could immediately fuse with them. External fertilisation requires vast numbers of gametes for a few embryos to survive. Reptiles and birds produce fewer eggs because of the protection afforded in nests guarded by parents. At the Jurassic fork in evolution which created mammalian genealogy, warm-blooded, lizard-like creatures called synapsids were still shedding large numbers of eggs until their wombs evolved with limited accommodation for fetuses. A bottleneck controlled by hormones allowed one or only a few ova to ripen at a time, although there were plenty more follicles in reserve that were wasted, at least until doctors came along to stimulate them with hormones.

Switching to internal fertilisation with gestation in a womb was a biological revolution of great subtlety. The eggs of sea urchins and frogs can tolerate vicissitudes of temperature and chemistry in their aquatic environment, but mammalian eggs have none of their flexibility. They need strictly controlled conditions to nurture them, a complexity compounded by the changing composition as they go at dawdling pace through the fallopian tubes to the uterus. John Rock and Miriam Menkin had no notion of the makeup of tubal fluids in the 1940s on which to base a formula for culturing human embryos and had to fall back on blood serum. The quest for perfect conditions still continues in IVF labs.

The prototypes were simple salt solutions, named by custom after the originator. Thus, Ringer's solution consisting of sodium, potassium, and calcium salts with lactate or glucose for energy was devised by a Victorian physiologist of that name. It is still used in hospitals to replenish water and electrolytes in the body via an intravenous catheter. On its own, it is inadequate for cells to survive for long, so the mouse embryos first cultured in Australia and Ruth Edwards' dishes in California were grown in a cocktail of Ringer's solution and serum. More research was needed to find a superior formula to enable the full span of development from fertilisation to the blastocyst stage.

The conditions for fertilisation differ from later embryos because they must satisfy the special needs of sperm as well as ova. If sperm stop swimming, there can be no intercourse between them. When Chang demanded a sperm tail with two pronuclei and polar bodies as conclusive evidence, earlier claims of achieving IVF were dismissed, including the one made by Pincus when he probably mistook parthenogenesis for fertilisation. A Parisian team led by the patrician-scientist Charles Thibault came close to fulfilling the strict criteria in the mid-1950s, extracting rabbit sperm from the uterus where they were capacitated. They watched fertilised eggs divide into two, then four and eight cells, et cetera, but ultimate proof required the birth of healthy kits, and that was left to Chang in 1959. When he transferred embryos conceived in vitro to doe rabbits, four of six became pregnant, and delivered 15 live young of both sexes.

That result convinced Bob that IVF had finally been achieved and more news was soon in coming. Chang repeated his success this time with hamsters after hardly any pause for sperm to capacitate, but not all species are the same. David Whittingham succeeded with mice in Philadelphia, bringing the technique to the Marshall Lab soon afterwards, but their sperm needed prior exposure to the uterus. By the time Bob got together with Patrick in 1968, IVF had only been achieved in three species, none of them closely related to us, and capacitation was necessary in two of the

165

three animals. No one knew in which camp human fertilisation would fall.

Capacitation was a riddle to Bob after the failure of his experiments in Baltimore and the UK. He asked Patrick to flush fresh sperm from the uterus of a woman the morning after she had intercourse with her husband, for they would surely be capacitated. It says something about a patient's trust and respect that she consented. Patrick not only collected the sperm but also supplied ovarian tissue from another operation for Bob to harvest ova. But when the cells were combined there was no fusion. They were running out of ideas of what to try next, which was unheard of for Bob.

However, there was consolation in Cambridge where students were making progress with animal embryology. Barry Bavister had greater success with hamsters than Chang ever had. A gregarious young man with a chin-strap beard, he called himself a high school dropout, although leaving the classroom from boredom rather than poor grades. After training as a lab technician, he realised a larger ambition to enrol in physiology at Cambridge where Bob's lectures inspired him to register for a PhD and Bunny steered him towards hamsters. They would be the star species of 1968.

Barry's first try to fertilise their ova in vitro produced mixed results. Sometimes a pair of pronuclei proclaimed success with a single sperm, but more often the eggs were penetrated by multiple sperm or none. He had diligently stuck to Chang's recipe, but the medium was far from optimal even in the hands of the Chinese American master. Benjamin Brackett in Athens, Georgia, had similar problems with other species until he kept sperm warm and stabilised the pH using bicarbonate with carbon dioxide. It was a formula that found wide application as the tenderness of conditions for IVF were better appreciated.[55]

Barry made the same discovery with phenol red, a chemical dye used to check the pH of swimming pools. It sometimes turned yellow, showing the culture medium was too acid, or purple if too alkaline; he wanted to match the dye colour produced by normal blood at pH 7.4. Few cell types tolerate much variation, and sperm are particularly sensitive to pH. In semen, they are bathed in a slightly alkaline fluid from buffering by salts and proteins. Barry guessed he would get more consistent results if he added bicarbonate to keep cells in the pink, and he did.

He obtained fertilisation rates of 75% or higher with the "magic fluid". There wasn't anything mysterious going on, of course; it was a rudimentary change to make cells happier, and the litmus test showed the way forward. He saw sperm thrashing tails more vigorously, and their heads released enzymes for the run-up to penetration. No secrets were kept in the Marshall Lab. Barry was eager to share his coup, and when Bob heard he thought there was a lesson for him. Could something as simple as pH unblock the road to human IVF? In the late summer of 1968, he asked Barry to collaborate with him.

Jean was sent to London the next time Molly Rose called for a specimen collection. Extracting ova was now routine and he expected to have several ripe ova from the tissue in a couple of days for a new IVF attempt using Barry's fluid. A semen specimen was obtained and spun gently in a centrifuge to separate a pellet of sperm for resuspending in fluid, not too concentrated that multiple sperm would penetrate, yet not so dilute that fertilisation would fail. The source of their sperm was never declared, and since there was no sperm bank and Bob would never ask students for a donation, it remains a mystery!

They kept the sperm warm for a couple of hours. It was a gamble to ignore capacitation but forced on them because exposing sperm to a female environment raised too many obstacles. Around midday, the sperm and ova were mixed in a dish and incubated for a few hours. Fertilisation in mammals takes a more leisurely course than Bob witnessed in sea urchins with Albert Tyler. He went home to dinner with his family, arranging to rendezvous with Barry outside the main gate to the laboratories later that evening.

It was dark when they returned, and lights were shining from few windows as the campus went to sleep. Finding the iron gate locked, Bob dug in his pockets for the key but couldn't find it. Keys weren't issued to students, but he asked Barry anyway. They were flummoxed. If they waited until morning it would be too late to see the first stages of fertilisation, or if the cells were dead, they would never know if the process had started. After investing time and precious material it was maddening to abandon the experiment, especially when it might be a long time before they could try again. They examined the row of sharp spikes on top of the gate and perimeter fence. This was not a time to be intimidated, so they scaled it, hoping not to get impaled or caught by a night watchman. After descending safely on the other side, they sauntered along the driveway chuckling at their boldness until they reached the physiology department where Bob had the right key.

They examined a dozen dishes in turn, each containing a single ovum and nine with swirling sperm. The other three served as controls to check the conditions weren't artificially activating them. Bob pipetted the first ovum on a glass slide under a microscope, using phase contrast optics for the best view. There was a fuzz of sperm stuck in the outer shell of the first one, but did any penetrate? He racked the focus up and down but couldn't see pronuclei, and there was only the original polar body and not a second one that appears after a fusion event. It was disappointing but there were eight more cells waiting to be examined at half-hour intervals. The next cell was negative too, and the third, and the fourth. He shook his head. Looking glum, he signalled Barry to try his luck.

It was past midnight when Barry peered down the scope. He immediately saw two polar bodies beside an ovum, and, more importantly, there were two pronuclei looking back like pearly eyes. He fell atypically silent, not wanting to look a fool by pronouncing results prematurely and trouncing his boss. Continuing to focus up and down, he suddenly burst out, "Bob, that's it!" The granular cytoplasm of ova looks uniform like a sandy beach, but he had noticed a sliver of something, like a beachcomber who spots a half-covered, shiny object that could mean buried treasure. It was a sperm tail! They hit the jackpot on the first night. Capacitation would not be an obstacle after all as sperm were competent soon after they were washed. Lost for words, they beamed at each other. Bob returned to the microscope seat to pore over the specimen for a long time. It was marvelous to think how the full instructions for making a whole body were combined before their eyes in something so tiny and deceptively simple, an object that in past imaginations was thought to contain a preformed person. His search confirmed there was only a single sperm tail, so it was a normal fertilisation, begging again the question from his student days at Bangor of why the one had made it and how the rest were excluded. When they examined the other dishes, they found more fertilised eggs. He called it a fabulous night; Barry claimed it was his finest day, pushing aside memories of his wedding day for a moment. They were bleary-eyed when they left the building and outside under twinkling stars the bracing air awoke them from their reverie to the sober knowledge that one golden night is not enough in science. But in the coming weeks they repeated the experiment several times and saw by the end of the year all stages of fertilisation in the 56 ova they collected, enough to write a paper. Eggs quickly died under the microscope lens, so they never knew if they could grow into embryos. That was the next step and one milestone was enough for a day.

Bob thought the paper deserved the wide attention offered by *Nature*. It was quickly accepted for publication and in his summary at the end he harked back to his *Lancet* paper, reminding readers that IVF was the first step of a grand agenda, and in a carefully crafted understatement at the end he anticipated it would come to the clinic.

Human oocytes have been matured and fertilised by spermatozoa in vitro. There may be certain clinical and scientific uses for human eggs fertilised by this process.[56]

He made Barry the second author and Patrick the third, and after Molly declined, he gave her fulsome praise in lectures. The honour of first author was given to Barry for their next paper, which provided more technical details, and Bob invited him to join a TV interview in London. Bunny discouraged him, anticipating a heated debate that could harm the reputation of a young scientist.

The press was gleeful when the paper coincided with St Valentine's Day in 1969. The editor broke the news ahead of publication in his journal to the *Times*. It stirred up criticism for ignoring the scientific protocol of waiting for a paper to come out before making a public announcement. While Bob had not done this, he had to face the storm alone. Although the *Times* celebrated the breakthrough, the competitive world of Fleet Street newspapers took a contrarian view, condemning IVF as an unnatural practice. A spokesman for the Roman Catholic Archbishop of Westminster said that if the products created and destroyed in a dish were indeed human beings then the researchers were murderers. Confused and divided, protestant clerics were more reluctant to give interviews.

The attacks continued with some journalists deriding the achievement for the feeble reason that Bob was not a medical doctor. The *Times* changed its stance in an editorial, declaring that money spent on IVF was wasted when there were more pressing problems, as if infertility didn't count as a kind of suffering. Bob was familiar with that rebuff and parried that infertile patients deserve sympathy. He was also ready to scotch the charge that IVF would cause birth defects, arguing the opposite, that genetic testing of embryos would avoid naturally occurring abnormalities and conquer inherited diseases. The idea was dismissed as science fiction.

He was appalled at the ignorance of human biology revealed by publicity, and the willingness of journalists to mislead the public with false connections to cloning and ectogenesis. Cartoonists added to the confusion. People across the age and social spectrum were rattled, and he never expected so much heat. He did not realise then that the episode foreshadowed bigger battles to come, like the opening shots on Fort Sumpter. But he could take heart from some encouragers. The *Daily Sketch* welcomed the hope it brought to childless couples, and he received letters urging him, "Please go on," and "Don't let the buggers stop you".

The opinions of men in ivory towers counted more for him than all the newspaper hacks: they were reviewers of his grants and papers. He imagined heads shaking in senior common rooms at Cambridge, especially after the physiology department was invaded by the press on the day of publication and phone calls jammed the switchboard. There was an outside broadcast van running cables up the flights of stairs to interview him, and snooping photographers snapped pictures inside labs until students ejected them. If the press thought they might see babies growing in bottles, they went away disappointed.

Perhaps hardest to endure was the cautious attitude of his mentor, Alan Beatty, who paid the sort of attention to scientific data an accountant gives to a financial balance sheet. He remembered Bob was always in haste and how hard it was to rein in his galloping enthusiasm. At a seminar, he explained to colleagues what their alumnus had claimed and summed up the expert opinion in the room in a letter to Bob.

I had certain criticisms ... I think most people felt that there was no absolute proof.[57]

He thought Bob should have waited longer to see if pairs of pronuclei fused in eggs, a stricter sign of the formation of a new genetic entity. He took issue with the confident title of the paper, which proclaimed human fertilisation, whereas the interior admitted the results were "preliminary". The letter ended on a conciliatory note, but he told a TV producer that IVF was unproven and not a British first. If Bob felt hurt by nit-picking, he never showed it.

As a national expert in the subject, Lord Rothschild was another party who could not resist needling the authors. In a letter to *Nature*, he protested there was no evidence the eggs could grow beyond the single cell stage and cautioned they might be parthenogenetic. Bob slung back with a cheeky reference to the frontispiece of his lordship's book in which the caption claimed the picture showed fertilisation. In fact, it merely revealed a sperm stuck in the outer shell of a rat's egg. Bob revelled, "Rothschild is hoist by his own petard".

History now accepts Bob's interpretation and acknowledges the paper as the first authentic account of human IVF. It seems a small thing 50 years later after millions of people have been conceived in vitro, but it was a turning point, not lightly achieved or without personal cost. He wasn't daunted by criticism and, instead, eager for the next step, a destination many people said he couldn't and shouldn't go.

12

OLDHAM

Bob parked outside the physiology department to run upstairs and help Jean organise for the journey to Oldham. There were boxes of equipment and books, lab coats and sterile glassware, and an ice box containing bottles of pink fluid she prepared the day before. They loaded them in the back of the Ford estate car, a brand he rented to acknowledge a generous benefactor. They packed pyjamas and toothbrushes as they would be away a few days for every trip from early in 1969, repeated as often as patients came to Oldham. The only pause was between the summer vacation and when his teaching duties ended in the Michaelmas term.

Oldham is nearly 200 miles north-west of Cambridge, which felt a longer road journey in those days, although there was the dubious compensation of having a fast driver who took shortcuts over the hills. Jean cowered beside him without a seat belt. They took a break at a transport café where he always chose a cheese and onion roll with a cup of tea to a background of the jukebox which often played *Blowing in the Wind*, a popular song of the day by another rebellious Bob. They were in a hurry, knowing Patrick got tetchy if they turned up even a few minutes late. He had a tight schedule in the operating theatre at the Oldham & District General Hospital, called "Boundary Park" because of proximity to the sports stadium.

As a star consultant, and the only doctor commanding attention outside the region, Patrick was held in deep respect and even affection by the managers. They gave unqualified support for his enterprise with laparoscopy, and now sanctioned his proposal to collect ova from patients stimulated with HMG. There was no hospital ethics committee then, but the board trusted him and would soon give the green light for fertilisation.

Bob converted a former sluice-room near the theatre into the semblance of a laboratory. There was barely enough space for two microscopes, a small centrifuge, incubator, and the gas tank under a bench, but it would do. Without filtered air, they wore face masks and constantly swabbed surfaces with alcohol to avoid infecting culture dishes. The hospital was unfailingly generous, providing clerical assistance and the costs of some hormone assays. Patrick's team was gracious. Nurses were willing to be called after hours, even past midnight in the closing stages of the project, with no expectations of compensation. They were surprised when Muriel occasionally handed each of them a fiver on a Saturday morning as a token of Patrick's gratitude.

The first patients were married women whom Patrick knew were trying to get pregnant. Although the younger ones had the best chance, he didn't turn away those nearing 40 if they could not adopt a child. In counselling them he was honest to the point of bluntness. No one had ever conceived with IVF, so they couldn't count on it, but even treatment failure helped to move progress along. Putting their faith in him, they happily signed consent forms for surgery.

He urged them not to tell even their family or close friends, and to brush off nosy questions, saying they came for routine tests. It was a wise precaution although the media got wind of the programme anyway. Some publicity was welcome if it attracted patients from further afield through the recommendation of a general practitioner, although he gently turned down requests from overseas. Women from out of town paid for their travel and lodging, but there were no professional fees. There was no shortage of eager couples for, as Sir William Osler remarked a century ago, the prime movers in human lives are to get and beget.

At the initial appointment, Patrick recorded their medical history and gave them a physical examination. Sperm counts and motility were checked in husbands while their wives would carry a much heavier burden the next time. He required a preliminary laparoscopy to diagnose the cause of infertility and clear any adhesions to make the ovaries more accessible. The first embryos would be for research, but this knowledge didn't deter patients, and they clung to the promise that another time they would be transferred for the chance of pregnancy. Some of the early volunteers didn't come seeking treatment for themselves but donated ova from a hysterectomy operation scheduled on a propitious day in their menstrual cycle. Suspecting ova ripened in vitro could never make a baby, Bob thought they were good for pilot studies.

They agreed to use hormones to stimulate more ova for patients who came for fertility treatment. The schedule required women to start treatment in Oldham a few days after their period with two or three injections of HMG a couple of days apart. Patrick was familiar with the drug which he had prescribed before for young women who stopped ovulating, but it was unknown territory to treat women with normal menstrual cycles whose infertility had other, often unknown, causes. He began with low doses, measuring oestrogens in urine to monitor how the ovaries were responding. Understanding the risks of overstimulation from memories of bloated ovaries in mice, Bob agreed the dose should be raised cautiously to a maximum of a dozen follicles. The process of kick-starting division in the ova required an injection of HCG around the tenth day of the cycle. Choosing the time to collect them was critical and Bob's studies of cultured ova predicted they would be ready about 33 hours later.

The staff worked in tandem in the theatre and lab. Bob's northern accent and friendly manner helped to ease him into hospital life despite lacking the status of a medical professional. He stood out from doctors without a tie and in baggy trousers; nurses and porters found him refreshingly different, even "lovable". Jean was also popular but kept a low profile to avoid treading on Muriel's turf, strictly adhering to her role as Bob's assistant and waited until called to collect a specimen.

At laparoscopy, the patient lay on a table with her pelvis filled with gas. Patrick pressed an eye against the lens of the laparoscope to manipulate tools poking through side ports in the skin. It was not a pretty sight, but the small wounds quickly healed, hardly leaving a scar. He anchored each ovary in turn with a gripper to examine the surface, hoping to see follicles bulging like grapes. His other hand steered a long needle attached to a draping catheter ending in a syringe held by a nurse. After puncturing a follicle, he called her to start the suction, and when it filled with fluid it was detached for Jean to take to Bob at the microscope. He emptied the specimen in a dish to check if they had caught anything while she returned to the theatre for the next follicle. The cycle repeated until all the large follicles were drained.

They mostly found blood and debris, not the fluffy mass of cells he wanted. It was disheartening to lose the fruit, blaming the clumsy method. They designed a new gadget with three ports drilled in the bung of a small glass jar. One connected to an electric vacuum pump that whirred in the background, another to a catheter attached to Patrick's long needle, and the third was a short stump of tubing for controlling suction by the on-off action of a gloved finger. It succeeded so wonderfully at low pressures that Bob described the invention in a short article for a gynaecology journal, although it was rejected by reviewers who failed to see the point.

The new system enabled a nurse to watch the advancing edge of follicle fluid running through the catheter to bubble inside the jar. She detached the jar for Jean to take away and connected another for the next follicle. Now Bob had the rewarding sight of clouds of cells in his dish and turned up the magnification to find ova buried inside. The fluffiest clouds had the best ova. He worked quickly to get them into the incubator. The rate of recovery from follicles rose from 36% to over 50% within a year, climbing even higher when the ultimate tools were developed. Surgeons today use a double-barreled needle to flush out any ova that get stuck inside follicles and control the pressure with a foot pedal.

Of 58 laparoscopies performed in 1969, over 80% yielded at least one ovum, and by October the teams were ready to try fertilisation for the last seven patients of the year. Husbands produced semen samples, looking rather sheepish as they handed over tubes to the lab. Bob or Jean spun them, washing the pelleted sperm with fresh medium before adjusting the concentration to 10,000 cells per millilitre, or more for poorly motile cells. Droplets of medium were covered with paraffin oil to avoid drying out and kept warm for 90 minutes, announced by the ring of a kitchen timer. It was time for sperm to mingle with ova. The nursing team had dispersed to other duties and the patient was resting in the recovery room when Patrick appeared at the lab door to enquire about progress if he wasn't already called away to an appointment.

Jean was much more than an extra pair of hands and carried out every procedure except handling ova and embryos, which

Bob reserved for himself. He loved it and from long practice was expert at drawing pipettes in a flame and sucking cells up in the fine tip with the most delicate pressure on a rubber bulb. Jean was dexterous too, but with the stakes so high Bob did not want her to carry responsibility for lost cells.

Culture techniques were a palaver before modern tools and gassed incubators. They used a glass vacuum desiccator, which you can imagine like a fishbowl with a tightly fitting lid and tap for filling with a mixture of carbon dioxide, oxygen, and nitrogen. An unconventional application for a vessel normally used for drying chemicals, it was small enough to fit in a warm incubator. Bob insisted on using vessels made with the purest glass and sealing the lid with a non-toxic grease. He never overlooked a detail, and obsessive care is still a hallmark of superior clinical embryology. He went too far, though, when he asked Patrick to switch from standard carbon dioxide for the pelvis to the gas mixture used in culture to avoid upsetting the pH around the ova. Since the gas was mostly nitrogen and under pressure, the women could be at risk from pulmonary embolism when they decompressed, like deep sea divers coming to the surface. He admitted it was a bad idea.

After the mixed gametes were safely stowed in a desiccator their work was over for the day. Bob boarded at a local hotel or stayed with his widowed mother in Manchester while Jean lodged with nurses on hospital premises.

The most exciting moment of the week was examining dishes early the following morning. At first glimpse, each ovum was surrounded by scores or hundreds of sperm, their tails still beating a slow rhythm that sometimes spun the ovum like a tiny planet. That didn't guarantee fertilisation. Bob had to turn up the magnification to check for a pair of pronuclei, which appear 12 to 14 hours after sperm entry and disappear before the split to make a 2-cell embryo. Among the first patients, only 20% produced embryos, but as they gained experience results improved to over 50%.

As Bob's only assistant and the beta observer of treasured mites, he left Jean in sole charge when he had to return to Cambridge. He had a family and students, papers and grants that needed his attention, as well as invitations to lecture overseas as far apart as the USA and India. The IVF project came on top of a punishing workload. He made slightly more trips to Oldham than she did, but she spent more time there, amounting to over a year across the decade, far in excess of his original estimate.

Healthy human embryos cleave into two cells by the second morning, and, fortuitously, they seldom block at that stage as in some animals. If they get so far, they have a good chance of reaching the 8-cell stage the next day, after which the trotting pace accelerates to a gallop to make a ball of smaller and smaller cells from the original mass. It was a huge relief for Bob and Patrick to find they were relatively easy to grow and heartening to know the rate was similar to embryos studied after natural intercourse by the Boston group. They thought embryos with the most symmetrical divisions and without cytoplasmic debris had the best chance of implantation. It was a reasonable assumption, although beauty contests are not entirely reliable, and an ugly embryo can sometimes make a bonny baby. As production of embryos became routine within a year, they were making break-neck progress.

It was mostly Jean's role to transcribe from notes jotted in the lab or theatre to hardback books.[58] Accurate records were vital, and she was as meticulous as in the lab, but the gravity of working with precious embryos never quashed her humour. On one page she added an unhappy looking emoji for a bad egg, and on the cover of a notebook Bob had labelled with his initials, subject, and date she inserted an extra word to tease him, "RGE *was* Human in 1969". Their relationship became informal and friendly, and she addressed him by his first name except in professional settings. He recognised her commitment and reliability, how hard she studied in her spare time for work that took her away from everything she loved at home and denied time for dating. She was the more detail-oriented of the two, which was vital for their goal, and with her nurse's heart could counsel patients from a woman's point of view. Bob declared the team became a "threesome", and he added her name as a coauthor to future publications.

One day in August 1970 while staying behind in Oldham after Bob returned to Cambridge, she called him unexpectedly. He could tell she was trembling. "Something's happening," she said. "You must come to look!" Two embryos from different patients that had reached the morula stage were swelling with fluid, like blisters. Bob knew they were blastocysts, the first ever grown in vitro and never seen alive before. Driving through the night without stopping, he found they were ballooned by the morning. There were slight thickenings inside to make a pole where he knew stem cells resided, like those he studied in rabbit blastocysts. The dream of regenerative medicine brightened that day.

When they had another pair of blastocysts in September, he sacrificed one to check the chromosomes, as he often did at younger stages. It was unethical to transfer embryos without some assurance of normality, if perverse to destroy what heartache and toil had created. Everyone agreed that some had to be sacrificed, for if the first baby had a serious abnormality IVF was finished. Those he tested always had the correct chromosome number.

Bob took the other blastocyst back to Cambridge in a bottle. It was evening when he walked into the lab, but students were still working. Putting the specimen under a microscope, he called them over to ask, "What do you think it is?" They looked puzzled and at each other. They were familiar with animal embryos, but this was different. Was Bob teasing them with a new species? And then it dawned, and the room hushed.

In under two years they succeeded in nursing eggs to blastocysts, and the best were vigorous, and surely had pregnancy potential. They were ready for the critical stage of implanting them in patients who would have amniocentesis for screening fetal chromosomes as a precaution if they became pregnant. The hospital authorities supported them, but lab space was far from ideal in a busy general hospital with little privacy. Besides, IVF was drawing attention from the press.

The managers offered accommodation at the Dr John Kershaw hospital five minutes away in the relative peace of suburban Royton. A tiny cottage hospital surrounded by lawns and flower borders founded by a local doctor, Kershaw's was a part-time clinic for general practitioners and a few in-patients for end of life care. It was hardly luxurious and far from the place you expect a medical revolution but offered more peace and hope.

On the ground floor there were three vacant rooms and a couple of beds for patients. Upstairs there was a bathroom and two small bedrooms for Bob and Jean to stay overnight. The box room was converted to a laboratory, a tiled room became an operating theatre, and between them the "gas room" was for administering anaesthesia. At about 12 by 7 feet, the lab was not much bigger than the one they left behind, but it sufficed and there was no room for clutter in tight space. On the bench between the incubator and a sterile flow hood housing a microscope and a warming plate, they stationed a weighing balance, pH meter, and osmometer. Jean could now prepare culture media in-house instead of bringing it from Cambridge. A visitor estimated the inventory cost the equivalent of around £10,000 today, thanks to Ford.

They had to equip the theatre from scratch since nothing could be taken from Boundary Park. Patrick gave Muriel £250 out of his private income to buy equipment, joking it might be better invested in the football pools. They were the "make-do generation" who knew scarcity as young men and women in wartime and rationing afterwards. He knew she had connections to beg for surplus equipment or buy second-hand, and she found an operating table and lights in one location and an anaesthetic machine and a trolley in another. The room was soon crammed with everything needed to reboot the programme, leaving little space for visiting observers. The only outsiders in those years were Joe Schulman from America and Ian Ferguson from a London hospital.

Bob celebrated the setting, believing that peace helped patients to get pregnant. Royton was too obscure a location for the London press to bother them. When a film crew for the Japanese Broadcasting Authority (NHK) made it as far as Cambridge, Bob was away in the north, but rather than return empty-handed they drove to his home address where they pointed a telephoto lens at Ruth pegging laundry outside on the line. When Bob complained he received an apology from the Japanese Ambassador's office. Would any other embassy be so courteous?

They expected even better results in the spruced-up facilities compared to the main hospital, so it was a shock when fewer embryos thrived in their dishes. Setbacks happen. It was a lesson that IVF was a technology on a knife edge. The pair tirelessly checked and tested everything they could think of, from chemical impurities to glassware, and they never discovered the cause.

Perhaps it was the lingering vapour of new paint because the results picked up.

It was December 1971 when they transferred the first embryo to a patient; she had the 169th laparoscopy in the series. Patrick disliked the word "transfer" because of its association with animals where embryos are gestated in surrogates instead of their own mothers. He preferred "replacement" or "replantation", although those words never stuck. In a remarkable coincidence, the first embryo transfers ever recorded in a species happened only a few miles away in 1890 at the family estate of Walter Heape, assisted by a Manchester surgeon. They produced a litter of rabbits that matched the genetic parents and looked obviously different to the birth mother.[59]

Embryo transfer in animals was routine by the 1970s, but the medical application presented new questions and challenges. Bob persuaded Patrick to use the procedure he had observed at the research farm where embryos were gently blown into the uterus through a catheter. Although trying the surgical route a few times, this was the method adopted. They wondered how many embryos should be transferred, since in the absence of freezing technology the surplus could only be used for research or wasted. Settling on one or two at a time, they avoided the risk of complications from multiple pregnancy, which became a burning issue when IVF was practised routinely around the world.

Another major question was when to schedule transfers. Chang said it was critical to synchronise the stage of embryos with their mother's cycle. The uterus was toxic when he placed rabbit embryos prematurely in the uterus, and if the transfer was delayed the window of receptivity closed and they perished. This was a prime reason for Bob to strive to grow blastocysts for the uterus, which was the proper place for them, but few embryos reached that stage and so they had to be transferred while they

185

were younger and still healthy. This posed the question of putting them in the fallopian tubes where they would be in synchrony with the environment, and that required laparoscopy. Patrick was loath to burden his patients with another operation. It was a dilemma saved by a quirk of human biology.

Few scientists scrabble around dusty archives, assuming they will learn nothing from dated literature, but the habit was serendipitous for Bob. He remembered an American paper from earlier in the century in which William Estes Jr transposed ovaries to the stump of an excised fallopian tube where it joins the uterus. On rare occasions, the grafts ovulated into the uterine cavity to enable women to get pregnant with no more ado than coitus. Could the human uterus be an exception to the rule of maternal-embryonic synchrony? It would be a bold step to transfer embryos prematurely to the uterus on such slim evidence, and there were no supporting data from animals until one of Bob's former colleagues found monkey embryos happily settle there after early arrival. The discovery is now taken for granted in clinical practice as embryos at almost any stage "take" in the uterus, rendering a more invasive procedure unnecessary.

However, after scores of cycles and juggling with medication, there was still no pregnancy by 1974. It was baffling after embryology was conquered so quickly. Everyone mourned and Bob felt the weight of responsibility as the initiator and driving force of the programme. He was spreading himself too thinly, working so industriously to keep his boats afloat that he became exhausted. It was more than a mortal should bear. A man not given to self-doubt internalised his feelings, his worries gnawing away at conscience. He hadn't helped their patients, only lifted hopes to be dashed later; he had led a fine team of colleagues on an idealistic quest to nowhere; he had sacrificed his family on that altar; he had wasted time and talent that might have been more productive elsewhere.

Against his own nature, he became irritable and discussed with Ruth if he should give up the quest. It was not just the technical hurdles, which he thought could be defeated with enough ingenuity and effort, but the taunts and opposition too. While still passionately believing it was ethical, he wondered if he was flogging a dead horse that was already moribund when he defended IVF three years earlier in Washington DC.

13

PROMETHEUS BOUND

Howard Jones was invited to a colloquium on advances in medical research in October of 1971, a time when research was coming under greater public and political scrutiny. The venue was the new Kennedy Institute of Ethics at Georgetown University in Washington DC. Sargent Shriver was an organiser and his wife Eunice, the sister of Jack Kennedy, was an advocate of people with intellectual disabilities. Bob declined an invitation because he had a meeting the next day in Tokyo, but Howard called from Baltimore to persuade him to stopover in DC on the way to Asia. It was an opportunity to discuss IVF with American thought-leaders and timely, although he did not know he would be transferring the first embryos to Oldham patients a few weeks later, shortly before Christmas.

Both men knew they were stepping into a lion's den. At a guest dinner the night before the meeting, they saw opponents seated around the table, representing theology and bioethics, law and politics. There was even a future saint and when Howard introduced himself to a petite lady in a grey smock, she replied, "Some people call me Mother Teresa".

Bob was the first speaker, perhaps because the organisers expected him to provoke riveting debate or he had to catch a plane later that day. Struggling with the fog of jetlag, he explained how medicine poorly served people with infertility, which he thought was an offence to social justice. If their earnest hopes were fulfilled, he was sure the children had wonderful prospects growing up in loving homes to become flourishing citizens. He told the assembly there were married couples waiting for IVF treatment, and in the past two years with his partners they had grown embryos to the blastocyst stage. The cells had a normal number of chromosomes, and the safety of conception by IVF was reassured by animal research. He sat down to wait for the attack.

In an institute founded by a famous Roman Catholic family, he expected hostility, but the first assault came from a Methodist from Mississippi, the Princeton Professor Paul Ramsey. The theologian did not mince his words. He accused IVF of breaching the sanctity of life and Bob of planning immoral experiments on living human beings. Ramsey was Bob's Polyphemus, wanting to wreck his voyage, and Scylla and Charybdis would soon try to block a passage through the straits to his destination. Not only did Ramsey excoriate the creation and destruction of embryos for scientific knowledge, he declared no standard was high enough to satisfy him that the innocents created by the technology would be safely delivered. He hated the Petri dish for threatening the role of Providence and had a low opinion of patients' ability to make moral judgments — they were too naïve and emotionally driven.

Those convictions were followed by another conservative voice, Leon Kass, a young doctor who would become nationally known in bioethics. He warned that babies would come to harm, and by opening the door to new forms of parenting, IVF threatened the family institution. There were higher priorities for research money, and it was dubious to recruit volunteers who did not stand to benefit.[60] When it was the turn of the DNA pioneer James Watson to speak, he expressed fear that mistakes were bound to happen with potentially lifelong impacts on health and ability. Repeating a warning he recently made in *The Atlantic* magazine, he said IVF would sow the seeds of cloning.

Bob shook his head. He expected the worst, but the accusation of unethical practice stung after he had thought so deeply on the subject. Their patients in Oldham were fully informed, some of them graduates or medical staff, and altruistic tissue donors understood their role for testing the safety of IVF.

If patients are to benefit, new methods must be perfected, often with the collaboration of people unlikely to gain from the research.[61]

He was not lambasted by the two other Brits at the meeting, but neither did they lend him much support. Having studied mouse embryos in Edinburgh, Anne McLaren predicted clinical IVF would have its day, though not for another 20 years. She cautioned Bob was going much too fast. Nor did the Cambridge veterinarian Roger Short object in principle to IVF, but he scolded Bob for sidestepping pilot studies in monkeys as an essential safety test.

Howard boomed against the threat of a moratorium, and a lawyer warned that hasty legislation never benefitted responsible research. Bob had allies, yet he knew how progress can be betrayed by a few people in elite positions who win over uninformed or undecided minds, a story as old as the heliocentric theory. It wasn't an entirely dispiriting day, though, as Ramsey's attack on his character and IVF won him sympathy. He was willing to be a loner in the liberty of honest convictions, confident that no one owns the truth, and had the satisfaction of a round of applause at the end of the session.

Scouts for British newspapers rushed the main points into print, sparking a flurry of letters to editors that revealed little pride in the countryman who would lead the world in reproductive medicine. Politicians, theologians, and doctors wrung their hands about the menace, and by asking why IVF was needed when babies could be adopted, they showed an ignorance of the obstacles faced by would-be parents. The most pitiless critics said infertile people had only themselves to blame. Robert Winston, a young London gynaecologist lately come to notice as a TV doctor, was sympathetic to patients, but he called IVF a "con" and commended tubal surgery. Years later, an amnesic press celebrated Professor Lord Winston as an IVF pioneer.

One of Bob's neighbours in Cambridge, Max Perutz, was the second nobelist to censure IVF. When someone becomes a laureate, the press crowns them with omniscience, although the prize is awarded for supreme distinction in a highly specialised field. Neither Perutz nor Watson had any expertise in human embryology. Bob wryly pointed out that molecular biologists had a cavalier attitude to the safety of recombinant DNA technology, and it was true in the early days there were no agreed safety standards. He might have expected backing from British luminaries he knew, but Waddington had migrated from embryology to human ecology, and Medawar stayed out of the fray.

While his peers acknowledged the man's creativity and knowledge, perhaps greater than anyone in his field, he was regarded suspiciously for not pursuing IVF more systematically with carefully controlled experiments, starting with animals. It is true that he switched protocols on impulse and trusted deductive intuition, because it had often served him well to perceive logical connections and implications. Peter Medawar, the boss Bob regretted he never had at the NIMR, captured the spirit of scientific creativity in an essay when he wrote: *Science progresses by imaginative scientists proposing ideas that are winnowed by others with a more critical cast of mind.*[62] Bob did indeed have a quiver of flighty ideas, and occasionally one of them got airborne.

Most scientists prefer to keep their heads down to avoid public controversy. That wasn't Bob's way. He once expounded a belief that scientists may have to make disclosures about their work and its social impact that may hurt them, maybe by stirring up public opinion and lobbying for legislation. It was a social obligation he learned from Waddington. If he looked flashy and self-aggrandising at the time, it is clearer now he was breaking new ground as a science communicator, and heads of universities today would applaud the publicity for their institutions.

After some blistering interviews, he became more cautious, understanding the media have different priorities and needed to satisfy a broad audience even if facts had to be trampled on. Trying to draw back from publicity for some peace and his family's sake, he forgot he had declined an invitation to appear in a BBC TV documentary about cloning and animal-human hybrids. He was relaxing at home with Ruth one evening with the box switched on when the programme was broadcast. It confirmed his deepest suspicions, opening with a newsreel of the atom bomb exploding over Hiroshima, then a camera panned from a street view to the windows of the Marshall Lab. The solemn voice of a narrator told that human embryos were being created inside and mentioned as an aside that Ernest Rutherford split the atom a short walk away at the Cavendish Laboratory. But the filmmakers missed the scoop because hanging on the wall behind the Edwards was a portrait of Grandpa Ernest, and his academic robes hung in the hall closet.

While Bob endured most attacks, Patrick fell victim too. He invited a film crew to watch surgery and interview him with an anonymous patient. He compared the help he offered the woman to a midwife assisting her delivery. He wasn't creating life but was merely an agent to bring her eggs and husband's sperm together, leaving the rest to nature. Patrick's account fell short of the sensation the producer wanted to present viewers as a battle between supporters of IVF versus tubal surgery. Patrick's side was portrayed as the wilder option that would release the genie of genetic engineering from Pandora's jar. He was horrified when a patient whose identity was so carefully concealed was tracked down and her personal details spilled into print with speculation about test-tube babies. The whole team was shocked and embarrassed by the breach of confidence. As their unofficial historian, Jean collected all the published stories in a folder, hoping they would be read with more glee than grief in future.

The transfer to Kershaw's was positive in many ways, but by 1971 Bob was feeling the strain of bridging two distant bases. He wanted one, preferably yoked to the University, which meant Patrick would have to move. This was not a light decision for a doctor with hundreds of devoted patients he would leave behind in Lancashire, but he wanted the alliance to succeed and dreamed of moving closer to London.

Bob asked the Ford Foundation to extend its grant for Patrick to join him in Cambridge. The request was declined with a recommendation to try the MRC, which was investing in obstetrics and gynaecology to improve the parlous state of research. For all its triumphs in science, Cambridge was barren ground for their patients and advancing the nascent technology. University dons resisted a clinical school, despite having a professor of physic since the reign of Henry VIII, and the old Addenbrooke's hospital desperately needed redevelopment. The local health authority was interested if Patrick brought a new income stream from fee-paying patients, and it offered him a place at the Newmarket general hospital, some ten miles away. At the same time, the director of the new MRC Clinical Research Centre in north London courted Bob for a senior post alongside clinicians, but he decided the sacrifice of Cambridge science and students was too high a price to pay.

The offer from the MRC did, however, encourage him to bid for an independent grant with Patrick based at the University. An official advised him to trim down an ambitious budget to under £10,000 per annum, still a significant sum, equivalent in today's money to £736,000 over five years. The application was reviewed by the Council on April Fool's Day.

Board members and external reviewers accepted Dr Edwards was an investigator of high scientific standing, energy, and originality. However, they had serious doubts about ethical aspects of his proposals, especially the implantation of embryos conceived by IVF, which was considered premature and too risky without safety studies in monkeys. Preimplantation genetic testing was too fanciful, complicated, and unnecessary. They also expressed reservations about using laparoscopy on experimental subjects.[63]

It was a devastating and humiliating blow to be so completely rejected by peers. The charge of dubious ethics was familiar but still painful, although in fairness to the board, his defence of this critical issue was wanting. When he read the report, Patrick turned his head without uttering a word at the paragraph about laparoscopy. He expected to be chastened since it hadn't yet won over all detractors.

It was said Bob's enthusiasm was running away with him, and Ramsey's barbs were repeated. Volunteers would be asked to undergo risky procedures without receiving benefits in return, and couples would likely make rash decisions from yearning for children. That the northern health board approved the research made no difference and was ignored.

Insistence on prior studies in monkeys was a sticking point that Bob refused to accept. Genetic affinity does not necessarily imply similar physiology. Their menstrual cycles were different, more seasonal than in women, follicles were too small for easy aspiration, and embryo transfer was tricky through the tortuous cervix of monkeys. Besides technical drawbacks, information about their embryology was scanty, the animals were expensive and potential carriers of dangerous zoonoses. By the time he could jump over those hurdles it would be too late to help women already in their thirties and forties. His doubts were justified later by the former student Barry Bavister who moved to America where he mastered IVF in rhesus monkeys in 1983, finding methods used in patients had to be modified for his animals.

Bob appealed for permission to submit a revised application, but the decision was final and that was that. It had unforeseen consequences because the MRC abandoned the chance to observe and guide IVF through tender stages to clinical application, leaving it to the private sector. It would take the birth of two babies conceived in Oldham and one in Australia to change attitudes, and then IVF would be embraced by the MRC with apologies for being too cautious.

Without a large grant, they had to manage on a shoestring budget and Bob continued to yo-yo between centres. They had money from the Ford Foundation, which granted over a million dollars over 17 years to 1980, but the foundation was susceptible to American sensibilities and forbade any acknowledgment of their support in publications about human embryology. He made a blunder by underestimating reactions at home and abroad. After abortion became legal, and with knowledge that emergency contraception and IUDs kill fertilised eggs, he assumed embryo research was acceptable.

They needed all the funding they could catch to grow the programme. Patrick dug in the pockets of his private practice and Bob donated honoraria from lectures to create a fund registered as a charity from 1973.[64] There is no clearer evidence that their goal was never driven by pecuniary ambition. The hospital authorities in Oldham and Manchester were unstinting supporters, a courageous stand against the opinions and policies of big shots in London. Into this patchwork came another source of income that was kept confidential until the benefactor's death in 2014.[65]

When Bob received an American letter offering money out of the blue in 1968, he thought it was a hoax. In fact, it was from the office of a wealthy Californian, Lillian Lincoln Howell. The first tranche from her foundation arrived around the time of his paper on sexing rabbit blastocysts. The coincidence could suggest she had a personal interest in heritable diseases, or perhaps she just wanted to support infertility research. Over nine years up to Louise Brown's birth, Ms Howell donated $95,000, representing nearly half a million in today's money.

The daughter of an entrepreneurial father, she opened a multilingual TV station in 1976 and gave money to education, women's issues, and the Asian immigrant community. Modest and shy of publicity, she met Bob privately on several occasions in both countries. He credited her with saving them in a dark hour. Two decades earlier, another philanthropic American funded the first great advance in women's reproductive health. Katherine McCormick, the wealthy daughter of the inventor of the mechanical reaper, collaborated with Margaret Sanger to drive development of the contraceptive pill by another scientist-doctor partnership, Drs Pincus and Rock.

Those men abandoned IVF in the 1940s, but Rock was delighted to hear his old project resurrected a decade later by Landrum B. Shettles, a Mississippian with a southern drawl and skittish manner at Columbia University. He wrote appreciatively in an anonymous editorial of an American journal.

The time may be rapidly approaching when the poor woman whose tubes had been excised, yet who still wants a baby, will rejoice that Dr Shettles will be able to extract an ovum from her ovary, probably not by laparotomy but through an operating telescope (which can be done – we have done it), then fertilize the egg in vitro by the husband's spermatozoa, and finally put it back in the uterus.[66]

Shettles had more ambition than aptitude in embryology. If Miriam Menkin had been his assistant, he might have left a better legacy and reputation. He made the error of publishing an alleged image of a human morula conceived in vitro that is now interpreted as a fragmented ovum, but journal reviewers in those days could be fooled as this object was almost unknown.

Without a regular supply of ova, Shettles switched to sex selection, bringing the "Shettles method" to wide attention through a best-selling book.[67] He claimed male sperm with a Y-chromosome swim faster than X-bearing females and are shorter lived, as if mirrors of other gender differences. People who wanted a boy should therefore have intercourse close to the time of ovulation so male sperm can be first in the dash to an ovum or choose an earlier rendezvous in the menstrual cycle for a girl. Andrology experts were never convinced. Drawn back to a sensational subject, he published a phoney-looking picture of a blastocyst to match one from the Oldham group in 1970. Bob knew the difference, although he never ridiculed the man, even wished him good luck.

Three years later, the Florida couple Doris and John Del-Zio contacted Shettles to ask if he could help them have a baby to bond their marriage. He called William Sweeney, an outstanding gynaecological surgeon at the New York Hospital.[68] It is likely that Sweeney used laparoscopy to retrieve Mrs Del-Zio's ova, and a pity he did not collaborate instead with the embryologist downstairs who once worked with Bob, namely, Julio Sirlin. The ova were conveyed in a tube hidden in a pocket on public transport uptown to Columbia's College of Physicians and Surgeons where Shettles had borrowed laboratory space. He mixed the ova with a sperm sample John produced in a public lavatory and placed the dish in an incubator. When Shettles bragged to staff he was making a test tube baby that day, they felt a duty to inform the chairman, Raymond Vande Wiele. He was furious at the unauthorised research by an unqualified doctor that could bring shame on the hospital's reputation and drained the tube in the sink.

Now it was the Del-Zios' turn to be wrathful as they became plaintiffs in a suit for $1.5 million. It took five years to come to court for killing their "baby", and in claiming a wrongful death their attorney tried to convince the judge that embryos are persons, a doubtful point that became a rallying call for opponents of IVF. He claimed in court the act of destruction denied America the first test-tube baby in the world, and by a stroke of irony Louise Brown was born in Britain less than three weeks later.

The court awarded the Del-Zios $50,000 for emotional anguish, which was a relief for hospital managers who feared it would be more. After he was fired from Columbia, Shettles moved to a clinic in Nevada that was reputedly trying to clone humans, and the same year his erstwhile coauthor, Daniel Rorvik, published a story about cloning an anonymous businessman called "Max" as if it had really happened.[69] Bob knew it was a spoof because mammalian cloning was impossible, or so it was generally believed until Dolly the sheep arrived.

The Del-Zio case was a setback for the reputation of IVF in America. There were plenty of outstanding researchers there, but at the time only one was engaged in human embryology open to scrutiny. He was the Belgian-trained doctor Pierre Soupart at Vanderbilt University in Nashville, Tennessee. Respected both sides of the Atlantic, Soupart worked painstakingly to observe the finest details of sperm invasion of ova. He embedded each egg in resin for cutting into potentially 2,500 of the thinnest sections for examination with an electron microscope. It was a mammoth task requiring enormous patience.[70]

The publicity from Oldham was firing up opposition from the pro-life movement to lobby the United States Congress. The Constitution protects freedom of procreation from unwarranted interference, but lawmakers had the power to strangle research by cutting off federal funds. When a government department reviewed the potential harms and benefits of IVF, its morality and the risks of runaway technology, the practice was approved in principle for married couples only, but a series of regulations from 1973 blocked research grants. Soupart's application to study chromosomes was delivered to the Ethics Advisory Board.[71] There were fingerprints of political jiggery-pokery to quietly suspend all research, and his application went into limbo for six years until he died in 1981.

Later the same year, the Joneses announced the birth of America's first IVF baby, Elizabeth Carr. This news followed hostility in conservative Virginia and efforts of the firebrand senator from North Carolina, Jesse Helms, to persuade Congress to bestow on embryos the same legal status as people. IVF would not be halted as it could advance in the private and not-for-profit sector. But America wasn't as friendly territory for this research as Britain, which had become a more secular society.

Bob never let the politics of reproduction drag him down, but the toll from working away from home and discouraging results weighed heavily. He was always interested in politics, ever ready to express convictions about social inequality, and in the winter of 1973-74 his homeland was in trouble, teetering with strikes by miners and railway workers. Edward Heath's government announced a three-day working week to conserve energy as power stations ran out of coal, and the OPEC oil crisis added to national misery when petrol stations ran dry. Bob's work was little affected, but he couldn't ignore the strikers, or the hardships endured by their families, not least because his late father worked in mines and railways. He felt called to serve his community and plunging into politics in Cambridge would be a counterweight to frustrated goals in Oldham.

Cambridge was then a different kind of place, a mix of intellectual conservatives and social activists in a compact city dominated by a university with a deep blue hinterland of rural Tories. A history of railways won sympathy for those workers, helping to make 1973 a political watershed as the electorate threw out the Tory administration after years in charge of the city council. As a candidate for the Newnham ward where he lived, Bob swept in with the Labour tide.[72] He won handsomely with 60% of the vote. It was another example of his perfect timing. He was lecturing in Rome when news of election reached him by cable, and he was re-elected three years later.

Labour colleagues remembered his energy and ideas, faithful attendance at meetings, and hearty canvassing on doorsteps during election campaigns. It was a time when central government encroached more on local affairs, a chronic bugbear of national life, and councillors were engaged in skirmishes with Westminster politicians and civil servants. Bob cared about the new policies for city schools. He had benefitted from a grammar school education and taught privileged undergraduates, but his heart was in making schools comprehensive to stir up the social mix and liberate children from an elementary test at age 11 that affected their prospects in life.

He earned a seat on the city board and as chairman of the finance committee transferred accounts from Barclays Bank because it supported apartheid in South Africa. His involvement with the development of the commercial centre of the city is still acknowledged on a plaque recording the opening by the Princess Anne. It was rumoured that neither he nor her brother, a Cambridge alumnus, liked the project. Camaraderie with like-minded people on the council was refreshing and satisfying to see policy unfolding to benefit citizens. He hadn't felt so positive in years, and after getting feet wet in local politics wanted deeper immersion.

The Labour party sought nominations in 1974 for a candidate for the parliamentary constituency. If elected a Member of Parliament he would have to leave science, probably for good because it is hard to catch up after prolonged absence. Ruth thought it was a poor deal for the family to exchange occasional absences in Oldham for the vagaries of parliamentary life in London. When he asked his mother, she too urged him to stick to science, as did Patrick and Jean, of course. He put his name forward anyway.

Pitted against a posh candidate, he narrowly lost the vote. The outcome might have been different if his research was not blazed in newspapers, but it would not have made any difference at the general election when a popular Conservative MP easily retained his seat. Had Bob won, he would have been a zealous and argumentative politician; Parliament needed people with a grasp of science and technology instead of conventional backgrounds in law and business. But he would have been passed over for a place in the Cabinet to stay as an ornery backbencher and thorn in the side of his prime minister.

He reviewed options after accepting defeat with equanimity. When he asked Jean if she wanted to continue IVF or switch to stem cells, she didn't hesitate, saying, "Let's keep going". There was a slump in the number of cases at Kershaw's from around 60 patients a year to about 40. They needed to regain momentum, and this was braced by three factors. First were the pleading letters of people who turned to them as a last resort to build their family. The second was the determination of Patrick's team and Jean's undaunted spirit. And the third was his critics, for Bob would never surrender to give them the satisfaction of victory. And, yet, to maintain the pace for a breakthrough, he also needed a place for occasional breaks to revive in peace and anonymity with his family.

A haven was advertised in Yorkshire in 1973. It was Bruntscar, the old stone farmhouse where Eleanor used to live and a short distance along the track from Broadrake where she grew up in the Bonnick home. It was an ideal setting for his family to share a love of the Dales, where older folk still remembered him and his brother dwelling among them 30 years earlier.

They rented the farmhouse for six years until they bought a farm of their own outside Cambridge. It was cold and drafty, facing the fate of other tumbling houses and barns in the district, so they applied for improvement grants to make it comfortable to stay in summer vacations and even midwinter. Ruth accepted the privations, knowing it would be prime time together and she could make friends in the dale. The children could bring pets and safely roam the fields. Bob befriended the Brennands at the next farm along the track and they embraced him as a fellow York-shireman but knew little of his other life. They didn't need to know, and he didn't want to tell. It was a place of memories where Bob could help the farmer with haymaking on dry days, repair walls, and dip sheep in stinking pools of antiseptic. Ambrose Brennand playfully chided, "You're a townie", and he answered, "Hell's teeth!" Those were happy times.

A vacation for him meant coming home to a farmhouse supper after a day filled with physical labour. He was only an hour from Oldham in his car, yet it seemed a world away, and without the internet or mobile devices he was out of reach, except by snail mail or calling his office from the telephone box on the country road. Reading and writing indoors on wet days, his gaze would occasionally drift out of the spattered window across fields to the viaduct where his Dad used to work. On dry days when not farming, he might be found kneeling alone in the dirt lost in private thoughts while he planted trees in an almost bare land-scape. It looked a futile endeavour, if reminiscent of Elzéard Buffier who sowed the barren heights of Provence.[73]

He never explained that passion, but it is a fitting image for the loneliest scientist in the world, and paradoxical for the gregarious and bloody-minded Yorkshireman who wanted to make babies in new ways. Shrewd operators choose safe and familiar routes to a successful career, but a path rarely taken can become a busy highway later. Misunderstood rebels pay a price for their choice until obstinacy and waywardness are hailed as genius. The visionary scientist J.B.S. Haldane who inspired Aldous Huxley's most famous novel defined this kind of figure in a 1923 lecture at the Heretic Society in Cambridge.

The chemical or physical inventor is always a Prometheus. There is no great invention, from fire to flying, which has not been hailed as an insult to some god. But if every physical and chemical invention is a blasphemy, every biological invention is a perversion.[74]

14

HARD ROAD

After the first couple of dazzling years in Oldham, Bob and Patrick were confident they would soon have a pregnancy, but for several more they wretchedly cast around like looking for a path in a foggy Yorkshire moor. There were no signposts and very few had travelled that way before. Time after time when they transferred embryos, they heard their patients' periods returned a fortnight later and pinned hopes on the next case. Was it the quality of embryos or the uterine lining that was most at fault? The seed-soil metaphor seemed rather apt; it was the kind of question farmers ask after their crops fail.

They checked the chromosomes, but was that effective, or even enough? It was easy to miscount if there was just one extra or missing chromosome when there were so few cells to screen. They didn't know that embryos can have a mixture of normal and abnormal cells and still be viable, and it was the unknowns that gave them the gravest worries. In Edinburgh, Waddington and Ruth Clayton found a mutation that rendered fruit flies peculiarly sensitive to heat at larval stages, turning antennae into monstrous legs that stuck out of their heads. Was that kind of phenomenon limited to insects or could temperature and chemicals in the culture medium cause lasting harm to human eggs? There are vulnerabilities and had they been known in the 1970s alarm bells would have rung.

The first evidence was when cow and sheep embryos grown in serum-rich medium occasionally made overgrown offspring, sometimes with internal abnormalities. This is the territory of epigenetics, involving special genes that are turned on or off depending on whether they are inherited from the mother or father ("imprinted"). Dual expression or none causes abnormalities or is fatal and explains parthenogenesis. A corresponding condition in humans is the Beckwith-Wiedemann syndrome, more common in children conceived by IVF for reasons still poorly understood, and fortunately rare. When you feel your way in the dark, as Bob did, you might never have started if you knew all the obstacles and hazards you might encounter on the way. His biggest scare was when Chang found cultured rat embryos had small eyes at birth. But when he heard that half the animals were affected his training in genetics told him the defect was not caused by culture but a sporadic mutation in the animal colony. Phew!

He continued juggling with the medium to improve fertilisation and growth to the blastocyst stage, calling John Paul in Glasgow for expert advice. Some of the best outcomes were with a medium developed for a completely different cell type (Ham's F10), but it was only a waypoint to matching natural conditions in the tubes. And it was agonising wresting clues from the few embryos available for research since most were destined for transfer to patients. Data were too scarce for rigorous statistics, so progress was guided by intuition or trial and error, mostly error. Students in the Marshall Lab would have found his struggle hard to appreciate because for every 100 healthy mouse embryos they made in a day he would be lucky to have 10 of mixed quality in a week.

While uncertainty existed about the best formula for culture medium, he was sure of its purity, buying the purest chemicals for Jean to dissolve in triple-distilled water, preferring the soft

Oldham source instead of calcareous Cambridge water. IVF clinics today choose commercial media instead of making it from scratch, but that convenience comes at the cost of losing control of the composition. It was the custom in Oldham to use serum from patients' blood as a supplement, but could it carry over to dishes of embryos the factors that made a woman infertile? They tried purified bovine albumen, even serum from fetal calves because it was good for embryo stem cells in Glasgow. This shocking choice preceded knowledge of mad cow disease from eating beef corrupted with prion proteins. When Jean prepared media, Bob cross-checked ingredients and dials on the instruments for measuring pH and osmotic strength, and as another safeguard they incubated mouse embryos to check the medium. They never stopped asking how to improve results, knowing that perfection is a mirage.

There were still no pregnancies. It might have helped if they turned older women away, but Patrick was loath to deny anyone a chance. Having grown confident in the quality of embryos, Bob had a gut feeling the problem lay in the soil instead of the seed. Perhaps the uterus was unreceptive to embryos in cycles disturbed by drugs and hormones. The prospects would surely be rosier if they were placed in the womb of another woman at the receptive time of her undisturbed cycle. It was a tantalising question of surrogacy, but it seemed a step too far and would give more ammunition to opponents.

As suspicion of disturbed cycles grew, they talked about keeping embryos in a freezer for suspended animation until patients returned to natural cycles. If David Whittingham could do it with mouse embryos, why would humans suffer a killing frost? David was sent spare embryos in tubes handed to railway staff who had no idea they were transporting such tiny passengers to London. When nothing came of the experiment Bob rented an automatic freezing machine, which annoyed staff as it made a baleful noise pumping liquid nitrogen and threatening to explode frozen vapour as it slowly cooled specimens. That trial was abandoned too. The breakthrough was made overseas six years later in 1977, but the first steps were taken at Kershaw's.

The procedure for transferring embryos came under scrutiny too late, for what could be simpler than blowing embryos from a catheter into the void of a womb? It was routine in farm animals. As an abdominal surgeon, Patrick was used to heavy-handed manipulations and lacked the deft touch doctors later found is important. Moreover, a stiff catheter can traumatise a tender tissue lining. Not until after Bourn Hall Clinic opened was it replaced by a soft and flexible device designed by John Webster in collaboration with a small company, quickly becoming adopted by other clinics.

A question often repeated and never satisfactorily answered is why the breakthrough for IVF took so long, involving hundreds of cases and consummate care. Is it facile, albeit true, to say the pioneers faced complex, poorly understood biology? Would an improved catheter have brought earlier success? Among many theories, they were on safe ground assuming embryos should harmonise with their environment. A farmer knows when to sow seeds, ploughing and fertilising the dirt in advance. Bob and Patrick had to sow viable embryos on receptive ground, too, but how would they make it more fertile?

One of the clues they latched onto was reported by patients who noticed their periods returned sooner than they were accustomed to. Instead of about a fortnight after ovulation or harvesting ova, it was often around 10 days. The difference is significant because embryos are impelled to produce HCG at the blastocyst stage for timely rescue of corpora lutea, the temporary source of progesterone from the ovaries. This biology is the theoretical basis for a contraceptive vaccine against HCG, and it didn't need a brainwave to wonder if artificial cycles were causing IVF to fail by shortening the phase when progesterone was needed.

They suspected HMG was the culprit because the hormonal drug takes over the menstrual cycle to grow extra follicles and produces excessive oestrogen. It boosts the hormone prolactin that can interfere with fertility and was a problem when it triggered a premature surge of LH that ovulated ova ahead of Patrick's timetable to retrieve them. Perhaps the corpora lutea failed to develop properly for making enough progesterone to build a juicy lining so embryos can implant in the uterus, or the glands switched off too soon.

They tried giving HCG injections to mimic the blastocyst hormone, but that didn't work, so Bob decided on the direct approach with progesterone itself. It would be needed for eight weeks until the placenta produces enough hormone. He was uneasy because the oil in which it is dissolved can cause painful scabbing from repeated injections, so he recommended switching to a synthetic progestin in a depot version that keeps hormone levels raised for days. Doctors already used it to prevent miscarriages. The drug was tested for over a year until one day he read with horror it can cause early pregnancy loss. They were giving infertile patients a contraceptive!

They had the unenviable task of repeatedly breaking bad news, becoming accustomed to silence at the other end of the telephone until an outburst of sobbing or anger. The only compensation was to try again, and when one method failed there was another up their sleeves to offer hope of breaking the chain of sorrow.

They abandoned HMG for a while to test clomiphene citrate (*Clomid*), a synthetic anti-oestrogen that stimulates the pituitary gland to release FSH and LH. It is a cheap drug with a proven safety record, although nausea and menopausal hot flashes were distressing side-effects and it generated fewer ova. The trial closed without benefit.

The years 1973 to 1975 were the most discouraging of the decade: the sowers were planting on barren ground. After a morning in the lab, Bob and Jean would occasionally take off for an hour or two on a fine day to drive to Saddleworth Moor, a wide expanse of heather above old industrial towns and villages nestled in valleys below. He felt happier inside Yorkshire borders under a big sky of scudding clouds and a breeze to clear mental cobwebs. The setting favoured discussion of ethical minefields they were navigating, and he could try ideas on her before approaching Patrick. Did pyruvate go off in the culture medium? Should they try to knock down prolactin levels? Would they be luckier switching to natural cycles? A host of other questions dangled in conversation. Always in the background, pressures bore down from patients who had faith in them.

The moor was a haunting place to ponder the value of children. Not far away there were boys and girls buried in the dirt, and one of them still rests somewhere. How can it be that people can destroy the crowning joy of life, plunging parents to the deepest grief we can know? But there were people like the Moors Murderers who lurked the streets of Manchester and a girl from Gorton was their first victim.[75]

The Oldham team didn't have to worry about competition from America now, but would not have the field to themselves for long. There was a challenge coming from further away in Australia.

The leader was tall and aquiline with long blonde hair and a suntan; someone you might think was a beach bum as he climbed out of a beaten-up Morris Minor in flip-flops and T-shirt. But if you continued to watch you would see him swinging through the doors of Monash University to be hailed by staff as their chairman of obstetrics and gynaecology. That was 41-year-old Carl Wood, already internationally respected for research in women's health in 1970. His attempts to bridge blocked fallopian tubes with pros-theses had come to nothing, like other medical plumbers, but he was receptive to new ideas.

When visiting a research farm outside Melbourne, a scientist advised him to consider IVF and embryo transfer to help patients. He said it was promising for the livestock industry and played to national strengths in reproductive science, but would it help patients? The radical technology was going to draw resistance in the religiously conservative state of Victoria, although it was also timely. There were fewer babies for adoption after abortion was legalised, and the fading stigma of illegitimacy meant gamete donation would be more acceptable. The conversation reminded Wood of a recent paper from a British group describing human IVF, and he heard rumours that it was also buzzing in other countries. By the time he had driven home he had plans to open IVF research in his department, and in the next few years that initiative pushed the Aussies ahead of the coming surge of IVF enthusiasts. He wanted to build a well-organised team, better equipped than the homespun programme in the north of England. When Bob heard about the competition, he regarded it with the same grace he showed to a rival cricket team. In a gentleman's game the best team wins.

Wood recruited Alex Lopata to convert the back of an office at the Queen Victoria Medical Centre into a laboratory. It was another example of an inauspicious start. Young women scheduled for routine surgery were asked if they would donate ova for research, starting at the end of 1971. Only one or two volunteered per week. Since more cases came through Ian

211

Johnston's service across town at the Royal Women's Hospital, he was invited to join the enterprise they called the "Melbourne Egg Project". Wood was knocking on an open door after Johnston recently returned from observing Patrick operating in Oldham and heard Bob acclaiming IVF at a conference. Ian converted a janitor's storeroom at the Women's to a laboratory and recruited the distinguished endocrinologist Jim Brown to consult about ovarian stimulation and measure hormones. They would ride hard to the finishing post for the prize of the first IVF baby. Only occasional contact was made with the British team as this was before the days of email or even fax, and the "Kangaroo route" involved five or six stops before the first jumbo jets crossed the hemispheres. The Aussie team had to work out methods from scratch with a little help from publications, driven by the enthusiasm that novelty inspires and pooled professional fees to pay for expenses.

They didn't have to wait long to celebrate. Fertilised ova grew to healthy-looking embryos, giving confidence to transfer them, although the first 15 cases failed to get pregnant. From the next patient at the Monash centre they collected immature ova during abdominal surgery (laparotomy instead of laparoscopy) that needed to ripen before insemination. Three days later one ferti-lised egg reached the 8-cell stage, and two weeks after it was transferred the woman had a positive pregnancy test.[76] Unhappily, her stitches needed repair and the next time she was tested it was negative and deemed a "biochemical pregnancy".

In 1973, the team rushed the report to the *Lancet* as the first presumptive pregnancy from IVF. The Brits were alarmed that Aussies were overtaking them, but on second thoughts Bob called the claim, "unbelievably fanciful". It sounded like sour grapes. He knew that ova matured in vitro stood little chance of develop-ment, and an awkward fact emerged later when the patient originally diagnosed with blocked tubes conceived spontaneously. There was a question whether conception happened the first time in vitro with a poor-quality egg or from a natural ovulation. In any case, the report drew wide attention to give IVF greater credibility, although austral euphoria deflated over the next seven years from an unbroken series of negative results.

Wood and Johnston split the programme to drive progress by competition, a policy that paid off to give world leadership for a few years after Louise Brown was born. The Ford Foundation supported Wood for identifying new contraceptive targets, but embryo research went under the funder's radar, the same as in Cambridge. He recruited Alan Trounson in 1977, a young scientist returning from Cambridge who had no more than a passing acquaintanceship with Bob. It was a decisive appointment. The advanced training received at the animal research station was transferrable, and Alan was confident reproduction in "two-legged sheep" was not fundamentally different. Doctors soon acknowledged the care and skill of embryologists were the most crucial ingredients for treating patients with IVF.

We soon realised it was the scientists (who appeared to be invisible) who made the progress, and really except for minor changes in the stimulation protocols and aspiration of oocytes we did "bugger all".[77]

The Aussies gave Bob and Patrick a scare but would eventually lose the race. They had the consolation of the third baby in the world, Candice Reed born in 1980, and nine more births in the next two years were tremendous achievements.

If the Oldham team assumed IVF was their exclusive domain in the UK, they had another jolt in July of 1974. Newspaper reporters called about a disclosure made at a meeting of the British Medical Association in London that came as much a surprise to them as doctors in the audience. One of the speakers, Douglas Bevis, announced three healthy children already existed in the UK or western Europe after embryo transplantation.[78]

Bevis was a known name. Medically qualified in Manchester with service as a naval surgeon in the last war, like Patrick, his contribution to treating rhesus disease in infants was notable, if more acknowledged overseas than in his home country. Despite his nickname, "Tiger", from playing rugby at school, he was a man of quiet charm not known to make outrageous claims. He was a professor in Leeds and only a short drive from Oldham, but he had no professional connections there.

The Oldham team was bewildered, not daring to deny the claim in case it was true or look resentful if they were scooped. Bob put on a brave face, welcoming the news. It was never clear if Bevis made a covert claim for the babies or conveyed hearsay, and when pressed for more information he hid under the cloak of patient privacy. The story fizzled out, attributed to fake news. The kindliest interpretation was that the man had fallen unwell or become delusional, and he won some sympathy when hostile publicity ruined his reputation, leaving him a broken man, his earlier achievements forgotten. There was a lesson for pioneers: IVF was perilous territory.

The Oldham team had its own problems when Patrick became a patient. Years of working on his feet for long hours leaning over an operating table strained his back and joints. One arthritic hip had been replaced and the other was giving him chronic pain and needed attention at the end of 1975, followed by convalescence with Sheena in the Barbados. The clinical programme slumped despite help from Gordon Falconer, a junior surgeon who stepped into his shoes. The downturn came shortly after news of Gladys Purdy's diagnosis of terminal cancer. Jean asked to be released to help her mother and support her father, which meant closing the laboratory for over six months. She was indispensable. This sad news broke after a blissful summer.

The Edwards family was on holiday at Bruntscar in the Dales. One afternoon when Bob was working outdoors, he noticed the postmistress's husband cycling away from the farmhouse too far away to hail. It was puzzling because mail was delivered in the mornings. The man left a telegram which Ruth, suspecting unwelcome news from Oldham, propped on the mantelshelf for when Bob came back for supper. After tearing it open, he held it up with a broad grin.

POSITIVE – STOP – RING ME URGENTLY – STOP – PATRICK

They had waited years for this day. His dinner postponed, he raced across the dale to a phone box outside the inn. When he got through to Patrick, he heard a patient had a positive pregnancy test. She was a local woman with a long history of infertility after giving birth to a boy and wanted a brother or sister for him. The pregnancy came from a blastocyst transfer, but Bob believed it was stopping depot injections that made the difference.

She was told to avoid heavy work and keep the news to herself and her husband. The pregnancy continued uneventfully until the 12th week when she had a routine scan at Boundary Park. Staring at the screen, Patrick furled his brow. The fetal sac looked higher than normal; he needed a closer look. To his horror, he saw an ectopic pregnancy from the embryo moving out of the womb into the stump of a tube. The poor woman was terribly distraught and the whole team felt gutted. After terminating the pregnancy, he opened the sac to find a perfectly formed fetus. The woman begged them through tears to try again. About 60% of patients had only one attempt, a few tried four to eight times, but she had a total of ten cycles and never became pregnant again.

Bob was sure the *Lancet* would be avid to publish this case, but a rejection notice declared the story was not novel three years after the Australian report. His persistence paid off again, though, and a brief article appeared in the journal. There were detractors who denied the conception was by IVF, suggesting the ovum escaped during laparoscopy, but Patrick could refute them as he had carefully dissected the tubes, finding them completely blocked. It was, however, a solemn lesson that changed his practice. In future, he removed or sealed diseased tubes to make ectopic pregnancy impossible and thus provide undeniable proof that any conception afterwards must have occurred from a transferred embryo.

It was no compensation to the couple, but the case was encouraging for research as the most convincing evidence to date that the culture environment was good for embryos, and this would surely not be the last pregnancy. Bob wondered if they had missed biochemical pregnancies in which embryos perished so early that periods came back on time. He had an archive of blood samples preserved from previous cases and now shipped them to London for a more sensitive test. A few results came back positive to confirm his suspicion. Implantation wasn't the insuperable obstacle they had begun to fear, and perhaps the losses were more in line with those occurring naturally. They felt relief from the news, and knew it was only a matter time until a pregnancy reached full term. It would take 457 treatment attempts for at least 282 women. To reach the climax they needed a new strategy.

It might have been on one of his moorland hikes or in conversation with Ruth when Bob first aired the idea of casting troublesome drugs aside to go with natural menstrual cycles. It sounded like an option borne of desperation, yet it had the attraction of working with nature instead of riding over it. Welcome news for patients, it would be a heavier burden on staff. They would yield control, needing to precisely time each "wild" cycle to grab the single ovum from a ripe follicle before it ovulated. The prospect was daunting. There was no room for error finding the ovum and growing it to the stage for transfer.

Patrick raised his eyebrows, knowing the stakes and understanding the gravity of the challenge. The greater strain would be on Bob and Jean who would be slaves to the whims of nature, analysing countless samples around the clock and monitoring eggs. When the nurses were asked, none chickened out.

It would have been harder to switch tactics before a Japanese company manufactured a sensitive new method for measuring the ovulatory hormone LH. The *Hi-Gonavis* test could produce a result in minutes in their lab, and by analysing urine from patients every three hours they hoped to pinpoint the initial rush of LH into the bloodstream. A phone call to Muriel then arranged Patrick's team to assemble for collecting the ovum 24 hours later, a safe margin before it popped out of its follicle spontaneously. The laboratory would be ready even past midnight, and Bob thought the quiet hours were fine as they harmonised with biorhythms. The plan was far from a guaranteed success.

Time was running out with only nine months to go until Patrick retired as a consultant in the NHS. His 65th birthday would fall in July 1978. He was pulling out the stops for this wild shot, and they would see 80 more patients before the programme was wound up. Bob was eager to stop traipsing up and down the country, and everyone felt weary. It was time to make or break.

15

BABY OF THE CENTURY

Lesley Brown was not the kind of woman a film director would cast for a leading role, but her background made the story of IVF more poignant and her character was critical for success against the odds. She had the courage and determination to fulfil nature's call to motherhood, and never lost a natural modesty when she became celebrated.

A rebellious teenager from a broken home, Lesley ran away from her grandmother's Bristol house in 1963. Her first boyfriend was in detention at a borstal when she met John Brown, a stocky 21-year-old with long sideburns and a West Country brogue.[79] It was in a seedy café near the docks where seamen picked up girls. He was lonely, longing for a nice girlfriend. When he struggled to balance a factory job with care for two infant daughters after his wife abandoned them, he arranged for one child to be adopted by relatives and the other went into a municipal care home. They were hard times.

When they got together, Lesley and John looked a perfect match, but he could not offer security from what he earned after leaving school barely literate at age 16.[80] They spent the first night together in a disused railway carriage, drifting from there into cheap digs. But when he found more permanent employment they got married and took his daughter Sharon out of care to make a family of three. Lesley was a kind stepmother but craved for a baby of her own and became desperate as years rolled by. She blamed herself because John had proved he was fertile and felt she would never be a "proper woman" if she could not become a real mother.

She had an operation at the Royal Infirmary to unblock her fallopian tubes, but more barren years followed. An application to adopt a child as a last resort was turned down by the agency. After nine years of trying for a baby, and now aged 29, she hoped for a miracle after being warned she had only one chance in a million, yet she persevered with stubborn faith in her luck. Feeling for her desperation, a female gynaecologist mentioned there was a doctor near Manchester testing a method that sounded like science fiction. It was the thinnest of straws, but Lesley grasped it, asking to be referred to the wizard in the north. He was Patrick Steptoe.

The couple opened a long-awaited letter from Steptoe's office one day in 1976 when they came home from a caravan holiday. They were invited to a consultation in Manchester. For a couple who rarely drifted far from home, the north of England seemed like the end of the earth, but nothing would stop a woman seeking meaning for her life. They were poor and had to bear the costs of travel and boarding if she was accepted as a patient, but by a strange coincidence John won £800 on the football pools the day the letter arrived.

Patrick's consulting room was in swanky St John Street, where a row of gracious Georgian townhouses in the city centre survived the hegemony of Victorian architecture. The entrance would have reminded them of a Harley Street clinic had they ever visited London. They sat quietly among posh private patients in the waiting room. When their turn came, Patrick leaned over a large desk in a pin-striped suit, examining her notes from the hospital in Bristol. He said her regular periods were good news, but she would need an exploratory laparoscopy, and John would have a sperm count before they could join his list. He warned the experimental trial was unsuccessful so far, but any children conceived would be normal and healthy. His manner conveyed intimidating authority, and while he had not promised them anything, they put their faith in him and left the office feeling ecstatic. She vowed to obey his order to give up smoking.

When she returned in February it was to Kershaw's cottage hospital, staying at a B&B in a district of abandoned mills and factories with broken windows. Her laparoscopy the following day confirmed Patrick's suspicion; he found one of her tubes was stuck to its ovary and the other was a stump buried in a veil of adhesions. She needed another operation to bring order to her pelvis and resuspend the ovaries to make them accessible for ovum collection. The prospect of surgery didn't frighten her, and staff admired the stoicism that made her an ideal patient. She had to wait another six months to reach the top of the list, and then, satisfied with the operation, he gave her the green light to become one of the first patients in the new series. She would come for natural cycle treatment in November, over a year after her first visit.

John accompanied her for an appointment scheduled two days before her menstrual calendar predicted she would ovulate. As they entered Kershaw's, Bob strode up to greet them in his customary way, holding out a hand for a brisk shake and quickly easing into chitchat. John liked blokes who were "natural" and didn't put on airs.

Lesley was shown her bed where a large jug of drinking water stood on a table with a jar to pee in every three hours. Bob or Jean took the fresh specimens to check for the first telltale spike of LH with the *Hi-Gonavis* test, when they would convey the news to the medical team for collecting her ovum. John had to do his "bit". After washing to remove seminal fluid, his sperm sample was diluted and checked to confirm the cells thrashed around like microscopic tadpoles. Meanwhile, the medical team prepared Lesley in the theatre next door.

She lay on the table covered in drapes until Patrick moved a flap to expose flesh and insert a needle to inflate her pelvis. He introduced the laparoscope through a small incision and made ports on both flanks for other instruments. Through the scope, he spied unripe follicles in the right ovary, and the opposite organ was obscure behind fresh adhesions. But when he broke the veil of connective tissue, he sighed at the sight of a plump follicle, all pink and blue like a ripe grape. A nurse waited for his nod to signal her to flick a switch to start a vacuum pump whirring. A rehearsed team needs few words.

He guided a long needle to impale the follicle. Another nurse started the suction, holding up the collection jar to watch amber fluid enter from the catheter until she detached it for Jean to take away. Bob was sitting at the microscope in a white coat and cap with a noisy current of air blowing in his face through a filter in the back of the sterile hood. He poured drops of fluid from the jar into a dish, which he gently swirled while examining clumps of cells. The conversation paused until he yelled at the overhead intercom: "No luck. Try again." There was still a chance to find the ovum if it was stuck somewhere. Patrick scraped the deflated follicle with the needle point and called for more suction.

Jean waited solemnly as Bob searched the contents of the second bottle. He burst out, "I've got a beauty!" The ovum was fully mature, only needing a short rest before meeting John's sperm. After the drama there were smiles all round. Was greater effort ever invested in making a baby, or a single cell more precious?

When Lesley awoke, Patrick came into the recovery room in a green cap and gown. "We were lucky this time," he whispered to her. "Nearly gave up on you." She heard the other patient left earlier in tears. Having carried grief privately, thinking her condition was peculiar and blaming herself, she now realised she wasn't alone.

Workdays for Bob and Jean alternated between fits of concentrated activity and intervals kicking their heels until it was time to check dishes. All the toil and trouble were soon forgotten when they saw Lesley's egg bristling with sperm in its shell, but had one gone further to fertilise it? Yes, it had! He saw two plump pronuclei lying side-by-side and ready to unite their genetic loads. The single cell represented the Browns' hope of breaking years of quiet desperation and the medical team's brightest hope after a fruitless decade. But would the egg survive for transfer to Lesley, and, if so, would it end like all the previous cases?

By the next evening the egg had split to make two cells, and the following morning it had divided again, still inside the shell that stops embryos from sticking to fallopian tubes or a dish. The team now faced the perennial question of whether to transfer the embryo while the going was good or wait for the blastocyst stage that had a better prospect of implantation, if it survived the extra two days in culture. Bob cautiously advised to transfer the embryo later the same day at the 8-cell stage.

Patrick had reserved a table from 8 PM at a local restaurant for Sheena's 57th birthday. He planned the transfer shortly before the dinner party, but Bob called an hour earlier to report there were only 6 cells. The Steptoes went to the restaurant to meet their friends and he chose the best bottle of wine in the house, but only drank water.

They departed for Kershaw's at 10 PM to find Bob, Jean, and Muriel lounging outside the lab. Lesley rested nearby. He was told the embryo had stalled. They sat together chatting until midnight when Bob checked the embryo again. It now had 8 cells.

Patrick quickly donned his blues and scrubbed while Muriel prepared a tray of instruments, including the duck-billed speculum and tenaculum needed for the transfer procedure. She helped Lesley to the lithotomy position under the glare of lights on the operating table, covering her with a drape. Patrick wore a gleaming flashlight suspended on a band above his spectacles as he sat on a low stool between her legs spread in stirrups. After swabbing and opening the vagina, he had a clear view of the pink cervix and its dark centre that marked the entrance to the uterus. He gently slid a guide catheter inside.

Bob took supreme care to suck the embryo from its dish into the tip of the catheter. He carried it as a dangling loop between outstretched arms with rare deliberation for a man normally in haste. Patrick took it in both hands, inserting the open end into the guide and advancing it for a calculated distance to the apex of the uterus. He gently squeezed the plunger on the syringe at the other end. Bob had stepped back with the onlookers and now came forward to take the catheter back to the lab to check the embryo was expelled.

It was a repeat of so many previous performances in that theatre with the same two players centre-stage, although Sheena would say it was more like repertory since the acts were never quite the same and each subject on the table had a different story. One thing was always repeated: it was a shared belief with every new case that it would be "the one". But, hitherto, almost every patient who reached this stage had a negative test later, turning hope for a triumphant act into another rehearsal.

Lesley and John were euphoric when they returned to their council house in Bristol. It is not unusual for women to feel they are pregnant soon after an embryo is placed in their embracing womb, even before their physiology recognises it. Two weeks later, fingers were crossed when her period passed its due date.

The pregnancy test was ambiguous at first but came back positive next time. Lesley had succeeded at her first try. Without a phone at home, Bob had to mail the news, warning her to avoid exertion with sport or Christmas shopping.

Dear Mrs Brown,
Just a short note to let you know that the early results on your blood and urine samples are very encouraging and indicate that you might be in early pregnancy ...[81]

Alone at home when the letter arrived, John tore it open when he saw the Cambridge postmark. Still dancing around the room when she came in hauling two heavy bags from shopping, he waved it at her. It was the best Christmas present ever. She blessed her luck but still didn't realise she was the first patient to get this far. It was a distinction that never mattered to either of them.

After the holiday, the former trickle of patients at Kershaw's turned to a flood. Besides those returning for another round, there were 16 new cases in January. The staff were under pressure, and it was only bearable because the curtain would come down in July. The small carpark was busy as staff and supplies shuttled back and forth all day; the laboratory light never went off, and the W.C. was constantly busy for urine collection. When Jean was on night duty, patients remembered how she crept into their room to collect jars, and if she saw them tossing and turning in bed gave them thumbs-up with an ivory smile at the door. It was vital to maintain morale, and her knowledge of Lesley's baby and two more pregnancies on the way was immensely encouraging and hard to keep secret.

High spirits were blown down when one of the pregnancies miscarried from an extra set of chromosomes making it triploid.

Bob may have missed an extra pronucleus if it was hard to see. The third pregnancy was luckier until at five months the woman went into premature labour on a walking tour in the Dales. She delivered a perfect baby boy, but too small to be saved.

A final group of 22 women arriving in May included the 32-year-old Grace Montgomery (née MacDonald) from Scotland who was returning for a second attempt.[82] The first time she came after browsing an article in the *Lancet* on the table of her doctor's waiting room and persuaded him to recommend her to Patrick. The side-effects of drugs were horrible the first time, so she was glad to come back for natural cycle treatment, and almost arrived too late when her hormones surged earlier than expected.

Patients who reached embryo transfer were asked to remain in the district until their pregnancy test. It was a policy that gave them an opportunity to meet others, so they became more than names on a list and could share stories of personal journeys and make friends. They called themselves the "Ovum Club" and hosted a party for Patrick's retirement.

Grace was the lucky one. Her ovum was found and fertilised, becoming a healthy embryo for Patrick to transfer to her. When coffee tasted repugnant, she guessed she was pregnant before the test confirmed it. Her joy was tempered by knowledge that at tender stages there is no guarantee of a happy outcome, and it was hard to share news with others going home disappointed. The absence of jealousy was amazing as they drifted home, bidding her, "Do it for us, Grace!"

It is hard to be a lonely survivor and the only saving grace for the rest was Patrick's assurance they could come back, although he could not say where or when. Many of them decided it was time for closure from exhaustion or advancing age, but the heart-ache remained, and some marriages failed under the strain of unconquered infertility. Perhaps when IVF became routine, they found satisfaction looking back at their contribution to progress, but privacy forbids naming them.

Sixteen weeks into her pregnancy, Lesley returned to Manchester to screen for chromosomes by amniocentesis and test her baby for neural tube defects. Gynaecology makes strange bed fellows as she had to wait among patients who had miscarried or came for an abortion. She was nervous because she had promised to have the pregnancy terminated if the baby was abnormal. But everything was fine, and she was told it would be a girl. She already felt bonded, and the sight of her baby on the scanner screen was immensely moving. The news was relayed to Patrick and Sheena on a Cunard cruise in the Caribbean, and that night they popped open a fine bottle of champagne.

Despite precautions to avoid leaks, a hospital mole passed intelligence to the Oldham *Chronicle*. From time to time, lurid headlines announced the baby would be born abnormal, or if she was safely delivered "Mr and Mrs X" and their doctors would become millionaires. Such fake news would be worse today from gossip and speculation spread by social media. Patrick was so worried about the strain on Lesley and risk of discovery he sent her to stay with his daughter Sally in Suffolk. Afterwards she moved in with her brother in Bristol.

The doctor who took care of her there noted a slightly elevated blood pressure that accounted for her swollen ankles. These were potential signs of pre-eclamptic toxaemia, a complication of late pregnancy that harms both mother and baby. At 32 weeks, long before her due date, Patrick booked her into the maternity block at Boundary Park under the pseudonym Rita Ferguson. Only two members of staff knew her real identity, and he kept her notes in his pocket for safety. Bob had caught reporters rifling through a hospital filing cabinet.

After another scan and X-ray, the fully formed baby was found to have stopped growing, increasing the fear that toxaemia reduced blood flow to her placenta. Every planned pregnancy is precious, but no adjective fitted this one. When the local newspaper got wind of the danger, it printed a headline that Mrs X would lose her baby. Lesley should never have seen it as it made her frantic. John threatened to dig out the mole, who would not fare well against him. There were journalists roaming the hospital disguised as workmen, and a pair dressed as a nun and priest asking nurses where they could comfort the patient. Unaccustomed to unsavoury attention, the hospital managers were slow to post guards, and apologised for their bad apple in the *Chronicle's* pocket (who was never identified). Normally a poised and self-confident doctor, Patrick called a senior colleague in London for reassurance in case Lesley had a medical emergency. Fortunately, her blood pressure stabilised, the baby started to grow again, and the risk of premature birth faded.

Advance preparations were made for the birth in case media attention turned into a tsunami. Patrick and Bob turned down offers to tell their side of the story to the media and advised the Browns to sell world rights to a single publisher so competitors would leave them alone. Advised against big deals from America, they focused on British contracts for the rights to newsprint and books, films and TV. A local solicitor was engaged to draft a contract with Associated Newspapers Ltd, the London company that owned the *Daily Mail*.[83] Although financial details were confidential, it did not stop speculation about deals of up to £350,000. The Browns vehemently denied astronomical sums, and they obviously spoke honestly because their lifestyle remained modest. They consented to a film of the birth and an interview afterwards through the Central Office of Information, a communications agency of government. The couple had come a long way from a grubby railway carriage to the limelight of international attention.

As the date of delivery drew close, media attention grew more intense, attracting TV crews and reporters from around the world who sent out scouts looking for unusual activity around the hospital. An anonymous caller tried to smoke Lesley out of the maternity block with a bomb warning. It was distressing to be the cause of a commotion that forced women out of beds in the labour ward or after operations, but after two hours with sniffer dogs the police gave the all-clear.

Patrick decided to deliver the baby by caesarean section. Some professional opinions have declared it was unnecessary, but he did not want to risk a lengthy birth in an extraordinary case. He set the date for the 29th July when a test of amniotic fluid proved the baby's lungs could fully expand for her first breath. He then brought it forward three days, and then finally chose Tuesday the 25th to foil the media and its slimy mole.

He visited her every day, and after finishing a ward round that Tuesday he checked her blood pressure and fetal heart for the last time. It was OK! That was when he told her this was the night. She shouldn't tell John when he came to kiss her goodnight, so he wouldn't betray his excitement. He would go back to the hotel where he was staying under the alias Ron Ferguson, conveyed by *Daily Mail* minders by lying down on the back seat with decoy drivers to mislead competitors. He didn't stop for a pint that night at the Turk's Head where the press harassed the landlord for information, nor did he expect to be called back to the hospital around 9 PM.

Bob was unaware of the revised date until Patrick telegrammed him. On holiday with his family at Bruntscar, he was dipping sheep with Ambrose Brennand. The distant roar of a motor bike along the track made him look up. That meant only one thing, so he headed back to read the message. Knowing little about his friend's other life, the farmer was dumbfounded when Bob appeared in fresh clothes shouting to watch the news the next morning.

Jean was waiting when he turned up at Boundary Park around 8 PM. John Webster was preparing to assist Patrick with the operation, and the anaesthetist and paediatrician had been called. But Muriel was returning from vacation at her sister's home in Cornwall, still expecting a later date for delivery, and had no phone connection to alert her. She would hear the news on the car radio as she drove into Manchester. After investing so much, it was a bitter disappointment to miss the birth of the century, and she refused to speak to Patrick for weeks. Edith Astell took her place as the senior nurse. Everything was ready except the drag of official paperwork. Patrick instructed the staff to guard theatre doors as a surgeon is master of his domain, and hospital managers despatched constables to patrol corridors and watch for peeping toms at windows who might trigger a chaotic invasion.

They knew that a nurse could innocently give the game away if she was told not to take Lesley's supper that night, for that would mean she was fasting in preparation for surgery, so they arranged a ruse. Sheena came pretending to be on a routine visit, pouring the tea down the sink and hiding Lesley's meal in her bag to take away. When the nurse returned, she was amazed Lesley had eaten so well and offered more, making it hard for the two women to conceal their smiles.

The Steptoes drove away together in his white Mercedes, hoping that scouts would notice and leave their stations until the next day. After a short break at home, they returned unnoticed through a side door during the busy hour for hospital visitors. Patrick left the locker room with John to convey Lesley from her private room. It was a strange scene as two doctors pushed a trolley along empty corridors after the hospital went to sleep. Patrick murmured, "They'll wish they had me in London now".

Medical staff gathered in the theatre wearing blues and greens, and behind their masks harboured private anxieties. They were skating on thin ice, but no one could be sure how thin. No baby had ever been born after conception in a dish. If she was the least abnormal, even from obviously natural causes, clinical IVF would be finished, and reputations ruined for everyone involved. There could no cover-up in front of press cameras and other witnesses.

The anaesthetist Finlay Campbell prepared Lesley with a muscle relaxant and sedative before intubating her for a mixture of oxygen and nitrous oxide to put her to sleep. Patrick stood squarely at the table with his team at their posts; Bob and Jean were out of sight. The crew from the government office and newspaper stood back with cameras pointed at the floodlit scene.

Patrick looked cooler than he felt. He had done the same operation countless times, always quick and never hasty. He made a long incision with a scalpel in Lesley's belly, controlling the blood seeping from the wound with the waft of an electrocautery. The peritoneal wall open, he pushed aside the empty bladder with a retractor. The swollen womb now revealed, he cut a letter-box opening in its lower segment from which milky amniotic liquor gushed out for a nurse to mop with a wad of gauze.

Plunging his hand inside to feel the baby's head, he gently eased it through the aperture and then gently hauled out the rest of the wet body. The pulsating cord was immediately clamped and divided. All eyes fastened on the baby, not the clock at 11.47 PM. Camera shutters and flashguns never fired faster, even at the Academy Awards.

Holding the baby in his arms, Patrick declared in a matter of fact way, "It's a girl". Everyone knew that already and waited for more momentous news as he quickly examined her. "It's a perfectly normal baby." They were the most memorable words of the day, celebrating the child for being whole and ordinary. Moments later she took a deep breath to let out one of the loudest yells ever heard there.

In a deep voice that hid relief, he said, "That's what I like to hear. Good lung development."

With her face wiped and airway sucked clear of mucus, a nurse carried her to the weighing scales. She registered 5 lb 12 oz, or 2.8 kilograms. A nurse nodded with a smile after pressing a stethoscope on her little chest. The baby was bonny, ruddy, chubby, and had good musculature. She continued crying as the paediatrician Don Hilson examined her for the first time in a series of tests, more than any other for an uneventful birth.

Patrick removed the afterbirth and closed the womb, but before stitching the skin wound, he did something remarkable. Gently lifting the organs to show witnesses, he proved Lesley had no tubes, so no one could deny that conception occurred outside the body. The new mother was wheeled away fast asleep in a trolley with a drip stand.

When the paediatrician finished, he passed the baby to Patrick who cradled her in a blanket. Bob stepped forward to take his turn, a broad grin hidden behind his mask. It is a rare scientist who makes a fundamental discovery and then runs all the way to an historic application. Jean was out of sight behind him, but Patrick curled his hand to urge her forward and laid his arm on her shoulder for the trio to stand together blinking at the staring floodlights.

Meanwhile, John Brown waited anxiously in another room with Sheena. She tried to distract him with mundane talk and joke about the TV series with her family name, Steptoe and Son.[84] A nurse burst in to tell him he had a beautiful, healthy baby girl. The

Browns' journey had been so long that the end made the brawny man speechless, and tears rolled down his cheeks. He kissed the women. When his daughter was brought, he was too scared to hold her for long. He worried he might drop her from shaking, saying over and over, "I can't believe it!"

It was the small hours of the morning when the Steptoes drove home through empty streets, though they couldn't sleep much that night. John Webster invited Bob and Jean to his hospital apartment across the road where his wife prepared a snack of cheese on toast. There was no champagne that night, and the only bubbles were in their heads.

Patrick visited Lesley early the next morning in her room. It was customary for nurses to bring new babies to their mother's bedside, but this time they insisted he have the pleasure. As he transferred the baby to her, she fell silent for a long time until she found the strength to say, "Thank you for my baby". The Browns wanted the name "Louise" and asked the Steptoes to choose her middle name, and it was "Joy". Some years later when an interviewer asked Patrick to recall the day, he stumbled for words and could only offer the colossal understatement that he would never have the same experience again.

The morning after delivery, Patrick and Bob sat side by side for live interviews on TV. The *Daily Mail* blazed the headline, "It's a Girl", followed the next day by, "And Here She is, the Lovely Louise". The *Daily Express* proclaimed, "The Men Who Made the Breakthrough", giving credit to the male duo and overlooking all the women who made the feat possible. Announcements were broadcast in English and multiple languages throughout the world, but most doctors were reluctant to comment until they assimilated what had happened.

Sammy Edwards, then a distribution manager at Manchester's *Evening News*, chuckled when he saw a freshly inked headline on his paper, "The All-British Miracle", about his younger brother's achievement. It was patriotic news to cheer a nation in the blues during the so-called "Winter of Discontent" when labour unions, refuse collectors, and gravediggers went on strike in the hard winter ahead.

Despite the leaks and rumours, the baby Louise took many people by surprise, even close confidantes of the pioneers. Howard and Georgeanna Jones were moving into a new home in Norfolk, Virginia, when a reporter turned up unexpectedly to interview them, and Jean Cohen was in his Parisian clinic when he heard news on the radio. Both parties would soon launch their own IVF clinics, while naysayers had to eat humble pie. Roger Short, now hailing IVF as a breakthrough, was invited to explain the significance and morality of IVF from John Knox's pulpit at St Giles Cathedral in Edinburgh. Afterwards in the vestry, an elderly lady whispered, "I've seldom seen the kirk so full. It's the rain, you know." Seldom has such a proud message been deflated so completely, but IVF would eventually become as familiar as weather forecasts.

The ambulance to take Lesley and Louise home was surrounded by a throng of reporters and cameramen before the driver could depart. Towards the end of a three-hour journey, a radio message warned a crowd had gathered in the Browns' street and cars blocked the junction, so he pulled up until the police cleared a passage. When he finally drove up and opened the back door, a microphone swung into Lesley's face on a long boom and a gang of reporters begged her for comments. She remained silent as she jostled with her husband to the front door and her driver carried baby Louise over heads.

Once indoors, John slammed and bolted the door. They moved to the back of the house like timid animals in a cage to avoid faces at the windows. It took several days for the hubbub to die down and telephoto lenses to withdraw from windows of neighbours who cashed in on the media frenzy. The Browns settled down to open hundreds of cards and gifts from well-wishers around the globe. Their lives would never be the same again. They never expected or sought celebrity status, they only wanted a baby, and four years later they had another girl, Natalie, also conceived at the first attempt.

The MacDonald baby Alastair was born in a Glasgow hospital in January 1979, but a snowstorm prevented Bob and Patrick from attending the delivery. During Grace's stay in the Oldham area she got to know the Browns, and the two families built a friend-ship that continues through their children. Lesley warned Grace she would also come under siege, and both families retreated to greater privacy at new addresses. Alastair was raised quietly so he would be treated the same as other children, but there was pride in having the world's second IVF baby and first boy. Grace was startled a few years later when she heard the rank was challenged.

On Christmas Day 1978, three weeks before Alastair was born, the magazine *Medical World News* reported an IVF baby was delivered three months earlier. If Oldham was never a scientific hub, Calcutta was even less likely. The sixth Prime Minister, Rajiv Gandhi, called it a "dying city", although it had a proud history as a nursery of creative minds. Was it credible that a lone Indian genius had succeeded through all the tricky steps?

The same year that Patrick and Bob got together, Subhas Mukherjee moved to Edinburgh to study reproductive endocrinology at a renowned research unit.[85] His training did not include embryology, nor did he visit Oldham. Mukherjee returned to India where he had a local reputation until the birth of the little girl with the pseudonym "Durga" brought him to notice.

Born 70 days after Louise, he said the girl was conceived in a dish and her embryo frozen before transfer, a double claim because it was not until five years later that the first cases of embryo freezing were announced in Australia and the Netherlands. For a frozen embryo, it meant the date of fertilisation was close to when Louise was conceived.

The status of priority is key in science and medicine, and a matter of professional pride. The dazzling news of an Indian birth prompted the West Bengal government to investigate the story. Mukherjee explained to the committee how he achieved the goal but could not release the names of Durga's parents who pleaded privacy. Infertility was shameful in their culture. The investigators were not persuaded by the evidence, accusing the doctor of fabricating the story. They forbade him from lecturing overseas, forcing him into another clinical service where they hoped the embarrassing case would be forgotten. He committed suicide three years later at age 50.

The tragic story would have faded except for T.C. Anand Kumar, the nation's premier reproductive biologist, a patriotic Indian trained in England and one of Bob's friends from his connection with the IPPF. He accepted the committee's report until he read the laboratory notes and met the parents and one of Muhkerjee's associates. He became convinced the man made an honest claim. He decided to surrender the prestige of being the scientist behind his country's first official IVF baby, born in 1986, to restore the man's reputation and transfer the credit.[86]

From the little we know about Durga's parents, their long history of trying for a baby was compounded by tubal disease and low sperm counts. The doctor's notes bear witness to a conscientious and skilful gynaecologist who had a colleague trained in freezing and thawing cells, but there was no record of pilot studies with animal or human embryos. The woman aged 31 was stimulated with HMG and five ova were recovered by accessing her ovaries via incisions in the vagina. The fertilised eggs were frozen for several weeks before thawing them one at a time for transfer in successive cycles. It was a smart strategy, one that Bob wanted to try when freezing technology became available.[87]

What can we make of this story so many years later? IVF is now routine and every stage in the complex process is better understood, but it was a huge challenge in the 1970s even for dedicated teams trained in specialised facilities, and most experts denied it was possible. Should Muhkerjee be hailed as a wronged pioneer who succeeded against the odds or was the child conceived naturally and he made an honest mistake?

Infertility is often assumed to be a permanent state if a couple has tried to conceive for years whereas it is often a matter of statistical probability. There are women whose periods stop at young ages only to have them revive spontaneously years later to offer a chance of motherhood. There are other cases where they become pregnant by natural intercourse after doctors diagnosed them with infertility and tried IVF, successfully or otherwise. We might wonder if in exceptional cases treatment can open the obstruction enough for gametes and embryos to pass through tubes. The Australian woman who had the biochemical pregnancy after IVF also had blocked tubes, yet she had a pregnancy later without medical assistance. Such cases occurring sporadically imply that unless tubes are sealed, as Patrick insisted, the possibility of fertilisation in the body is hard to rule out absolutely.

Science offers greater authority than clinical notes and the memories of witnesses, but it is silent in this case because there are no tests to prove if a subject was conceived in vitro. It is the most wonderful thing about IVF that babies are indistinguishable in biology or genetics to the rest of us. This has allowed Durga's story to become promoted from a shameful claim to a brilliant achievement, and where the question is considered settled it is a matter of national pride. Bob knew the story but did not comment publicly, neither therefore will this writer cast an opinion, but let readers draw their own conclusions.

16

MANOR BORN

It was hard to accuse IVF of being a wild idea after Louise and Alastair, yet their births were regarded by stubborn detractors as singularly lucky breaks. Few people imagined it would join the pantheon of medical breakthroughs, but doubts faded as more babies were announced.

One icy night in January 1979, Bob and Patrick travelled to London to give prestigious lectures at the Royal College of Obstetricians & Gynaecologists. The meeting hall was packed with members and fellows of the college, and seats reserved for Sheena and Ruth who brought their families and friends. Howard Jones flew in from Virginia, two embryologists came from Australia, and another pair from France. The audience hushed as the speakers took the podium in turn. They could now look down at familiar faces: college grandees who once dashed Patrick's hopes of a practice in London and men who turned down Bob's MRC grant. It was an immensely satisfying occasion calling on the greatest restraint to avoid looking smug.

After speeches that left listeners spellbound everyone rose to give a standing ovation, the first since the college's royal charter. Most opposition dissolved that night because IVF was not so risky as pessimists maintained; it was an excellent option for patients with blocked tubes and had potential for overcoming other problems. It was a triumphal night except for whisperings that investors had gagged Bob from declaring the prized recipes of culture media. It was never characteristic of either man to hold back information, so the criticism blew over.

The first two births marked the end of the beginning. Invitations poured in for Bob and Patrick to speak at glitzy dinners and conferences, but these were distractions from their path. Although everything was different nothing had changed. Where would they make a new clinic after winding up operations at Kershaw's?

When Patrick retired the previous July, he lost the privileges of a surgeon, although he was still in Rochdale and seeing private patients. Ruth was glad to have Bob back in the fold, though he was often overseas on peregrinations that earned him record air miles. Arguably the foremost reproductive scientist in the world, and certainly the most famous, his acclaim was not yet universal. There was still smouldering opposition, if expressed more discreetly, and dons in his department sneered at the ambition to open a fertility clinic.

He had two fallow years after Louise was born, but only as far as IVF was concerned. It was not Bob's nature to wait for something to turn up; he had contracts for two books along with conference travel, teaching, and research. The first book was autobiographical with alternating chapters written by Patrick. *A Matter of Life* had the freshness of recent history. The second, published the same year in 1980, was the vastly ambitious *Conception in the Human Female*, a compendium of over 1,000 pages about female biology and reproductive health that colleagues held in biblical awe. It demonstrated he was as skilful a craftsman with the pen as a pipette. He drafted it in a cluttered room at the farmhouse while Jean scuttled around libraries for him and his long-suffering secretary Barbara typed up scrawled notes and revisions he grafted with tape.

The Edwards had recently moved from Gough Way to a 60-acre farm outside the city in the village of Dry Drayton. They had many happy years after renovating the damp Victorian farmhouse. It was Bob's dream to own a farm but fell to Ruth's practical head to make it prosper while raising their daughters and returning to work in the lab. They wanted to use the hodgepodge of fields for livestock, make new paths, fences, and stiles, and dig a pond for stocking with fish. The land was transformed into a haven to enjoy with their family, which grew to 12 grandchildren. He resumed a mission to plant trees that finally numbered thousands on previously rough grazing land, earning him the name "tree man" from neighbours who watched him in a woolly hat and raincoat planting saplings in the fall and watering them in summer drought.

Cattle and goats arrived, a livery service was opened, and a small menagerie of fur and feather roamed the yard. The Edwards were not seeking a living from farming; it was more a hobby and fulfilment of a boy's dream. He was enormously proud the day he helped to foal a mare, but it was Ruth who cared for most of the animals, and her scientific background was handy. She improved the stock of pedigree Angora goats using artificial insemination, and a veterinarian helped to transfer high quality embryos to "scrub" goats. Sweaters knitted from fleeces were shown at exhibitions and sold at craft fairs. Duck End Farm was a lively expression of their love of animals and eclectic interests.

At various times of day, Bob could be seen wearing a collar and tie or overalls. His red truck parked outside the department with bales of straw in the back was emblematic of a man who strained to live several lives at once—university professor and clinic director, writer and publisher, politician and farmer. He said with a wry smile he never knew anyone worth cloning including himself, but it is the only way to achieve such vast ambition.

Ruth never tied a ball and chain on his leg, though sometimes wished she had. He carried the workload of two or three able people, needed little sleep, and dozed off with a pile of papers on the eiderdown at night. He had a gift for tuning out of intense mental activity to recharge energy, but never really did — nor could — put out of mind an agonising decision.

He needed another clinic to resume the partnership with Patrick and regain the lead they were losing to the Aussies. After the first ten babies, the Melbourne teams generously opened doors to train the world. In America, Howard and Georgeanna Jones with Lucinda Veeck as their embryologist were expecting their first baby at the end of 1981. There was progress, too, in France, Germany, Austria, Japan, and Israel. The Brits believed that if their government had enough national pride, they would open a clinic for the public, so they were flabbergasted when the Department of Health turned them down. The MRC had refused them before on the grounds that IVF was clinical, and now the NHS used the excuse it was research and too expensive.

Jean had tried to persuade them to stay in Oldham, but it was too late for that. Bob was tired of the journey and Patrick was retired and ready to move. Cambridge was a better prospect since a clinical school opened in 1976, and there was accommodation in the sprawling Addenbrooke's hospital. He dreamt of modern facilities close to home, but the hospital offered two rooms, an antiquated operating theatre on an upper floor, and a "shed" outside for a lab. Tramping up and down stairs with dishes would be far worse than before. Cambridge missed an opportunity.

There was only one other option, but going private ran against Bob's principles, and Patrick was committed to the NHS too. Neither of them had the business experience or connections to investors to open a private clinic, so Bob contacted the editor at the *Daily Mail* who had offered to help if they ran into difficulties. The offer was still open, and the editor asked if they had any premises in mind. Building from scratch would delay opening services, so Bob despatched Jean to search the property market while he finished his textbook. She pored over lists at estate agents and scoured the district for empty mansions, factories, and offices. None of them fitted, including a 400-year-old Jacobean hall.

The hall of ancient bricks and tall chimneys stood four-square on a raised mound that once commanded a view over a moat. It had a stable block and a chapel, plus 20 acres of lawns and gardens. Only eight miles from the city, it was one of the architectural gems of the county set at the heart of the tiny village of Bourn and next to the medieval church of Saints Helena and Mary. It was Bourn Hall and she could not get it out of her head.

When she laid the prospectus on Bob's desk, she watched to see his response as he turned the pages and examined the pictures. The owner was asking £250,000, a fortune in those days for a building with Grade 2 listing that made renovations more expensive. It wasn't what they had in mind, yet they had to see it.

It was no less beautiful than illustrated. As they stood on the threshold, their backs to manicured shrubberies and lawns mown with military precision, there was a carved family shield over the lintel with the Huguenot motto, *Jour de ma Vie*, roughly translated, "A day is like my whole life". The owner Major King swung open the heavy oak door, the picture of an old army officer with an accent redolent of a privileged class Bob shunned when he was in the service. As they followed him on a tour of the hall and adjacent buildings, they saw chandeliers and moulded ceilings, oak wainscoting and leaded windows, Persian carpets and a roaring log fire to take the nip out of frigid air. The furnishings and decoration were from a bygone era, and there was precious little upgrading since electricity was brought in from the street. It was a museum piece, hard to imagine as a licensed clinic, so they dared not give their hearts away.

When they told Patrick, he agreed they should ask if Associated Newspapers was interested in the property. It was and sent a surveyor to evaluate and draft proposals for conversion. The plans were extremely detailed and exuberantly ambitious. The hall needed redecoration, re-plumbing, re-wiring, and all the mod-cons for surgery and laboratories. There would be a canteen and dining room for patients and staff, and menus that could grace a 4-star restaurant. Rooms would be provided for resident staff and a customised home was planned at the bottom of the driveway for the Steptoes, for which Patrick wanted to copy the floorplan of the Joneses' home in Virginia.

It was euphoric news after a barren year. With the architect's plans sent to the county planning office, tenders were invited from construction companies. Progress was whizzing along when Bob received an unexpected phone call from London in April 1979. That was all it took to return the hall to hush. Their sponsors had pulled out, fearing a baby could be born with an abnormality. *April is the cruellest month, breeding lilacs out of the dead land.*[88]

After the struggle to pick the fruits of autumn and survive winter's hibernation, hope died in the spring. They persuaded the company to delay an auction for a month to give time to find another investor. Alan Dexter, a financier with experience in hospital projects, became their lifeguard although he knew no more about IVF than what he had read in newspapers. He advised them to raise money in the City of London, but it was hard to generate interest for an unprecedented project, especially if led by a scientist and a retired doctor with only two babies. Competitors in Australia and America had less difficulty finding angel investors than Alan ever had in the country where

IVF was born. A notice in the *Financial Times* finally led to a private equity company willing to help on condition that Bob and Patrick demonstrated faith in the enterprise by digging in their own pockets. They wanted Alan, too, as a savvy businessman.

The hall started to hum again with workmen. Since it would take two years to finish the main building, they rented portacabins to launch the clinic as soon as possible. The prefabricated shells provided accommodation for patients with adjacent rooms for hormone analysis, sperm preparation, embryology, and an operating room designed by Muriel. Jean planned the embryology lab, including a communicating hatch for passing culture dishes between rooms, a feature copied elsewhere. The hormone lab was first to transfer into the old hall where it occupied part of the stable block with remnants of mangers still hanging on walls. Some services moved much later to a new block yet to be built. Patrick and Sheena never got their custom-home, although a thatched cottage in the village was a charming alternative.

Clinical services opened without any fanfare in October 1980. Patrick was the medical director and Bob scientific director while Alan managed the business and Jean had the honorific title of technical director. A festive outdoor party with fireworks was delayed until bonfire night in November when Bob groomed the lawn with an old tractor and Patrick entertained families by dressing up as the scarecrow Worzel Gummidge.

The programme unfolded as a facsimile of what they left at Kershaw's. They had to chart the whims of natural cycles for Patrick to collect the single ovum for Bob and Jean to combine with sperm to warm in desiccators. Bob was torn between the fear of changing anything lest the results suffer versus the impulse for research to find improvements. Jean's training as a nurse kept him from wild experimentation, and the balance paid off better than expected after a two-year gap.

The first two patients each had an embryo for Patrick to transfer in late October. In the next fortnight, most of the 21 new cases had an ovum successfully recovered, although not all fertilised. It was not long afterwards when Bob walked into Alan's office holding aloft a vessel of yellow liquid. Alan said it was too early for a glass of Chardonnay. It was urine. One of the first two patients was pregnant. It was a spectacular start and they were back in business. Patrick opened a bottle of chilled champagne to celebrate with them, and a few weeks later there was more news as progress gathered momentum. By the first anniversary of opening, they could boast over 60 ongoing pregnancies and five births. Jean raised a flag on the pole in the back green every time a patient called to announce a baby.

Mechanical diggers and men in boiler suits were familiar sights around the hall, while medical care went on inside portacabins. It was a happy and productive scene indoors and outdoors. Only Bob was worried. There was dust blowing from the windy fens, noise from low flying jets for which he harangued a USAF station, and he grumbled when farmers burnt stubble in their fields. After so much effort to prevent contamination he wanted to avoid anything that might spoil results. Concerned about the effects of light on biorhythms, he installed blackout curtains in patients' rooms, and after hearing that tungsten light hurt hamster embryos, he fitted microscopes with red filters that turned everything green in the eyes of staff after using them. He forbade photographing embryos and urged the team to return dishes quickly to the incubator to avoid chilling. When so little was known, he left no stone unturned in case it could improve results.

Services for patients were open 365 days a year, staffed by three shifts of nurses around the clock. The embryology lab buzzed from 6 AM to midnight. Heavy workloads were signs of success but blinded them to a looming problem on the bottom line. Alan was alarmed when the balance sheet tilted to the red as fee income was eroded by service costs and mortgage debt when the bank rate hovered around 17%. The other directors were oblivious. Patrick gave free treatment to couples with limited means, and Bob wanted the best equipment and more embryologists. They needed more patients to avoid bankruptcy, but it was hard to contact people on the list carried over from Oldham. Suddenly, it dawned that childless women go out to work, and when they started calling in the evenings the appointments calendar began to fill.

Patients came from across the British Isles and in equal numbers from overseas in the first couple of years. They stayed for at least a week, usually paying in cash because a cheque made to Bourn Hall meant only one thing and they wanted their presence to be secret. The press sniffed around the village for gossip and rumours about celebrity patients, and the broad apron of lawn held them at bay as the moat had kept hostile forces out long ago. The pro-life lobby called LIFE was frustrated when the horrors it imagined could not be confirmed, and didn't arrange street protests like those troubling the Jones Institute in Virginia.[89] The hall was a home for a happy family headed by Fathers Patrick and Bob who managed operations with a light touch, even bringing food hampers to workers on Christmas Day.

The drudgery of charting menstrual cycles to predict the day of ovum collection was abandoned when the hall switched to stimulated cycles following the lead of Australian and American groups. Clomiphene and HMG offered the tremendous advantages of conveniently timing collection and boosting the potential harvest of eggs. It was never clear why they failed at

Kershaw's, but the benefits were undeniable now, and this was the first notable change in practice at the hall.

The rising number of patients and intensity of embryology work stole time Bob needed for other responsibilities. He hired three young biologists in 1982, starting with Simon Fishel who earned his PhD in the Marshall Lab, then Carol Fehilly who studied goat-sheep chimaeras ("geeps") across town, and Jacques Cohen who had experience with cell culture and freezing in Rotterdam. They were the generation of brave new embryologists, including Alex Lopata and Alan Trounson in Australia, Lucinda Veeck in America, and Jacques Testart in France, among a few others. They had broader responsibilities than embryologists today and greater liberty before new regulations, accreditation, and paperwork changed their job forever. Apart from those lucky enough to have Bob and Jean as coaches, they learned from journals and conferences as well as trial and error. Before commercial services were available, they had to make and test culture media, fabricate their own tools and small equipment, chemically analyse specimens, keep clinical records, and even design laboratories. They had to be inquisitive and prepared to experiment to raise pregnancy rates above a dismal 15 to 20%.

Those men and women (mostly women in future) became founders of a biomedical discipline that is exceptional because they were science graduates with patients, albeit microscopic ones, and made key decisions with medically qualified colleagues. Bob was the founder of the new specialty and its guiding genius. A man of restless curiosity who loved to crack a mystery, he was always far more than Patrick's clinical embryologist in any modern sense. As for Jean, she had a unique role as his assistant and was an archetype for clinical embryologists who, more like physicians and engineers than basic scientists, have duties to patients and skills to identify and fix clinical problems.

With his new trio, Bob could concentrate on other things, while Jean withdrew from the embryology lab, although still the oracle for information and willing to give a helping hand. Still responsible for making and checking culture media together, they never lost the attention to detail they had at the beginning. She continued to be the record-keeper, her assistants verifying data in notebooks so there would never be a scandalous mix-up of gametes or embryos at the hall.

They needed more doctors and nurses as the service grew. John Webster came down from Oldham as the first and most experienced of the crew who could substitute for Patrick, now hiding an ailment. Muriel Harris brought some of her original team from Lancashire and was appointed matron, residing in the stable block. They didn't realise they were pioneers of another new specialty, and fertility nursing has taken over some responsibilities from doctors as nurse practitioners adjust medications and even transfer embryos in some centres. Muriel still had an adventurous spirit and could be seen in a Piper aircraft looping the loop overhead, although prowess in acrobatics was not matched in navigation, not at least on the day she got lost in traffic over Stansted International Airport.

One more brand of professional staff emerged at Bourn Hall. Busy doctors and nurses had difficulty finding enough time to counsel patients, and this would become mandated when Britain passed a law to regulate IVF. Bob persuaded Tim Appleton to be the first fertility counsellor, a role he added to existing jobs as a physiology lecturer and an ordained priest in the Church of England. Tim fulfilled it superbly, setting a high standard from the start. Counselling was not only for people with strong religious convictions, it helped others to negotiate the complexities and ethics of medical treatment. Tim would also officiate when the time came for funerals of two of the clinic's founders.

The team assembled to review clinical cases and discuss research every lunch hour. No one was excluded. Patrick sat at the head of the table like a sleepy owl in immaculately preened plumage until he abruptly broke the silence with an astute comment to show he was paying attention all the time. Bob would rush in from the university to dominate discussion between munches on a cheese and onion roll. He never let sloppy arguments pass, despite contributing plenty of his own whacky ideas. It was always a positive experience, educational and never intimidating. In respecting, even inviting, lucid criticism of his suggestions, others found the confidence to speak up. If the clinical pregnancy rate fell back, everyone contributed to the inquest and no theory was too trite. It usually led to a fit of scrubbing and fresh batches of medium, but the causes of fluctuating results were often unidentified, and still are. IVF still has its mysteries. Throughout proceedings, Patrick and Bob, affectionately nicknamed Steppy and the Boss behind their backs, respected the other's expertise, and if they were ever heard arguing behind closed doors both came out smiling.

The meetings sizzled from mixing staff, but otherwise professional turf was respected. Bob was the only non-medic who could casually walk into the surgical arena, whereas embryologists held junior doctors at bay where they feared endangerment of their sanctum sanctorum. One day when a group of American doctors came as observers, a sperm sample was being prepared when a visitor rested his behind on the edge of a sterile flow cabinet, knocking over a methanol burner that burst into flames around his feet. The embryologists now savoured their prejudice, yet Bob, the obsessive boss, would later laugh off the incendiary incident.

By the fifth year, 30 patients passed through the service every week and 1,000 babies had been born, more than the rest of the world combined. Photographs of cute children sent by doting parents crowded the noticeboards. Treatment given to early patients was now outdated by better technology, raising the pregnancy rate towards 30% per cycle. The hall had already replaced desiccators with incubators automatically controlling carbon dioxide, but still preferred home-brew culture medium to commercial products. Never very accurate, *Hi-Gonavis* was traded for a better assay for LH, and a whole slew of hormones was measured by Colin Howles, who joined the hall after training in sheep endocrinology. Staff who started in academic careers were sometimes snubbed by former colleagues for deserting "pure science", and a few like Colin moved on to the expanding corporate world of fertility. Growing in leaps and bounds, IVF opened new professional channels.

Breathtaking changes were happening in the clinical domain too. Ultrasound scanning for follicle growth replaced round-the-clock urine collections for oestrogens and provided a faster way of collecting ova than laparoscopy. New combinations of hormones were tried and a drug that mimicked the brain hormone GnRH avoided cancellation of cycles from premature ovulation. Patrick was not so old school that he couldn't embrace novelty, but he was seen less in scrubs. He was often away for engagements and Bob, too, was showered with invitations and awards. It was with special pride when they appeared together for honorary doctorates at Hull University, and Bob received two more from Yorkshire universities and another from Cambridge.

The hall hosted a symposium in 1981 for doctors and embryologists from Europe, Australia, and America, securing its reputation as a world centre, and so successfully that it was repeated. People wanted to see the first clinic and were eager to learn how others practised IVF before methods became standard. They wanted to know what Bob was thinking and would try next, for there was nothing too secret to share. IVF was growing into a family of technologies for tackling the most intractable problems, now called assisted reproductive technologies (ARTs), and discussion continued late into the evenings. The proceedings were edited for a book by Bob and Jean.[90] This remarkable spirit lasted more than a decade until the field became crowded, competitive, and commercial.

Bob initiated, or at least predicted, nearly all the major break-throughs that would come. He knew his studies of rabbit blasto-cysts would lead to preimplantation embryo testing (PGT), and the embryo stem cells he studied in Glasgow were auguries for regenerative medicine. He proposed injecting sperm into ova for the unsolved problem of extremely low sperm counts, a break-through that came in 1991 in Brussels and is universally known as ICSI.

Other centres ran ahead with ideas. He was frustrated that he didn't have more facilities and staff as he wanted Bourn Hall to win every time. He had unique snags. His barrister warned to avoid exciting research that might cause adverse publicity to jeopardise libel suits at the high court brought against newspapers and the British Medical Association for falsely reporting research (he won them all). It lost him a lead with frozen embryos, although not for long because the hall announced its first "frosty baby" in 1984. A "time-warp twin" was subsequently born from an embryo conceived simultaneously and stored in the freezer.

Not every prediction has come to pass, of course, although some dangle a little lower. He said the time would come when sperm are made from skin cells, so no man is denied the chance of genetic fatherhood. He suspected the best embryos for patients had the heartiest appetite for carbohydrates and drove at break-neck speed to York wearing an extra sweater and a hat with the air-conditioning full on to keep them cool until culture fluids could be measured in Henry Leese's lab. A non-invasive test of embryos would garner praise from foes of IVF but, alas, the theory remains an orphan until better biomarkers are found.

There were plenty of other hunches and hypotheses at the time. One of them was a strange belief that "helper embryos" can boost success without risking multiple pregnancy and another was that a womb rested in a pseudo-menopausal state before IVF improved implantation. They appear hair-brained now but were taken seriously, at least when uttered on Bob's lips. He wasn't shy to admit his mistakes for the important thing was to have ideas and the guts to test them. Unfazed by missteps, he knew every wobbly stone on a path leads to a firmer stride across the lake of ignorance.

17

EGGS & ETHICS

Liberties won in the turbulent 1960s cast old verities and moral beliefs in new moulds that impacted fertility medicine in the coming decades. When does life begin? Is it precious from the start? Should nascent lives ever be used as a means to an end? And who decides what type of life is worth living?

Bob understood it was not enough to say IVF was justified as a fulfilment of a human want or need. People had to be convinced it was ethical and, if necessary, opponents had to be beaten down for the sake of social justice. He expected a fight. Although the subject was medicine it wasn't just for doctors to make decisions; researchers had responsibilities as innovators. But they must not run too far ahead in enthusiasm or for personal glory, succumbing to the kind of pride in Mary Shelley's creation story. He believed scientists must sometimes leave their bench to engage in bioethics, a vague and nameless subject before the word was coined around 1970.

As the power of biology and genetics rose, elite committees and political masters still made key decisions about the processes and fruits of research. In medicine, it was senior doctors and hospital ethics committees (where they existed) who held authority over patient care and medical experiments, guided by the Helsinki Declaration and the Nuremberg Code. But times were changing. Trust in authority was eroded by the Vietnam War. Revelations of abusive treatment of disadvantaged research subjects in the Tuskegee syphilis study led to more accusations against medicine, which had enjoyed privileged status. The public began to challenge the paternalism and assumed omniscience of medical providers and experts, and patients asked tough questions about their medical condition and treatment. One day they would have access to personal data and information at their fingertips online, and although this has some drawbacks it is surely always better to have knowledge than live in ignorance.

The changing mood of society encouraged the founding of a brains trust called the Hasting's Center in 1969 and the following year the Kennedy Center for Ethics where Bob was called to debate IVF. British hospital ethics committees were established, and later the Nuffield Council on Bioethics. The old guard hated to surrender ancient privileges but had to retreat as professionals were forced to be more accountable for information the public was entitled to and often paid for.

Bob was swimming with the tide when he stirred up ethical debates in the 1970s, although dragged by rip currents when he argued a fertility revolution was coming. He had no formal qualifications in bioethics for, unlike French students who are taught Montaigne, Sartre and so on, it is rare for British science students to attend a philosophy class. Bob's mentor Conrad Waddington was a heavy-weight intellectual whose example fired him to more than a dabbling interest in British philosophy. His socialism grew symbiotically with a care for social justice, springing from the utilitarianism of Jeremy Bentham and John Stuart Mill. Calling himself a consequentialist, his ethics were not set in stone, like the Ten Commandments, but defined by the outcome of actions. A good act is known from its benefit. He was suspicious of easy answers or appeals to nature. Rules based on cultural norms and dogma (deontology) were foreign to him. He agreed with Bertrand Russell and Freddie Ayer that no philosophy or religion should claim superiority, and moral assertions are only expressions of attitude, never of fact. Bioethics accommodates plenty of rhetoric but no experts.

His public entry into bioethics and dawning interest in law were heralded by a casual meeting in 1969, triggered by his daughters riding bikes around their neighbourhood. The girls started chatting to children from the Sharpe family. As one thing leads to another, Ruth became friendly with Mrs Sharpe and invited the family over to one of the parties they hosted for staff and students. As a visiting academic lawyer from George Washington University, David Sharpe and Bob had little in common, but the conversation turned to embryology. Bob asked if federal laws in America could encumber IVF. The answer was no. He wondered if state laws affected reproductive choice. That needed a longer answer.

The dialogue continued after the Sharpes went home, and by 1971 the pair was ready to submit a joint paper to *Nature*. It was the first airing of ethical and legal aspects of IVF to address a wide readership and was a tour de force. Reviewing the benefits and risks seven years before IVF was actualised, they anticipated issues that would be debated later in parliaments, professions, and the Vatican. They called for an official body from diverse backgrounds to consider the implications, lead public debate, serve as watchdogs, and advise researchers. They warned heavy-handed laws and regulations would hinder progress. The paper attracted scant attention because IVF was dismissed as a fantasy, and it took the birth of Louise Brown to stir governments to action. They published one more article together in 1992 about a rogue American fertility doctor. It was a court case confirming fears that as treatment options evolved in a competitive market-place extravagant claims would sell products of dubious value.

Bob hoped their first paper would shield from future head-winds, but they were more ferocious than he expected. After the British abortion law of 1967 and the U.S. Supreme Court ruling Roe versus Wade gave women the legal right to abortion, he thought controversies would be light and quickly forgotten. If half the embryos conceived in the body die, most without the mother's knowledge or marked by a solemn rite, why would the fate of a few mites in vitro matter?

The paper appeared the same year as Paul Ramsey's attack on him at the Kennedy Center. The Princeton professor, famous for defending the Just War and harangued by pacificists in the Vietnam era, made his mark in medical ethics as an incisive thinker and a formidable—some said ruthless—debater. His beliefs about genetic testing, euthanasia, and organ transplantation were strictly pro-life, and he wanted to demolish moral arguments for IVF in his lecture. He published it later, more moderate in print according to people who heard it, causing a stir when he steered away from a shocking admission.

If Aldous Huxley had any insight into our times, perhaps one can express the paradoxical and the macabre "hope" that the first example of the production of a child by in vitro fertilization and embryo transplant will prove to be a bad result — and that it will be well advertised, not hidden from view! I do not actually believe that the good to come from public revulsion in such an event would justify the impairment of that child. But, then, for the same reasons, neither is the manipulation of embryos a procedure that can possibly be morally justified.[91]

Perhaps Professor Ramsey's heart would have softened if he met Louise Brown later or lived to see grown-up children of Bob's former patients stop him in the street to thank him for their lives. Bob took two years to formulate a reply in 1974, explaining the biology behind IVF and couching arguments in compassion for patients. He repudiated Ramsey and the more reasoned criticisms of Leon Kass, the doctor appointed by President Bush in 2002 to review stem cell bioethics. The conference in Washington was a rehearsal for battles that would pit progressive convictions against conservative beliefs, casting reason and science against religion and tradition, something which has parallels in culture wars today. Bob was confident that optimism would triumph over pessimism.

The Roman Catholic Church was never likely to be a friend, although there was an unconfirmed rumour that Paul VI welcomed the Brown baby's safe delivery as he lay dying at the Castel Gandolfo. Wiggle room exists even within strict doctrines. For one, should the biblical exhortation to bring new life into the world override the ancient veto of masturbation? For another, can conception by IVF be more acceptable if it occurs in a natural cycle, like the Browns? Then there are no spare embryos to worry about and it mirrors the rhythm method of contraception, declared licit in the encyclical *Humanae Vitae*.

There was, however, the deep problem that making babies without sex conflicts with unyielding belief in sex as the only way. The taboo against breaking the link between sex and reproduction was coupled with strict teaching about ensoulment from the moment of genetic union, like the divine spark from God's finger animating Adam depicted in a fresco on the ceiling of the Sistine Chapel. It was hard for Bob to reconcile this belief with what he understood from biology, although the church was not always implacable. For centuries, Christendom accepted animation commenced *after* the union of man and woman, even weeks later. As a faithful Aristotelian, Thomas Aquinas accepted three types of soul unfolding successively in the womb: first a vegetable soul, then an animal soul, and finally a rational soul on the 40th day in males (40 days later in females). The theology of progressive ensoulment, or "personhood" in today's parlance, is more consistent with embryology than the doctrine that has ruled since 1869.

Presenting views in 1983 at the Vatican, Bob emphasised the union of male and female chromosomes is but one milestone in a continuum beginning when gametes form and running the course of pregnancy. For the first couple of days, molecules formed in the ovum before ovulation drive development until parental genes kick in.

During discussion of embryo research, words like "potential", "dignity", and "sanctity" made the going tough because there were no agreed definitions or understanding of what they meant. If it was difficult to find common ground about elemental IVF, how much harder it would be in future as the march of science challenged more precious beliefs and doctrines. How should embryos be regarded if they can be made from skin cells? These questions were not yet on the table, but one day fixed notions about cellular potency would collapse, and shocks from every new discovery in embryology would be grist for the burgeoning field of bioethics.

Two years later, Howard and Georgeanna Jones were invited to the Pontifical Academy of Sciences at the Vatican for a meeting with moral theologians. They discussed the strange moral space occupied by embryos in a dish, somewhere between mere organic entities and personhood. Sensing there was backing for IVF in the room, the Joneses were astonished at the power of Monsignor Carlo Caffarra, a future cardinal who had the ear of a conservative pope. He declared the method illicit because "conjugal love" was missing, supposing love can never be represented by conjugating gametes in a Petri dish. That he prevailed against a majority was apparent when *Donum Vitae* banned IVF in 1987, even for natural cycles. *Dignitas Personae* has updated instructions for later technologies. The GIFT operation, no longer widely practised, occupied a grey area, but genetic testing of embryos (PGT) became a casualty. Nevertheless, Catholic doctrine is regularly ignored, sometimes with the support of a parish priest, in the same way that people quietly embrace contraception while remaining faithful adherents of their church.

The Roman Church is less monolithic than it appears. Bernard Häring, a theologian of charitable disposition who endorsed birth control, drew a line at the first glimmers of sentient life marked by emergence of grey matter, which occurs past the time embryos are viable in vitro. His definition had the satisfaction of symmetry with brain death at the other end of the life span and consistency with John Locke's depiction of humans as thinking creatures capable of self-reflection. The double meaning of conception ("a thought") is no coincidence. Bob was happier with this reasoning but refused to be pinned down to a date when human life deserves full human rights.

Anglican prelates carried more sway for him because senior bishops sitting in the House of Lords would vote one day on legislation for IVF and were still divided on the matter. He never found a greater ally than the Reverend Professor Gordon Dunstan, a theologian who became chaplain to H.M. the Queen. Bob was flexible, embracing accomplices wherever he found them, and called Gordon one of the most wonderful men he ever knew. The priest wrote that moral philosophers are artificers who craft ethics, not reading them on stone tablets.[92] He saw nothing unethical at Kershaw's, and from attending lectures and conferences he knew more about embryology than most gynaecologists, carrying his erudition modestly.

Bob wanted to open an ethics committee at Bourn Hall as soon as possible. More than a wise act, it spread responsibility borne hitherto by the two directors, who were vulnerable to lawsuits from opponents. The first chairman was Alan Dexter and Jean Purdy was the secretary with membership of doctors and scientists plus a local bishop. There was no lay representation then, but nor was it a rubber stamp as they debated everything from embryo freezing to egg donation, postmenopausal mother-hood to treating single patients.[93] The commercial reputation of surrogacy repelled Bob, but he came to welcome other arrange-ments and, through IVF, it offered a commissioning woman with intact ovaries a genetic link to her child. The hall was first in Europe to offer this kind of biological contract, which he felt was more of an issue for the law than ethics.

Images of embryos in magazines and newspapers were novelties to the public, as drawings of human fetuses by Samuel Söemmerring were in the 18th century. They were powerful arousers of debate in polite society and dispelled the absurd myth of preformation in eggs or sperm as an endless series of homunculi, like Russian dolls. According to another German, Ernst Haeckel, development in the womb recapitulated human evolution: from amphibian to fish to reptile to bird and our final form. Of course, if at the four-week stage we look like a fish it does not mean we should be treated like one. Biology should not be the sole instructor of ethical behaviour.

Schooling in the physiognomy of unborn life reached a new pitch when the Swedish photographer Lennart Nilsson used flex-ible endoscopes like Patrick Steptoe's tools. As the awe of devel-opment kept growing and revealing ever more moving details of anatomy, his pictures were bound to affect attitudes to new life. Foes of abortion adopted them for campaigns to make all prenatal stages sacrosanct, but conflation of early embryology with fetal stages disappeared from the responsible media in the 1980s. Showing embryos as tiny undifferentiated aliens bearing no morphological resemblance to later stages helped to sway the public to accept reproductive technology.

As more clinics opened, not all with fine reputations, the Thatcher government felt bound to regulate the technology. In 1982, it set up a committee of enquiry chaired by Dame (later Baroness) Mary Warnock, a moral philosopher at Oxford with experience on committees for special education and animal experiments. They handed her a hot potato. Five women and eleven men from the professions joined with only one scientist, Anne McLaren. Gordon Dunstan wasn't available and, of course, she could not have Bob. No gamekeeper who ever wrote the rules for a hunting estate ever consulted a poacher, even if the man knew the woods better than others.

Mary's committee met bimonthly for two years and at venues around the country to consult the public and local experts, including those at Bourn Hall. It was an exercise in direct democracy based on a principle that people have a right to inform decisions on controversial matters. The agenda never strayed far from standard IVF to hot topics that soon came over the horizon, like surrogacy and fertility care for LGBT people. Civil servants cautioned her to avoid stepping on slippery slopes and the subject of abortion completely, which could unravel existing legislation.

Anne was a dominant figure as an embryologist and articulate spokesperson for science. Mary asked her to give members a primer in human embryology at their first meeting. No one raised objections to natural cycle IVF, but stimulated cycles presented the thorny problem of what to do with surplus embryos not transferred to the mother or donated to another couple. Was it ethical to summarily dispose of them, or to use them in research? People ranked embryos differently, some regarded them close to gametes, others almost equal to fetuses. Bob insisted clinical

263

treatment was unethical unless it was based on sound embryo research.

Anne swayed members to liberal conclusions, including most crucially a recommendation to allow embryo research for up to 14 days after fertilisation (not counting time in the freezer). It left a margin of several days after the blastocyst stage when it was impossible to keep embryos alive in vitro (but no longer true).[94] Her rationale was the appearance of a primitive streak a week after implantation. It marks a new phase of cell migration and the origination of three germ layers for making body parts. This is the latest time an embryo can split to make identical twins, considered a definition of individuation. Bob thought a firm date was arbitrary, but to be effective and enforceable, laws and regulations cannot have fuzzy borders.

New discoveries continued to blow up in the faces of the committee as IVF was getting into its stride. Embryo freezing was one, and another was a male fertility test from fertilising hamster ova with human sperm. It was hard for lay members to keep up, so they listened quietly with poker-faces. Eventually, they needed settlement to draft a report for 1984.

The Warnock Report backed IVF treatment and research with 63 specific recommendations.[95] It approved egg donation and freezing methods. Embryo research was accepted for advancing knowledge provided there was informed consent from the genetic parents, a cardinal principle of bioethics. Three dissenting members submitted a minority report. It was agreed unanimously that patients should be offered counselling, children from donated gametes or embryos legitimised, and genetically unrelated rearing males registered as legal fathers. They banned cloning experiments and flushing embryos from wombs to donate for other women.

One of the most far-reaching recommendations and in the spirit of the age was the creation of a QUANGO.[96] The body would have broad representation to reassure the public only approved work was carried out and only in licensed facilities. The report crafted for the needs of patients and to satisfy practitioners attracted a mixture of commendation for a thorough and sensitive job as well as the criticism the moral philosopher in charge was destroying morality.

Bob said it was too harsh to impose criminal penalties for non-compliance, and the 14-day rule would block the study of biochemical pregnancies. More surprisingly for someone who usually forged ahead, he was uneasy about embryos specifically created for research *if* there was never any intention to use them for treatment. Was he bowing to Kantian philosophy? Was the absence of intent a justification for an otherwise wicked act? In striving to be ethical, Bob could make unnatural bedfellows. In the Catholic church, the principle of the double effect allows the shortening of life by drugs if they are intended to relieve pain. Bob often used spare embryos in research because it was better to do something with them for good than nothing at all. It was consistent with his consequentialism, but the Curia would have none of that.

When the report reached the House of Commons the same year, he was in the Stranger's Gallery looking down on unusual numbers of Members for a Friday. Warnock had opponents in both main parties who hoped to repeat their earlier success when they stirred up the House of Lords. During the debate, they tried to catch the Speaker's eye to give long and passionate speeches. The Labour MP for Oldham West and Royton, Michael Meacher, stood up to praise the Warnock committee, urging the House to accept its recommendations. When it came to the turn of the Tory Sir Bernard Braine, he said, "never in all that time (35 years as an MP) have I approached any subject with a greater sense of fear than this". He affirmed his belief in the sanctity of life from fertilisation, finding support in scripture from the prophet Jeremiah. Heads nodded in agreement on both sides of the aisle. The hostile forces were organised to give Warnock a thrashing.

Frustrated by slow progress in parliament, the MRC and Royal College of Obstetricians and Gynaecologists assembled an unofficial body with the support of a government minister to reassure the public. There would be a sheriff in town for the wild west of reproductive technology, as the media described it. Without the force of law, the voluntary authority could not offer protection from exploitation, yet most clinics adhered to the guidelines which served as a model for a future statutory body.

Feelings ran high and the government, fearing for its reputation, hoped the subject would fade to oblivion in the churning mill of parliamentary business. But Enoch Powell's bolt from the blue ensured this would not be so. A nativist who would have called himself a Eurosceptic today, he quit the Tories for taking the country into the EEC (now the EU) to join the Ulster Unionists. He tabled a private members bill called *Unborn Children (Protection)* because it did not need government sponsorship and then summoned his oratorial skill to melt the glacial pace of legislation.[97] He didn't want to ban IVF but thought every embryo should have a chance to make a baby and never be a research subject.

Opening shots of the campaign were fired in the House of Lords by the 17th Duke of Norfolk, a Roman Catholic and big howitzer in the Conservative benches. He shared Braine's belief that personhood begins at fertilisation, so IVF was repugnant. He lashed out at the neologism "pre-embryo" bandied about on both sides of the Atlantic, saying it was an invention to make the exploitation of helpless human beings seem respectable. The expression has some biological justification since a complete body originates from a minority of cells that are hard to identify at tender stages, the rest make the placenta and outer membranes. Embryos were, however, always called embryos. Bob agreed with the old duke, if only on this point, acknowledging that it was a shabby way of shrugging off a serious moral question. What was totally unacceptable to him in the Powell bill was the proposed restriction on access to fertility services that implied patients would need a license to procreate and deny help for needy cases. In his opinion, it was an affront to civil liberties. There would be hindrance, too, for research on genetic testing (PGT) for which animals were poor substitutes.

He invited Powell to Bourn Hall where Bob and Patrick faced the intimidating presence across the vast expanse of Patrick's desk. They were old hands explaining the technology, and having come so far, believed the tide was turning in their favour. Hundreds of babies had been born in the UK, mostly from their clinic, and there were more around the globe every day. After listening closely, Powell left without giving a clue to his thoughts, unless silence revealed he was not for turning.

The political turbulence continued for more months. A hostile campaign by the LIFE organisation gained two million signatures. There were warnings that people with birth defects would feel more stigmatised, and fears of creeping genetic engineering. The word "eugenic" was lobbed like a grenade to explode liberal goals. Jerome Lejeune, the doctor who found the cause of Down's syndrome and a confidante of the Pope, came from Paris to assure people PGT would never work and money was better spent helping disabled people to have fulfilling lives. The pro-research lobby responded by launching Progress, an educational platform with members from the professions, politics and a surprising mix of pro-choice women's groups and disability charities that preferred PGT to abortion.[98] Old quarrels gained new force as appeals on one side for justice and reproductive autonomy were countered by accusations of scientific hubris and murdering embryos on the other. It was an emotional, even hysterical, time that made government ministers fret; European politicians anxiously watched if the theatre would cross the English Channel. At its second reading, the Powell bill won by 238 to 66 votes, and if it won again it would go to the Lords where there were guaranteed supporters to turn it into a law of the land.

The government thought the bill was imperfect and so it was a relief when it ran out of parliamentary time and lawmakers could focus instead on the surrogacy service recently opened in London on an American business model. The agency was whipping up public feelings and the media hounded a commissioning couple when "Baby Cotton" was born after gestating in a surrogate mother. The government swiftly drafted a bill to ban commercial surrogacy, passed with cross-party support in July 1985. It wisely avoided interfering with private arrangements people have always made without exchanging money, for how can private bedrooms be policed?

Bob was doubly happy because the hubbub had the adventitious effect of taking attention away from the Powell bill, if only temporarily. Powell himself helped to undermine it for when he relaxed a formerly hard attitude it set him at odds with sterner supporters. Perhaps he remembered a warning at Bourn Hall that PGT needed embryo research to bring it to application. He believed PGT was preferable to genetic diagnosis later in pregnancy when parents make the agonising decision to terminate a fetus found to be abnormal after they started to bond. He was torn by the logical dilemma that if doctors have a clinical duty to avoid transferring abnormal embryos then the law must allow them to detect the problem, and that required the study of embryos. Powell was portrayed as an arch enemy by the pro-research lobby, but he had done PGT a good turn by giving it more credibility, and it was timely as molecular biology offered new levers that doctors could use.

The government was eager now for legislation to end the bickering. Bob was fearful if clumsy regulations hampered Britain's place in the vanguard of the field. There were new laws in the Australian state of Victoria where an incongruous alliance of religious fundamentalists and feminists threatened to prohibit world class research. There was more obstruction in other states, and in Germany the *Embryo Protection Act* in 1990 virtually closed PGT research. Italy was still a European haven for experimentation until a restrictive law in 2004 forced doctors to create no more than three embryos at a time and all to be transferred at once and never frozen (since overturned in the courts). America was unencumbered by these politics girdling IVF, although when national laws were flouted people travelled abroad for treatment forbidden at home.

There was slight easing of conflict between warring forces in the UK through exhaustion. The prospect of a more liberal law received an unexpected boost in 1990 from a scientific break-through in London. Preimplantation genetic testing (PGT) had arrived. Alan Handyside had audaciously amplified DNA to identify the sex of embryos to avoid implanting males where a family history put them at risk of inheriting dreaded diseases. The wide broadcast of this story triggered a surge of correspondence to parliamentarians urging them to support research. It was reminiscent of the 1960s when the thalidomide tragedy helped to launch prenatal screening.

The case was announced with perfect timing only five days before the House of Commons was due to vote on the *Human*

Fertilisation and Embryology Bill. Freed from the pressure of party whips to follow their conscience and spurred by the story of two unaffected baby girls, MPs passed the bill with a majority of 171. It included the key provision of 14 days for research. The defeated side had to be satisfied there would be inspectors to check the law was observed.

Throughout the fiery debates about the moral status of human embryos, the ethics of sacrificing animal lives to develop and test the technology hardly turned a hair. Countless thousands of mice perished, and even calls to use monkeys didn't raise hackles. This was in a country renowned for animal lovers. The anti-vivisection movement got underway in the mid-Victorian period when rural people started migrating to cities where the business of raising animals for food and hunting were left behind. Descartes' depiction of animals as dull automatons was replaced by Landseer's portraits of Queen Victoria's faithful pets and later bookshelves bowed under the weight of stories about faithful dogs, heroic rabbits, and naughty toads. The ethical treatment of animals became a national passion. So how then did Bob, a man of deep ethical sensibility, regard them on his path paved with experiments? It is a conundrum that bothers many young biologists coming to their subject from a love of animals, and an unsettling issue for philosophers too.

The Princeton philosopher Peter Singer has spoken up for IVF, but as a champion of animal rights he denounces the prejudice and injustices of "speciesism". He challenges the raw chauvinism of our species. Animals didn't mean nothing to Bob, but if God called him to account for all the animals he used, he would have been a spirited apologist. Without them, reproductive health care would be impoverished, and drugs would lose their first safety screen. Before studying human cells, he "sacrificed" animals for experiments, a term once reserved for a gift to a deity and now preferred to the blunt word, "kill". He could claim his treatment was mild, little more than controlled breeding or a routine procedure for a veterinarian, and he never killed as many mice as a barn owl catches in a year (about 1,000). That kind of defence might not convince every animal rights advocate, of course. Our relationship and exploitation of animals is delicate if we stop to think about it, and like the politics of human embryos it still divides people of conscience.

It was the ethics of patient care that dominated Bob's head, but his heart ruled an attitude to animals, as it does for many of us who are not closely involved in the animal production industry. From boyhood he wanted to be a farmer, but when he bought steers for his own farm and goaded them into a truck bound for the slaughterhouse, he saw sad individuals looking back through the bars. While he didn't regret the mouse carcasses that helped to understand how to build human families, he stopped raising animals for meat and became a zealous vegetarian. It was more a sentimental reaction than an ethical decision, though he could capitulate if he caught the aroma of crispy bacon in a frying pan.

18

HEARTBREAK HALL

Bourn Hall achieved more distinction in the 1980s than it ever had in the previous four centuries. As the first clinic of its kind, it was the place to go for treatment or learn the intricacies of IVF, and couples came from everywhere in the early days. A glossy brochure featured the practitioners who had the longest track records in the world, offering a Rolls-Royce service in an aristocratic setting. Patients dined in the ancient hall and met its famous pioneers. A serene environment that felt more like a health spa than a medical clinic favoured conception by helping the psyche. Bourn Hall was synonymous with IVF, and providing it stayed at the forefront of technology it was secure in the future. But no one noticed storm clouds gathering that heralded lightning strikes.

It was not only the firm principle but the self-confidence of the directors that made them willing to share the fruits of experience. They didn't conceal clinical or laboratory details that could help other specialists, including potential rivals, and patented none of their inventions. The Bourn team constantly published research in journals and at conferences, and if a discovery failed to get into print it was for lack of time to write another paper. They welcomed qualified observers to learn techniques in-house, and there were no non-compete clauses in the contracts of new recruits.[99] These were coveted jobs and there were no secrets to betray anyway. It was Bob's liberal philosophy and Patrick backed it.

The next clinic to open was in London, also for private patients, but in 1983 the first public service opened in Manchester, not far from their former base in Oldham. Soon, there would be a rush for contracts to treat NHS patients, although public funding was patchy, depending on the attitude of local health authorities rather than central government. Infertility was always a low priority.[100]

A new breed of clinician was emerging, the fertility entrepreneur who had a head for business besides qualifications in medicine. It was inevitable where a poverty of state investment exists alongside an unfettered fertility marketplace that a commercial ethos would thrive. It is a trend that has grown over time, most vigorously in the United States where IVF was originally most controversial. The poor cannot afford access to expensive treatment except through public subsidies or insurance, and the Browns might never have had children together if they had not enrolled in a free trial at Kershaw's. Bourn Hall was a torchbearer as IVF became commercialised, though not a hard-nosed business.

In the first years, patients from, say, Paris and New York flew to Heathrow Airport for a two-hour taxi ride to the hall in the depths of the countryside. As clinics opened around the world, they no longer needed to go, and foreign accents and languages were less often heard. The speed of change and power of market forces took the directors by surprise. They assumed their premium service and name would always attract patients, so they missed the opportunity to plant the famous brand as early satellite clinics around the globe, apart from a couple in London.

It is easy to be smart in hindsight, which is always 20/20 vision. The clinic ran by the seat of its pants, serving medical needs, conducting research, training visitors, and organising conferences. There was little time to ponder how the market was changing and where it would lead. Fertility care was a highly demanding service where every case was unique, involving a team of up to five kinds of professional staff. To stay ahead in the field, the hall had to keep running faster, like the Red Queen.

... it takes all the running you can do, to keep in the same place. If you want to get somewhere else, you must run at least twice as fast as that![101]

The pace was strenuous but had none of the joylessness of a spinning treadmill. It felt more like a runner's high. Few people half Bob's age had the same vitality or stayed as cheerful under constant strain, which can explain why he underestimated staff burnout and transfer to less stressful and better remunerated jobs. The first three embryologists he hired, as well as John Webster, left for understandable reasons within a few weeks of each other around 1985. It was a crushing blow for the hall and especially for Bob who prized loyalty, but he got over the hurt and didn't hold grudges. There were junior staff to make a smooth transition, and no shortage of well-qualified applicants to fill vacancies, but the disruption revealed an unexpected volatility in IVF.

Despite upsets over staff changes, it was another year to celebrate. Bob was promoted at last to a full professorship of human reproduction at the University. It was late recognition of merit, coming a year after election as a Fellow of the Royal Society of London and only four years from the watershed age of 65 when he had to retire from the chair. Two years later, Patrick would receive the same honour in London, rare for a non-scientist, but in 1985 their attention was focused on a new flagship.

The long-awaited new block opened, matching the old hall next door in red bricks and Georgian-style windows. As it went up, the builders wanted to cut down a fine old plane tree close by, but Bob doggedly resisted. Where they imagined heavy boughs smashing a new wall, he could only see the lovely grey bole and graceful limbs. It fell in a storm one day, a bad omen.

Patrick knew what a modern medical suite needed and spared no expense. There would be 40 beds for in-patients, two fully equipped operating theatres, a large embryology laboratory, ancillary rooms for research and instruments, storage space for frozen embryos and sperm, and a quiet area for staff to relax. When plans were drawn up, laparoscopy was still king, but it was already losing ground to ultrasonography by the opening date. Scanning was a major innovation and hugely beneficial for patients since the combined probe and needle could access the ovaries via the vagina to withdraw ova, only needing mild analgesia. It says something about a man who made his reputation with laparoscopy that he could set it aside for another technique 30 years later. But when bedded accommodation was redundant, surplus space in the block had to find new uses.

Now in his seventies, time and toil took a toll on Steppy. Still the final arbiter of medical decisions, he transferred surgeries to other doctors. After two hip operations in Oldham, one of his joints needed replacing again. He hid knowledge of prostate cancer for years in case the news hurt their efforts to find investors for the hall, and afterwards for the sake of its reputation. After making two great innovations in medicine and building a renowned clinic, he deserved some blissful years to enjoy with Sheena, but the final ones were harrowing. They started with a calamity as they were sailing home from New York. The ocean swell caused Sheena to fall and hit her head on the deck, causing a subdural haematoma from which she never fully recovered.

Patrick cut back on travel to care for her at home and soldiered on at work. It was hard to imagine the clinic without him, but no one guessed the youngest founder would predecease him.

Clinical embryology was not just a job for Jean, it was her life and Bourn Hall was her joy. She spent less time in the lab since new embryologists arrived in 1982, becoming more involved in paperwork, but people who saw her leaning into her work or looking up with a smile never guessed she was suffering from chronic pain. She only confided in a friend when she needed help to get to the hospital. That was enough to bear, but there was more, and one spring day in 1983 she noticed an irregular mole on her shoulder. A dermatologist sent a biopsy to a pathologist who returned the bleak report that she had malignant melanoma and needed surgery and chemotherapy. She pasted the letter in the last page of her scrapbook of IVF history with a sardonic caption in bright red letters: "Possibly the best news you'll have all week".

If her two bosses knew the diagnosis, they understood the prognosis and kept her secret, so she could continue working as if nothing had changed. Her colleagues were family after her parents died. She was single and refused to mope at home. It was an aggressive cancer which spread widely and after 18 months she could no longer hide her condition from others. Bob converted an attic room in the hall to a bedsit with furniture from her house, so she could be involved with the team for the remaining three months. Tim Appleton marveled at her stoicism, how she said she was lucky to know how much time she had left so she could concentrate on important things. She collapsed in the clinic and died on 16 March 1985 in hospital. She was only 39.

Mourners gathered on a cold, wet day at the graveside at the Anglican church in Grantchester, a pretty village outside Cambridge she loved. Bob was heartbroken after they had been through so much together over 17 years. A *Times* obituary said to be composed by him praised her contributions. She was involved in the conception of 500 babies at Bourn Hall as well as the two in Oldham, had coauthored 26 papers, some of them landmark contributions to science. Hanging in the main staircase was a tapestry she made of storks flying over Bourn Hall with babies hanging in cradles from their beaks. It was an icon of her devotion and unaccountably vanished one day.

After years of cordial relations with the Oldham Health Authority, Bob fought over the wording of a brass plaque celebrating pioneers of IVF in their hospital.

[Jean Purdy] *travelled with me for ten years and contributed as much as I did to the project. Indeed, I regard her as an equal contributor to PC and myself.*[102]

The managers insisted on only acknowledging the two men and "their supporting staff". He held the same principle as in sport that the entire winning team should be paraded before a crowd, even if the captain or coach carries the cup. There were other women missing from the story besides Jean, notably Muriel and Ruth. Bob didn't live to see the decision reversed by future managers, nor a new headstone in Grantchester churchyard engraved to acknowledge a significant life.[103]

Patrick looked frail as he leaned on his cane at the funeral. Within two years, he moved with Sheena to be closer to her family in Canterbury and to enjoy cathedral music. The number of babies conceived at the hall reached the first 1,000 in December 1987, and around that time he and Bob received letters from Whitehall asking if they would accept the royal honour of Commander of the British Empire (CBE). It was a middling tribute compared to

Bob's award from the French President, but prophets are often celebrated more elsewhere than in their own country. Admirers were vexed that others received more noble titles for holding a public office or as celebrities, but that is the British system, and those who make the appointments may have decided that neither man was an establishment type, one of the virtues their friends and colleagues most respected. Bob would not want a higher honour for the sake of dignity as that ran against his principles, yet he always fought for fair play. As for Patrick, he was disappointed to miss a knighthood, but nevertheless looked forward to meeting his queen at Buckingham Palace in three months. He died at age 75, a few days before the investiture. It was with a mixture of sorrow and pride that Bob represented them, looking incongruent that day in morning dress and an Ascot top hat to people who knew him. There was still a farm boy inside.

On the day Patrick died, nine-year-old Alastair MacDonald was watching Scottish TV when he recognised Patrick's face on the screen and ran sobbing to his mother, "Uncle Patrick's died". For him and the Brown girls, Patrick and Bob were like uncles who visited from time to time and sent them birthday cards and gifts. Alastair was too young to know about IVF, but as his mother explained the mystery, he understood why his grandparents often said he was a special child. His school friends now saw his name linked to Louise and cheekily asked how he got out of the test-tube, but it was good humored. IVF was losing its stigma.

Patrick's body was brought to the old church beside Bourn Hall for burial. Mourners filling the pews included the Edwards and Brown families, colleagues, patients, and friends from overseas. Bob and Sheena celebrated his life at the hall the next year when 600 parents brought their IVF children and erected a plaque for him outside the new block. Sheena passed away within the year, and their daughter who hid Lesley Brown during her pregnancy died in a road accident two years later, closing the Steptoe family's involvement with IVF.

This was another grievous loss that Bob stifled by immersing himself in work, and after retiring from the university he launched a new journal to add to everything else on his plate. But the man who helped to build other families was also the "glue" for his own. It didn't matter if his calendar was already full, for if he was in North America, he always took a side trip to his brother Harry and his nephew Dean often accompanied him on a lecture tour or for an award ceremony.

He felt the clinic was in safe hands when he was away as Steppy had given the rudder to Patrick Taylor. The two Patricks had known each other since the younger one went to learn laparoscopy in Oldham in the early 1970s, sent by his sagacious supervisor in Belfast. A competent and popular young doctor, Pat had boundless admiration for his namesake. It was there that he met a hyperactive Bob Edwards but, unconvinced that IVF would work, he took a routine job in Canadian obstetrics and gynaecology. On a return trip to see his ailing mother in Northern Ireland in 1978, he was watching TV when a newsflash announced the birth of Louise Brown. It changed his mind. With a generous subsidy from the Alberta government, he opened an IVF service which thrived until a change in political winds made it uneconomic. It was propitious in 1986 when a call came from Bourn Hall asking if he was interested in becoming deputy medical director. There was a hint he would step into Steptoe's shoes one day. The hall family embraced him, making him confident in the decision, although in turning down an invitation to join the financial board there would be no advance warning of a terrible shock.

Pat was hardly two years in the job when Bob walked into his office with the numbing news that the clinic was sold. The staff assembled in the boardroom to hear that Ares-Serono, the Geneva-based supplier of fertility drugs, now owned the premises and business. To outward appearances the hall was successful, attracting a steady stream of fee-paying patients, but the divisional manager of the company noticed orders were slipping and worried that the failure of a showpiece clinic could hurt drug sales. Besides saving the clinic from bankruptcy, there was a perceived advantage of vertical integration of production into a single stream: from harvesting the raw material (urine) to drug manufacture (HMG) to patient delivery (Bourn Hall). There would be joint management with the Hallam Clinic in London's Harley Street, previously bought from the family of Bridget Mason, a general practitioner and director of a lean and lucrative donor insemination service.

Dr Mason made her inaugural visit to the hall in August, followed by Serono head Fabio Bertarelli, who landed on the back lawn in a helicopter. Instead of putting the staff at ease, she proceeded to inspect them with a proprietorial air, calling every member of staff for interview to question their job description and dictate new roles. One of them ruefully asked why she hadn't come on a broomstick. Pat was recruited for perching on the top branch of the tree, but a takeover pruned him down to branch manager. He soon gave notice of his return to Canada where he resumed medical practice and wrote a series of successful novels about an Irish country doctor with two characters modelled on Patrick and Bob.[104]

The new owners launched a stringent review of finances and set new priorities. They protected medical services and converted the new block into a clinical trial centre but were not interested in basic research. Bob was gutted. He agreed to stay on as scientific director for two more years until his deputy, the son-in-law of college friend John Slee, took over and later became managing director. Working most days in his editorial office in the stable block, Bob had one last novelty to offer the hall. In partnership with the staff doctor Kay Elder, he opened a programme of workshops to train physicians and scientists in fertility medicine. It attracted people from far afield and was supported by a new medical director, Peter Brinsden, an alumnus of St. George's Hospital and former naval surgeon, like Steptoe.

Peter previously had a brief stint at the hall before moving to a huge IVF programme in London, returning in 1990 in time to celebrate the birth of its 2,500th baby, named Robert Patrick Peter.[105] He soon learned there were more changes afoot. The Bourn-Hallam union was dissolved for the Hallam to become the London Women's Clinic, and Bertarelli's heirs divested their stake, putting the hall up for sale. There was never a dull moment, but it never sank in a roller-coaster history.

The story of Bourn Hall is like a plant that sprouts vegetatively to generate new editions of itself. In its latest manifestation, the historic hall continues to provide excellent services in new ways in the same matchless setting, but it was never a perfect scaffold for a modern clinic. If the income swallowed by overhead costs had been invested in research and development, Bob could have fertilised more of his original ideas. When he purchased the hall, he allowed his heart to rule his head, and none of his other roles ever gave him so much grief and rapture. But one seldom regrets — and never forgets — a first love.

19

SPREAD THE GOOD NEWS

Gynaecology and obstetrics is the specialty for the most important transition in our lives, yet it was backward compared with, say, internal medicine or neurosurgery. Obstetricians were nicknamed baby-catchers, and the urban slang for gynaecologists is unprintable. There were brave pioneers, of course, but most practitioners were content with gradual evolution afforded by new surgical instruments and drugs. But by the 1960s, waves of technology washed up on the shores of the specialty, beginning with endoscopy and ultrasound before the high tide of IVF gathered reproduction and genetics in a frothy union.

Suddenly, there was more to fertility medicine than tempera-ture charts, sperm counts, old-time surgeries, and praying for luck. One technology after another rolled up, introducing acro-nyms now familiar — IVF, ART, ICSI, PGT, and GIFT. Technology was building families in radical ways. A subject that used to attract small audiences became hot, and seats had to be taken early to avoid standing at the back of an auditorium to hear a pioneer on stage like a pop star. The appetite for new knowledge and skills was voracious and, at least for a while, the spirit of cooperation was outstanding.

Conference presentations and journal papers are the seminal plasma for researchers to spread the news, and a mushrooming field needs more of them. A fertility society had existed in

America since 1944 with its own journal, but there was nothing comparable elsewhere. European doctors submitting papers there felt disadvantaged. They needed their own platform.

After two small meetings, British and European doctors organised a world congress on IVF and embryo transfer in 1984 at Helsinki's Finlandia Hall, a cubist style building of white marble overlooking Töölönlahti Bay. The 600 registrants barely filled a third of the main auditorium, but they made up for empty seats with their enthusiasm, talking about science and medicine into the twilight after 11 PM. It was the birthplace of a new society that would draw audiences from six continents and hold conferences filling the largest halls on the continent. Even the wildest optimists didn't foresee that growth at a special meeting called by Bob and the French gynaecologist Jean Cohen on the final day. Only three dozen turned up to listen.

The two men first met in 1968 at a conference in Bulgaria where they fell into conversation after arriving too early for the reception. Bob told him about IVF. Staggered by the idea, Jean wondered if the man was a prophet or potty. Some 16 years later his clinic produced the second IVF baby in France. This was another close partnership Bob struck with a clinician, rare then for a scientist. The pair inspired the Helsinki audience with a dream of founding a new society to combine specialists trained in science or medicine. They elected Bob as chairman for two years and chose the name European Society for Human Reproduction, soon known throughout the world as ESHRE since Bob insisted on adding an E for Embryology. He wanted a secure status for embryologists.

He would not be satisfied with a talk-shop. He wanted ESHRE to have annual conferences and symposia, practicals, and training courses. Two months earlier when he visited Jean Cohen's 16th arrondissement apartment he had a twinkle in his eye when he suggested a European journal in the English language as an alternative to America's *Fertility & Sterility*. It would be challenging to win support across the professional and language barriers of the continent, but they would try. The trickiest part when the time came would be getting the cooperation of a rival society.

A Belgian lawyer drafted the constitution and by-laws for ESHRE as a non-profit organization, its scope ranging from gametes to mid-gestation. A ginger group met in London at the Westmoreland Hotel, then owned by a gambling company. With under £2,000 in the bank the society was born in penury, but that didn't quash the excitement of the founders. Bob wanted fair representation of the society's officers across the continent and was eager to break with the traditional caste system in medicine. Distinguished members and famous institutions would not have special privileges, and he hoped low fees would encourage students to join. The principles were a facsimile of Bob's ideals.

The first conference was planned for Bonn in 1985. Jean made the first announcement at the opening ceremony of the European Congress on Sterility (ESCO) in Monte Carlo. It didn't go down well. ESHRE was treading on ESCO's turf, and there was not enough money from commercial sponsors to go around. He suggested merging the two societies, but ESHRE was the upstart with a democratic constitution and ESCO was an autocracy under its founder Kurt Semm. A man of grace and charm, Jean Cohen now found himself in a lion's den. As discussion with ESCO officers dragged into the evening, dinners were abandoned until Semm and his confederates finally agreed to go to the Bonn meeting.

Semm was an influential gynaecologist who adopted laparos-copy early on. He grasped the potential of IVF soon after Louise Brown's birth, inviting Patrick to speak at a conference he organised in Venice a few weeks later. A strong personality, he could ruffle feathers like Bob and Pincus, who had their famous spat in the city a decade earlier.

At the next meeting of the ESHRE committee, Bob was granted permission to start a new journal. He pleaded too busy to be the editor but relented when he was promised an editorial board of men and (he insisted) women. He only had a shoestring budget and an office in the stable block at Bourn Hall, a homespun beginning but he was confident of riding to success. But which publisher would they choose, or would they go alone? There were three major firms publishing reproduction, and as members of the committee had different loyalties to the firms the discussion became intense. They finally opted for IRL Press, a company incorporated into Oxford University Press three years later. IRL agreed to print and distribute a bimonthly journal of 80 pages per issue. Bob wrangled for a short contract and a 50-50 split of profits up to the first £100,000. The company fought back, knowing the market was small and a new journal was unlikely to make a profit in less than five years. He had to yield but was determined not to be a pushover when the contract came up for renewal.

The committee arranged the Bonn meeting at the Fondation Universitaire in Brussels, an academic club for alumni like others in London and NYC. Creaky floorboards, oak wainscoting, and an unappetising menu afforded a fitting air of pecuniary prudence. The officers only received reimbursement for coach class travel and out-of-pocket expenses, and to keep the budget in the black they needed grants from drug companies. Commercial support was oxygen needed for conferences to breathe.

They gambled that people would turn up for the conference, so it was with great relief that the register reached 650 and the society added 250 more members. ESHRE was rolling, which Bob took as a green light to put his foot on the gas pedal. He arranged extra workshops led by experts on ovum collection, embryo freezing, immunology, transgenic animals, and anything else he could think of. As technology evolved, an ethics committee was needed to steer the society through anticipated storms. Growing in stature, governments were now calling ESHRE for advice as they drafted legislation for IVF.

The new journal called *Human Reproduction* appeared as a pilot issue of 5,000 copies in January 1986. Subscriptions fell short of expectations and there was an alarming paucity of papers because the mailbox was empty almost every morning. They needed at least five new papers a week to fill an issue. Bob urged his colleagues and former students to submit their best work, and stalked conference halls to tap the shoulders of lecturers. He was hard to resist.

He was determined it would not be another stuffy academic journal. He looked for novel, even edgy, science and published a news and views section about legislation and social issues. Lennart Nilsson provided an eye-catching image of a fetus for the front cover, but subscriptions still fell 40% below target so he had to roll out another advertising campaign.

There were many calls on his time, but the journal was his priority and he refused to be a rubber stamp. He had an office staff of two assistants and a part-time graduate student but read every paper on receipt and sent it out to two expert reviewers he knew, which was almost everyone of any seniority around the world. He had raw memories of when his own papers were rejected and reviewers sniped at data from under the cloak of anonymity, so he was determined to be an advocate of authors, especially new-bies. He even redrafted papers from overseas if they were written in poor English and if he liked the content. Hungry for top science, he might overrule reviewers if a paper presented an imaginative theory or a new angle on an old problem. Reviewers could be surprised and even irritated by the waste of time if he ignored their recommendation. He worried if he lost a paper to a rival journal it might be important later and trusted the march of science would roll over any published work that became suspect. He pushed staff, reviewers, and himself to get papers published fast and ahead of the competition, accepting the risk of haste causing an error of judgment, like the day he took a bend too fast in his old Jaguar.

Approved manuscripts were marked up for the printer to set to type. Galley proofs came back a few weeks later for checking in the office and by authors. The entire process from receipt of a paper to its appearance in print was agonisingly slow, taking the best part of a year and aggravated by dilly-dallying reviewers. Bob wanted to blow up the antique process to rebuild it from ground level.

The journal was thriving in its third year with papers now received from beyond Europe, although it was not yet in profit. Bob had more high-quality contributions than pages allowed by the publisher but was loath to see them lost. IRL was irate when he deliberately exceeded the agreed limit of 120 pages and tried to make amends by asking American friends and companies to subscribe to the journal. It wasn't his last quarrel with the company or the only ruckus he caused.

Kurt Semm agreed to make an alliance between ESCO and ESHRE for a joint congress in Budapest in September 1987, although privately bristling at his partners' conflicting interests and half-hearted efforts that threatened to scuttle the meeting. To make it financially viable he needed to have more people on the register. Bob visited to calm the waters, throwing Dr Semm a bone by offering him the honour of the opening lecture.

The gesture was effective until he asked ESHRE to host another congress, this time in Cambridge and three months before

Budapest. This news so enraged Semm that it almost broke an already brittle relationship. Unsullied, Bob wrote to reassure him of his full commitment, and by a combination of diplomacy and advertising the Hungarian meeting did not turn into the disaster feared. A pacified Semm even agreed to arrange another one.

The Cambridge meeting was a bigger success. As chairman and host, Bob stood at the entrance to offer a handshake as participants arrived, many of them wanting to pose with him for their "Bob picture" to take home. Mary Warnock spoke about ethics of embryo research and Luc Montagnier on the emerging AIDS epidemic in a sumptuous three-day programme of lectures attended by 850 specialists. Patrick presented clinical data from the hall and played Haydn and his own piano composition to a full audience one evening. Thirty companies rented booths to advertise surgical instruments, laboratory equipment, and drugs; not so much commerce that it distracted people from lectures. Understanding the benefits of publicity, Bob set aside a room for the press to interview speakers. Although never a close fraternal relationship, town and gown were happy working together for the largest conference ever in the city centre, and both benefitted financially. Organised with barely a year of lead time, Bob paid too little regard to the society's budget but took responsibility afterwards to solve the deficit.

While never a man fettered by convention, some hallmarks of achievement were too valuable to ignore. Academic and medical journals are rated annually by Thomson Reuters with an impact factor to reflect the frequency authors are cited in other papers. It is a rough scale of quality and significance. Bob carefully watched how *Human Reproduction* was doing against the competition. As a relatively small field, reproductive science and medicine doesn't attract a broad readership like *Nature* or the *New England Journal of Medicine* and cannot expect a high score, but it is the position in the hierarchy of its peers that matters. His journal climbed higher each year until it became #1 in obstetrics and gynaecology, a crowning success helped by publication of landmark papers from European innovators of the ICSI technique. He had worked tirelessly to make it the leading title and a masterpiece for ESHRE. The publisher was delighted as it had 3,000 subscribers now.

With favourable winds blowing his argosy to warmer waters in 1994, Bob asked ESHRE to let the journal sail free of a commercial publishing firm. It provoked another tense meeting. Some of his colleagues conceded, if only in principle, but after a vote was cast against him, he had to lick his wounds and find compensation in negotiating tough terms with Oxford.

It was time to grasp novel technology. He encouraged authors to submit their work on floppy disks and offered CD-ROMs for publishing supplementary data to quench his gripes about fixed numbers of pages and expensive colour plates. The novelties were popular with authors, and the society was delighted as its coffers filled, but success breeds problems as well as blessings. The journal was bursting at the seams. Moreover, it had gathered an eclectic range of subjects, turning into a chimaera with medicine as a head, biology for a body, and review articles in the tail. His radical remedy was to amputate the title to create two new journals. *Human Reproduction* remained the core and the other two concentrated on molecular biology or review articles, both launched in 1995. Adding a specialist review journal was a crafty move because it would attract more readers and earn a higher impact factor. Bob edited the trio in the stable block until the following year when he moved a short distance to Moor Barns farmhouse where they continued an unassailable lead.

Able to boast a handsome profit when the contract came for renewal in 1999, Bob was sure he could become an independent publisher this time. The editorial office had already taken on much of the production work, yet Oxford continued to enjoy a large share of revenue. But pleading for autonomy was to no avail, and the executive committee invited tenders from six companies, finally settling on Oxford again. Bob made a panicky call to the chairman of ESHRE in Greece to convince him they would be better off going alone, but he was pushing against the tide. Even journals that began as independent operations with unpaid academic editors were being impelled into the arms of publishing giants from the economies of scale, advertising, and marketing networks. The rival journal *Fertility & Sterility* was already managed by a Dutch company.

His doggedness scared the committee, for who could replace him? He was frustrated by their timidity and angry at being steamrollered into a decision. He reached for the atom bomb. Collecting signatures from supporters, he wanted to table a motion for independent publishing at the society's AGM when several thousand members attended. There was no mistaking his fervour, or the risk of a public quarrel with the society's most eminent member, chief architect of its success, and captain of its journals. Civil war could break out. Since most committee members poorly understood the publishing industry, they chose the political way out of handing it to a special task force. It aimed to settle the argument with Bob in Capri, an island with a long history of struggle, a painful commission as some members were his close colleagues.

An external consultant warned them technology was going to upend traditional ways of publishing. Journals might move to the Web and libraries form cartels to shrink subscriptions. They were uncharted waters, and the financial health of ESHRE bound to its journals was at stake. The task force decided the safest course was to renew the contract, but when everyone thought the matter was settled and Bob had acquiesced, he refused to accept the decision.

Editorial staff were paid by the publisher, not the society, so they were now thoroughly frightened about their future. They knew he wouldn't be careless with their interests; he had discussed their concerns individually and given them a small raise from his own pocket in 1993 when salaries were frozen. While not wanting to shoot a broadside at their beloved boss, he could not provide the assurances they desperately needed, so they sent a joint appeal to the chairman of ESHRE. That was all it took to break the impasse. Bob's plan was not sustainable without their support. At last the ink dried on a contract to re-engage Oxford.

No one expected the drama was over. Bob had declared it was beyond the ability of one person to manage three journals across a vast range of subjects. He had endured for the joy of winning in his own way and managing them as he thought fit. He gave three-month's notice of his resignation, laying out reasons in an editorial.

It is with regret that I have decided to resign from the editorship of Human Reproduction and its sister journals from April 30 this year. I strongly believe that scientists and clinicians should organise their own publishing affairs and had hoped to free the journals from financial and other constraints imposed by publishing through a publishing house. It is my failure to persuade others of the benefits of this course of action that precipitated my resignation.[106]

It was the end of an era. The pros and cons of independence were no longer up for debate, and a new editor was appointed for each journal. Feelings were hurt on both sides and Bob cut himself adrift from the society.

The first spring of a new century was a time to collect his thoughts while mowing meadows in his tractor and helping Ruth in the farmhouse. It would be a mistake to assume he switched off when engaged in mundane jobs. There was always something over the hill to command his interest, and this might be the time to fulfil a hope that first took root seven years earlier.

At that time, he investigated the internet as a platform for publishing papers and conference proceedings. It was a vision led by an instinct he often relied on, and it is hard now to remember how radical an idea it was before Google, Amazon, and the dot-com boom. The Web and service providers for email were brand new. On visits to the university computing centre, he asked IT experts to forecast how digital technology would evolve. He had used the media for distributing CDs, but that was all. Could he deliver a journal instantaneously to desktops, even making content free for scholars and impecunious students everywhere? By the year 2000, it was clear that digital publishing was coming, and he wanted to be one of the first to launch that boat.

He converted the top floor of an outbuilding at Duck End Farm to an office for a new enterprise. Ruth was delighted he would be around the home every day, although not as a man of 75 years who yearns to potter around a garden or occasionally disappear to the golf course. He had a serious intent and was rallying supporters for his new journal. He would be at the helm as manager, editor, author, and publisher rolled into one. He would compete for the best papers with his previous journals which were still supported by an international society and based at Moor Barns farmhouse two miles down the lane.[107] He would be David against Goliath, using his name and connections for a slingshot.

A business plan was prepared by a financial advisor and a dozen loyal friends and colleagues opened their wallets to invest £400,000 of their own money in the company. They called the journal *Reproductive Biomedicine Online*. It was first in its field to go primarily online, and one of the first web-based academic journals in the world.

The startup funding paid for equipment, licences, and the salary of an assistant who came back for another demanding role.[108] The first issue of what became known informally as "Bob's journal" was soon online. Besides original research and reviews, he wanted news and opinion pieces, conference papers, politico-legal announcements, even obituary notices. There was the novelty that every full paper had a portrait and short biography of the first author (or second if the first was shy). He could now publish as many pages as he wanted with lightning speed.[109]

But who would buy it? He was wading into unplumbed waters, wanting to disrupt the tradition of paid subscriptions. Instead, his authors, or the organisations funding their research, would pay up front to publish their work, making it accessible to every reader who connected to the journal's website. He couldn't avoid imposing subscriptions completely, though, as he needed some income to pay an editorial office, but this came close to ideal.

Few editors had this vision at the turn of the century, although plenty grumbled about the system in which we pay twice, once for the research and a second time for it to be printed. Library budgets strained under the burden of escalating numbers and costs of journals. Science publishing grew out of the university presses of Oxford and Cambridge in the 16th century to become a multi-billion-dollar industry now dominated by five companies that monopolise half the world's science journals. Regarded at worst as parasites enjoying a free lunch from the labour of editors and reviewers, they require authors to transfer copyright as a condition of publication. Vast profits have been made from the fruit of scientists and scholars paid from the public purse or by research charities and institutions. If a researcher wants to consult a journal not available in the library, or an inquisitive layperson enquires what research is paid by his or her taxes, they find access to journal webpages blocked by a paywall. The fee for a single article is often around £25 or $30, even for work published donkey's years ago.

Commercial journals and the companies behind them claim they have delivered value to science for a long time and are understandably anxious about changes afoot affecting their bottom line. Major research funders have started to insist grantholders publish papers for "open access". Since 2009, the NIH has required authors to upload papers to the National Library of Medicine within 12 months of publication. Heavyweight British charity the Wellcome Trust is pioneering deeper changes, and a Russian woman was so incensed by paywalls she pirated millions of papers for the public to download free.[110] Although ever so eager to spread scientific knowledge, Bob would have recoiled from a Robin Hood who hacked journal websites. He would be sad, too, to see how bogus internet journals tempt unsuspecting authors to submit their research or act as unpaid consultants.

It would be false to portray Bob as a dour workaholic with no time for leisure or recreation. He took his family to Europe for holidays, although they always had an educational element. The farm was a gathering place for three generations of Edwards and their friends, a large company assembling for Bob and Ruth's golden wedding anniversary in 2006. They had a party on the lawn, a cricket match in a meadow, and tours of the plantation in his red truck where he named a special tree for every grandchild. Grandad Bob was a larger than life character, regarded with a mixture of awe and bewilderment as he tried to explain stem cells to children of primary school age.

On workdays, he sometimes slipped away from the office to have lunch at Churchill College or have a dram of malt whisky in his local pub at the end of the day. A senior fellow at Churchill since 1979, he enjoyed the lack of a high table that separates students from dons in some old colleges. He could natter about anything before retiring to the common room for a glass of port. Churchill was a good fit. Named for Sir Winston at its foundation in 1958, it is a progressive institution, the first all-male college in the university to admit women, and a hub for science and technology with many American friends and patrons. After retiring from his university chair, the college council elected him an Extraordinary Fellow, a title reserved for the highest achievers and never more fittingly given.

He was still travelling to lecture and receive prizes in four continents, sometimes staying only one night. The elder statesman of science stood out in a crowd in his signature white jacket for people to find him for a portrait. Notable engagements included Buckingham Palace, the Egyptian Ministry of Health, and the Palais de la Légion d'Honneur in Paris. On a flight to New York to collect another award, the medical director of Bourn Hall noticed him dozing in coach class, so he called the cabin staff to warn that a distinguished passenger cramped in the back was at risk of a DVT. Bob moved reluctantly to a club seat and, now fully awake, regaled him with science for the rest of the journey, jotting down remembered references for his companion to read later. He never lost the thrill of learning or sharing knowledge, but there was something different. He didn't engage in much banter about national politics now, perhaps because the party he supported and at one time represented had changed to "New Labour".

He returned to New York in September 2001 for the most illustrious award to date but had an earlier engagement in midtown Manhattan. His former embryologist Jacques Cohen had organised a conference for a guild of reproductive scientists of which Bob was its patron. It was the 11th day of the month and, after the seats filled in a large ballroom for proceedings to begin, Jacques told the assembly to swiftly disperse and avoid downtown, under attack by al-Qaeda. He recalled Bob was sombre but stayed cool while stranded in the city until evacuated to Montreal for a flight home.

He was back later the same week in the Big Apple, now in the throes of recovery, but after the horrendous attack only his Canadian nephew could represent the family. It was for the Lasker Award, said to be America's Nobel Prize and often foretells a call from Stockholm. Although qualified for the basic research award, it was for clinical accomplishment that he was recognised. It was exceptional for someone who wasn't medically qualified and disappointing that Patrick could not share it. In a speech presenting the award, Joseph Goldstein compared Bob's achievements to Darwin and Wallace's 1858 paper as "defining events in the history of human society". Bob casually brushed off the great compliment. James Watson came over to shake his hand 30 years after their tense encounter at the Kennedy Center. Four years later, Watson visited Bourn Hall where he admitted he had underestimated IVF.

Bob had more engagements before his final call to North America six years later, where he gave the opening lecture at a world congress in Montreal. A hall packed with specialists anticipated the father of their field would review the history of IVF and share ideas they could try in their own labs and clinics. Instead, he talked about salamanders.

A bemused audience dominated by gynaecologists would have drifted out of the room from a less eminent speaker upon hearing a subject so remote to their interests. Bob held their attention, explaining how salamanders have lessons for medicine.

The amphibian with an inscrutable smile like a Buddha and a body resembling an overgrown tadpole was his new love. He gave the neotenous Mexican axolotl a starring role in the lecture, as he did in the last paper he wrote in his journal. He was fascinated by its ability to regrow limbs after amputation and repair damaged organs, an inspirational model for researchers to find ways of fixing broken bodies that supersede transplants and prostheses. Those in the audience who knew him recognised the Edwards karma, the curiosity and commitment that always drove him to novelty, and the reluctance to look back. Why talk more about IVF when it was a settled matter, or about genetic testing and stem cells when they became crowded fields? Salamanders would have their day, although Bob would not live to see it.

His name alongside Patrick Steptoe's is forever linked with IVF, but both men are fading from public consciousness, even among the patients and professionals who benefit from their legacy. Apart from a handful of universal geniuses, scientists and doctors are more forgettable than artists, writers, and musicians. Elvis is more celebrated than Ehrlich, and Byron than Babbage, despite the more tangible benefits of scientific discovery and application. An obvious reason is that the arts have more immediate appeal and are more accessible to laypeople, but there is another reason for creeping amnesia. The works of artists are unique whereas behind every scientific pioneer there is a line of proxies, for if one man or woman doesn't find a gem under a stone another will come along to kick it over for the prize. And, yet, a scientific pioneer deserves respect for more than precedence. He or she brings benefits to application sooner, and the character of the discoverer and manner of discovery can affect how a breakthrough is received and accepted by society.

The champions of reproductive technology had to be especially resolute because no reception is sterner than when deeply held beliefs are contested, or the role of Providence is threatened. Those who still remember the crusade for a fertility revolution know that opposition did not evaporate in a whimper. They will tell you about lonely struggles and demonisation, as well as the perspicacity and persistence of those who conquered. After the early breakthroughs, the task of regulating a mustang technology fell to other people, while Bob found a new role spreading good news to benefit families around the world for a vast legacy.

BOUNDLESS REVOLUTION

At this writing, it is 40 years since the first IVF baby was born, and 50 since Bob Edwards and Barry Bavister fertilised human eggs in a dish. After unfolding history, it seems timely to ask how the revolution is going and where research is heading.

Language seems a trivial place to begin, but new expressions and abbreviations are signs of a flourishing technology, like computer jargon. IVF was originally an acronym used by specialists, but after Louise Brown it entered the public domain of conversations and novels, TV and theatre, parliaments and colleges, and much more. In the beginning, it only had the elemental meaning of uniting one ovum with one sperm outside the body, but now IVF encompasses a family of ARTs.

The first breakthrough was the hardest and the loneliest, but like others it gathered speed from the invention of better tools and techniques as practitioners shared knowledge, and enterprise served the growing industry. What had taken a decade of endeavour by a small team became routine, though it still required a close partnership between two cultures, one claiming clinical authority and the other asserting scientific superiority.

Fifty years ago, most causes of infertility were unknown, the blame mostly laid on women instead of admitting either sexual partner can be responsible, or the problem is occasionally a biological incompatibility. Fallopian tubes blocked by pelvic inflammation were well-known, and their failure to yield easily to surgical remedies encouraged efforts to bypass obstructions by embryo transfer. That was how the revolution in clinical IVF began, and applications have fanned out to serve couples and singles with infertility as well as genetic testing, fertility preservation, surrogacy, sex selection, and mitochondrial disease. They now evoke dreams and nightmares of genetically modified babies. A technique that started as a single instrument became a whole orchestra.

An idea conceived in America was born in the UK. When newspapers announced the arrivals of Louise and Alastair as "miracle babies" they implied we were unlikely to see many more, and even the biggest cheerleaders of IVF didn't foresee the future. Not so long ago, the tiny wards Bob and Jean nurtured in a desiccator were the only human embryos alive on the planet outside the body, whereas today more than half a million grow in controlled environments every week. Millions more are asleep in freezers awaiting their destiny. Most people know someone who has benefitted or read about celebrities with IVF children, women like Emma Thompson, Celine Dion, and Michelle Obama. Such news struggles for headlines nowadays, and no one is astounded at a woman past 50 with a new baby for they know a donor egg made it possible. Our species is unable to stay in a state of amazement for long as we rapidly absorb novelty.

One of the benefits of familiarity is the wearing down of the misleading and pejorative label "test-tube baby". It should not stick on children who are ordinary. According to most reports, they are as healthy as those conceived by the "wild" method, and their prospects of reaching a vigorous old age are likely to be the same. They might even be better than average considering the utmost care poured on them in formative years by parents who feared they would never have children.

It would be dishonest to ignore side-effects of IVF treatment, its costs, frequent failures, and the rare mix-up in labs. Every technology has a history of setbacks and glitches, but it often solves the problems it created. The first patients needed to be anaesthetised for laparoscopy, but this surgery was soon replaced by ultrasound as an office-procedure which carries the tiniest risk. Multiple pregnancies were once a common hazard because it was tempting to transfer many embryos, even ten or more, when IVF was inefficient and frozen storage unavailable. It could mean the wretched decision to "reduce" some fetuses to protect the rest when more implanted than expected. A competitive marketplace drove this regrettable practice as clinics vied for better pregnancy rates, but since improvements in embryology and the introduction of regulations the number of embryos transferred has fallen towards the goal of singleton births without sacrificing acceptable success rates.

Average rates around the world now hover around 25-30% for a live birth rate of over 20% per treatment cycle. It is not easy to explain why they are much higher in some clinics than others. Selection of "easy" cases is a factor, but differences in clinical experience and tender loving care in the lab probably contribute to the gap, which will shrink when IVF is more automated. Some of the hardest cases are presented by women who, on every ground except fertility, are in the prime of life but take longer to conceive, often needing egg donation after 40 years of age. That is far from an ideal solution for the enigmatic problem of ageing.

A success rate of one in four for a hysterectomy or vasectomy would be grounds for dismissing the surgeon, yet the same rate for IVF is allowed on the excuse that it takes an average of four menstrual cycles for a healthy young couple to conceive naturally. Does that mean technology has already reached a biological limit and no further improvement is possible? It is a flawed analogy because baselines are not comparable. Multiple ova are collected during standard treatment with hormones whereas there is only one ovum in a menstrual cycle, and collective data suggest fewer than one in 20 ova in IVF cycles produce a baby. That is not a huge improvement on natural cycle IVF in the last cohort of patients at Kershaw's fifty years ago (2.5%). Greater investment in research can raise pregnancy rates above the current creeping rate.

The technology has grown from a single procedure to a range of services, some of which were exotic and now considered standards of care. Since their inception in the early 1990s, ICSI and PGT have made tremendous strides in conquering male infertility, inherited diseases, and chromosome disorders. When standard IVF treatment fails, the huge disappointment and waste encourages doctors and patients to desperately try other techniques, often turning to ICSI or PGT. When they are not justified on strict scientific grounds, these techniques join the list of so-called "add-ons" to offer timid hopes of a better outcome for an additional fee.[111] Other add-ons include yoga and acupuncture for calming nerves, assisted hatching, endometrial scratching, and immunological modulation. The list keeps growing.

Critics complain they are not evidence-based, add to patients' financial burden, and accuse the least justified options of being no better than snake oil. Defenders reply they are following a traditional path of progress, pointing out with some justification that standard services today would be unavailable if they had required testing as rigorously as drugs. Bob often depended on intuition and guesswork to advance the field, although he had obstacles that are hard to imagine today. He did, however, recognise an uneasy alliance between the scientific method and medical practice.

As research in a cottage hospital laid the original foundations of IVF, the never-ending mining of knowledge in universities and by discovery research in companies will frame the future. Manual skills will be redundant as embryologists reach for more automation, and the steady "hands" of robots make fine surgeons. The Human Genome Project released gigabytes of data for detecting every conceivable mutation in an embryonic cell to avoid transmitting disease, while machine-learning algorithms hail a future of personalised medicine to guide clinical decision-making. Will developing countries fall behind in this hi-tech future or IVF follow the track of smartphones, becoming affordable everywhere, even the poorest areas in Africa? Bob fostered ideas for low-tech solutions in his journal, and where standard treatment is unaffordable less efficient technologies are acceptable.

The future will not be babies grown in bottles, not for a very long time, nor will it be cloning. It is more likely to be greater reproductive liberty, socially and biologically unless suppressed by political tyranny. It could include the dazzling possibility of making ovaries and testes redundant for fertility, just as treatment with synthetic steroids made them unnecessary for hormone production. Why? For one thing, it will make ova abundant for fertility treatment and preservation, as well as research. The idea of cultivating gamete precursors in vitro planted 30 years ago by a Maine scientist and in the author's Edinburgh lab is now dramatically blossoming with human cells. More amazing scenarios are ahead. Researchers in Kyoto turned back the biological clock of ordinary somatic cells to the primitive IPS cell type which they rolled forward to create competent gametes of both sexes, from which they made baby mice. A technique that works in mice is likely to be adapted to make human gametes, and if the cells are proven healthy who will ban people from using their own for a goal dear to their hearts?

There is a corollary that methods for making gametes de novo can be spliced with an extra step to genetically engineer them. Aldous Huxley's London Hatchery changed the form of babies epigenetically to serve a social caste system, but it was a process that had to be repeated in every generation because the modifications were not inherited. But genetic changes made at tender stages of gamete formation or in early embryos are incorporated for future lineages. This is called germ line modification. Some say it is alarming, others say alluring. The pioneers of IVF only wanted to mimic nature in the Petri dish, not tamper with it.

The state-of-the-art tool for cutting and pasting DNA letters is CRISPR/Cas9. Far from Frankenstein science, it offers immense potential for agriculture and treating diseases, even combatting some effects of climate change, but when it was used in China in 2018 to edit the genome of human embryos for spurious reasons it generated universal revulsion. There was renewed talk of a slippery slope.

Biologists are not fond of the expression "designer baby" or its image. It is the spectre of producing people with "enhanced" genomes, like depictions in the movie Gattaca. The term has been attached to sober stories of "saviour siblings". In the first case, a boy was conceived by IVF to save an older sister who had inherited Fanconi anaemia from both parents carrying the recessive mutation. His embryo was selected for transfer from a bunch after two tests: first to confirm he didn't have the mutation, and then to check he was a good genetic match for injecting healthy blood from his placental cord into his sister to colonise her bone marrow. There was a rumble about the ethics of making new lives for others to benefit, inspiring a popular book, but Bob was ecstatic when her life was saved.[112]

The case ignited fears of making bespoke children. Poorly informed writers claimed that parents would choose genes from a menu to enhance intelligence, physiognomy, and athleticism, the characteristics an egotistic species prizes for vanity sake and social advantages.

Bob knew it was a fallacy but died too soon to realise that CRISPR-like methods might one day correct inherited mutations at conception and render PGT redundant. All technology is prologue. Instead of screening embryos by PGT to eliminate those with genetic faults, a missing or incorrect DNA character would be replaced, rather like the nifty spellchecker used to correct typos in this chapter. This is consistent with compassionate medicine, and Bob's consequentialism would approve an action that had a beneficial outcome for a child and avoided destruction of embryos.

He would recoil from more extensive changes in the genome, especially if they were purely "cosmetic" because that would conflict with his egalitarianism. To take the metaphor further, if the account of his life was embellished by grafting in fictitious matter to make him look more heroic it could make his story incongruent and historians would condemn the attempt as hubris. Besides, the more complex the trait the higher the hurdle for genetic manipulation because many genes are involved with multiple effects ("pleiotrophic") in a deep genetic architecture honed by natural selection that moulded bodies over generations to fit their environment. Attempts to improve or redesign the human fabric are likely face unacceptable trade-offs. We need people like Bob who grasp these issues and can navigate a wise path.

Science was not something he regarded in isolation from society, but commerce was alien to him. A startup at Kershaw's cottage hospital was the biomedical equivalent of a fabled garage in Silicon Valley where industries grew into global corporations. The current trend to absorb IVF clinics into conglomerates offers commercial and professional advantages of scale for venture capitalists to swoop to the multi-billion-dollar industry. What was made in-house in the pioneer era is now manufactured in a factory, and as new tools and equipment are developed the long reign of desiccator jars, Petri dishes, and pipettes ends.

If the ghosts of the original pioneers strolled through the vast convention halls today, they would be amazed to see reproductive medicine making great strides and how conferences are ever more dependent on commercial sponsorship. Companies display their fancy goods in glitzy booths of exhibition halls, like showrooms for luxury cars. This is an unseen background for buyers of fertility treatment who can mostly only afford a second-hand "Honda". Bob understood the difference as the son of a working-class family and serial owner of old cars! It used to be said that children were the gift of love and nature and that remains true except for the unfortunate minority for whom they cost the earth. A cycle of IVF is costly even before add-ons, and patients count themselves lucky if they succeed the first time or benefit from insurance or government subsidy. Fertility medicine is highly commercialised and nothing evinces that fact more than the marketing of special deals ("money back guarantee", et cetera) and egg freezing for social reasons.

Hampered only by the limits of science, the dilemma of unmet need, and an uncertain political system, the fertility trade will inevitably move forward.[113]

IVF has come a long way since the nativity scene in Oldham where a small team of professional staff made-do with second-hand equipment and profit was the last thing on their mind. The revolution in fertility care never stops rolling forward, driven by a biosocial imperative that cannot be denied when parenthood is a definition of a fulfilled life. The number of clinics in Western countries rose to plateau after the 2008 global financial crisis and is slowly increasing again. The biggest growth is in China, India, and other medium-income countries, and Costa Rica was the last country in the world with a ban on IVF, revoked in 2016. Around 10% of new babies are conceived in vitro where the state fully pays for treatment, like Denmark. What started with one amazing birth has blossomed to eight million in the world today, and by the end of the century hundreds of millions of people will owe their existence to IVF, either directly by conception or as the children or grandchildren of IVF babies.[114]

Not a bad record, Edwards! A family man himself, he found great satisfaction knowing the families he helped to build were thriving and welcomed them back to reunions at Bourn Hall. He was proud of research that laid foundations for other laboratories to build deeper knowledge and offer better treatment. It was always the hope of a brighter future that drove him, but the most precious day was in the past, that shining night when he first peered through a microscope at a human embryo in a dish. No other sight ever inspired greater awe.

Epilogue

Letting Go

I was back in Cambridge in 2018 after a ten-year gap. I heard Bob and Ruth had some golden times before a hard passage to their rest. Too late to share their triumphs, I came to hear accounts from people who were witnesses.

It was a dank October morning under the arch of the porters' lodge at Christ's College. Stone walls hushed the hubbub from buses and taxis sweeping past on St Andrew's Street. In the last week of the undergraduate vacation before students tumbled back for the Michaelmas term, there was still a veneer of monastic peace in the quadrangle beside the vine-crusted chapel. The college has a tradition in embryology reaching back over a century and is only a couple of blocks from the Marshall Lab where Bob worked. Francis Marshall and Sir Alan Parkes were fellows there, and Charles Darwin was a theology student deeply interested in animal breeding. I waited to meet the latest heir to the tradition.

This musing was broken by a tap on my shoulder. It was Martin Johnson snuggled inside a heavy jacket with a smile I remembered from my first day in Cambridge when he was already blazing a career. I followed him to the third court, past the garden where Milton's mulberry tree still flourishes, to climb a narrow staircase to his room. I was eager to hear about the Nobel ceremony, and wanted to know how the story ended. The last time I saw Bob he looked frail and time was running out for the Prize, but unexpected news made our hearts merry in 2010.

"How did you hear about it?" I asked him.

"It started like any other day, but when I drove up to the journal office Ruth was waiting with her daughters. They were bursting to share news. I hadn't heard the radio that morning, so they had the pleasure of telling me they had a call from Stockholm. No further explanation needed."

The Nobel Assembly announces prizewinners annually on the first Monday in October. Even candidates who know they are on the shortlist are often dazed if they have been waiting for years with fading hopes. The call may come through at breakfast or be transferred by a spouse to the winner tending roses in the garden or sitting in a bathtub. The Edwards family was stunned, and as a solo recipient the accolade seemed even more glorious. Bob was nominated many times for over a decade, and at 85 years old he was only two years junior to Peyton Rous of Johns Hopkins University, the longest ever waiting laureate in physiology or medicine.

The day was turned upside down, and the home became a whirlwind of activity. Journalists tried to get through by phone, friends and colleagues waited for an open line, and arrangements began for the ceremony in December. But the man at the centre of the story was bemused by the fuss. Recently out of hospital, there was no question of going to Stockholm to collect the prize in person. Ruth would represent him along with their daughters and grandchildren, his Canadian nephew, and close colleagues. But who would give the special lecture? She shunned that kind of limelight, just as she never disclosed contributions to her husband's fame.

"He asked me to speak for him," Martin said. "I suggested Richard Gardner, but Bob was hard to resist even then."

As the date approached and Martin was putting the finishing touches to the lecture, Bob fell gravely ill with a chest infection. The family considered cancelling the trip to Sweden, but a round of antibiotics restored his strength. Never given posthumously, the call came just in time, though too late for Patrick Steptoe or Gregory Pincus in an earlier decade. The Nobel Committee graciously invited Patrick's son and daughter-in-law, both professors of health psychology in London.

The family flew out with Martin to stay all expenses paid at the Grand Hôtel in Stockholm, like a six-storey palace on the waterfront. Out of their windows they saw luxury cruisers and schooners berthed below and the old town of Gamla Stan across the icy water. It was bitterly cold.

The lectures were given on the Tuesday at the Karolinska Institute. Held in a large hall of tiered stalls, they were open for the public to hear the laureates and Martin present concise histories of their subjects from a podium draped with the image of Alfred Nobel on a blue baize. The overflowing audience watched on closed circuit TV. On the following two days, they visited an art gallery and museum, also attending a reception at the British Ambassador's residence. The relentless pace exhausted Ruth, now 80 years old, who didn't know she was ailing. In the rush between venues, she was often waylaid by people greeting her, including some mothers with IVF children.

The prize-giving ceremony was held in the concert hall on the Friday. The King and Queen led a procession of Swedish dignitaries dressed to the nines, the women in long gowns glittering with jewellery and men in tuxedos and white bow ties. The pageantry was like a royal wedding, so alien to the laureates used to offices and laboratories and one still at home. The prizewinners were announced in turn between musical interludes by the Royal Stockholm Philharmonic Orchestra. Professor Höög introduced

Bob's prize, declaring that IVF was one of the great medical advances of our age and a miracle for childless couples.

Nobel Prizes have sometimes attracted sneers if given for arcane research that has no obvious impact on ordinary lives. The discovery of a new elemental particle or gravity waves gives more of a cerebral thrill than the hope raised by new knowledge in, say, neuroscience or immunology. But even in medicine there is a long incubation period between a fundamental breakthrough and its clinical application. The authentic description of the DNA molecule and fertilisation of eggs in vitro were the first of many steps until millions of people could benefit from the discoveries.

King Gustaf stood on a dais to present laureates with a box containing the gold medal. When it was Ruth's turn, people in the front seats saw how she trembled when she turned to face the audience in her long black gown, firmly gripping the heavy box as they rose to give an ovation. Everyone knew she was there for Bob, but few people understood she was much more than his wife. After returning to her seat, a soprano sang the aria *Non più mesta* ("No longer sad beside the fire"). Bob loved opera.

Afterwards, the ceremony closed with the national anthem and the Edwards party was conveyed in a motorcade through streets of waving pedestrians to a banquet at the City Hall, a vast building of orange stone and colonnades. Hundreds of people sat at long tables covered in white linen arranged like the ribs on a sternum from a bird's eye view. The tables were lavishly arranged with silver cutlery and glasses for several courses that lasted four hours. Ruth sat with VIPs at the top table.

When the meal was over, one of the pair of physicists who discovered graphene came over to Ruth for a personal homage that made her speechless. He said it was a greater privilege to meet the granddaughter of Rutherford than receive his physics prize. He is a professor in Manchester where Rutherford once

314

worked, Bob grew up, and Patrick had a consulting room. It was a proud day for the city.

The last event of the week was a reception at the palace, but Ruth was too tired to attend. She wanted to go home to give Bob the medal and diploma in a private celebration with a special cake. People said it was a shame he missed the pinnacle of a rainbow career, and it was sad as he would have loved the lectures and debates. The man who found a care for certain kinds of suffering now needed care for himself, but there was a compensation for his absence as it granted Ruth a share of the acclaim she deserved, if only for a day and reluctantly.

An obituary in the *New York Times* claimed an illness robbed him of the knowledge he had won a Nobel Prize. It was a question that gnawed at me. Had it come too late for him to enjoy? His life was so singular that I wondered if he was the first recipient who was unaware of the great honour. Martin had an answer.

"For sure, he knew. He reminded me with a cheeky smile every time I saw him." I felt even better when Bob's daughters confirmed his impression.

I asked him why the prize was delayed until millions of babies were born and Louise Brown was 32 years old. The first Swedish IVF baby arrived in 1982 and objections from the Vatican were unlikely to carry weight in a country of Lutherans and people who don't profess religion. It was rumoured that an influential paediatrician blamed IVF for soaring numbers of multiple pregnancies, but that problem was disappearing. What was the obstacle?

Martin was also puzzled until he asked an official. He was told they waited until the first generation of children grew up and had their own healthy families. That made sense, despite Alfred Nobel's will granting prizes "to those who, *during the preceding year*, shall have conferred the greatest benefit to mankind" [emphasis added]. The committee was wary because the 1949 prize for leucotomy (lobotomy) backfired when the operation was found to do more harm than good. The Brown family was in the vanguard of the next generation as Louise and her sister Natalie have six sons and daughters between them, all conceived naturally. If that generation is secure, it is unlikely to be different further down the line.

Bob's home country now felt obligated to match the honours he had from overseas. The following year on the Queen's official birthday, he was made a knight bachelor, although too unwell to attend the investiture. A civil servant contacts the candidate before a public announcement is made to avoid the embarrassment of an invitation turned down, which has famous precedents. Ruth helped him to a decision, but it was hard. Although her father was a knight and her grandfather a peer in the House of Lords, Bob was an avowed socialist and egalitarian, although never declared himself a republican. How would he have felt if he was addressed "Sir Bob" on the streets of Gorton? We will never know, but the title pleased his family and admirers.

It was a strange time of presence and absence. Politics had its day, philosophy had its say, and science wouldn't stay because it always moves forward. The man who rode them all with restless energy and loved to talk was withdrawing to the great peace.

The farm was scaled down in recent years, and Lady Ruth wandered the grounds more as a naturalist now than a farmer. After tumultuous years as Bob's wife and collaborator she took up a gentle interest in the lepidoptera, but it wasn't for long. She was losing weight and feeling something was wrong. It was pancreatic cancer.

Bob died a year later, on 10 April 2013. He was 87 years old. A service of thanksgiving was held in the chapel of Churchill College. Another former fellow, Francis Crick, harangued the college when it was new in 1960 because he said an institution of learning and scholarship was no place for a chapel. Bob wasn't a man of conventional religious belief, but there was something spiritual about his humanity and hunger for knowledge, and he understood the comfort of ritual and had mourned colleagues in churches.

After the service, his grandchildren laid flowers on the coffin and mourners paused for an exhibition of his work in the college. On the inward journey to the chapel rolling dark clouds broke into a hailstorm, but when the congregation left for a reception at Bourn Hall the sun came out to make the day glorious. I imagined freshly groomed lawns, daffodils nodding in the borders, and trees bursting with buds. Only a stubborn spirit would be down-cast there, and Bob would be glad to know that inside the hall the programme he planted still thrives. That was Ruth's last visit to the hall. With him gone, and now worn out by an illness that had no cure, she stopped taking medication, dying at home six months later.[115] Once a place of bustling activity and intellectual fervour, the farmhouse fell silent.

I called the hall to ask my friend Kay if we could visit the farm together to refresh my memory of the place and people. When we turned into the courtyard, the farmhouse looked gaunt without the people who gave it vitality, but lights burned in an upper room of the outbuilding. Bob's journal was busy publishing research from doctors and scientists around the globe.

I imagined the farmhouse as a replica of a place he spent a formative year in the Dales and where he had brought his family for holidays. One was bone-cold and hewn from quarries in the fells, the other was made of bricks from local clay. One was enclosed by drystone walls in a wild landscape, the other bordered by neat hedgerows in drained fenland. One was the

317

homeland of hill-farmers, the other close to an ancient university and hi-tech companies. It was a long way between farmhouses.

After stroking a lone horse in the stable and nosing around the barn, we circled to the backyard where the old willow tree wept autumn leaves. I peered in the conservatory window, cupping my eyes to avoid the reflection. The furnishings hadn't changed, like a time capsule. It was easy to imagine him leaning back in the wicker chair with an impish grin, beckoning to come inside for another episode of salamander stories. It was hard to accept that someone so physically and mentally robust, a man whose presence we still felt, was no longer around.

He was a man, take him for all in all,
I shall not look upon his like again.[116]

We continued to wander around the farm. Fields had grown into woods, and the trees had the first tints of red and gold. Somewhere among them was Lizzie's pear tree, Harry's conker tree, and others he named for grandchildren. I strained to understand his passion for trees, which he never explained. It began 50 years ago with planting the sterile steppes around Broadrake and continued at the farm where he planted thousands more with his own hands. They are over 40 feet tall now: oak, beech, and other species I can't identify, although if he had been our tutor the names would have rolled off his tongue with lessons in taxonomy and silviculture. He was always fully immersed in things he cared about. I heard the first thing he did coming home to hot weather from a lengthy trip was to give his baby trees a drink with fatherly care. If future owners are as careful, they will flower and fruit, passing a genetic baton to future generations that will stand long after the pioneers have fallen, and the planter's name is forgotten.

Some day when they are in voice
And tossing so as to scare
The white clouds over them on.
I shall have less to say,
But I shall be gone.[117]

A passion for trees seems an eccentric footnote for the last page of the story of the Father of IVF, but it is a tempting motif to draw some threads together. He wasn't a mystic but there is a mystique at the centre of every contemplative head that struggles for knowledge, order, and the hope of renewal which the "tree of life" has represented down the ages. It is totemic. He was the "tree man" to his neighbours, and the "life man" to patients. He found in physical labour not only rest from intellectual pursuit but a grounding richer than his ancestors ever had from clawing sterile coal. In toil there can be stillness to reflect on the cycle of life as *the fire and the rose are one.*[118]

His arc grew out of a mother's ambition, needed a wife's sacrificial love, and the alignment of luck and talent to realise a mission that was incredible and mocked before it was celebrated. It was a brave hope to plant saplings in heavy clay and transfer fertilised eggs to barren wombs. He would never live to see those babies growing up to have their own and couldn't help them in rough weather. But there was solace in the knowledge that sturdy growth from loving care would protect them from storms as they heave at their anchors to become founders of a flourishing succession.

Gallery

Broadrake farmhouse, North Yorkshire (2017).
(Source: the author)

Ribbledale viaduct viewed from Broadrake (2017).
(Courtesy of Mike Farrington)

Sheena Simon Campus, Whitworth Street (formerly
Manchester Central High School for Boys).
(Courtesy of Lauren Evans and Professor Daniel Brison)

University College of North Wales, Main Arts Building
(now Bangor University).
(Courtesy of Bangor University Archives)

Lieutenant Robert Edwards on board ship (1948).
(Copyright unknown, image courtesy of Edwards family)

Edwards in army uniform (late 1940s).
(Courtesy of the Edwards family)

John Slee visiting the Edinburgh Zoo with the Edwards (1963).
(Courtesy of the Edwards family)

Institute of Animal Genetics, Edinburgh (2017).
(Source: the author)

Charcoal sketch of Conrad Waddington (1905-1975).
(Courtesy of the University of Edinburgh)

Bob Edwards at the Institute of Animal Genetics (1955).
(Courtesy of the University of Edinburgh)

Sirlin and Edwards in Edinburgh (early 1950s).
(Copyright unknown, image courtesy of Sirlin family)

Ruth Fowler as a graduate student in Edinburgh (1950s).
(Copyright unknown, image courtesy of Edwards family)

Lord Ernest Rutherford (1871-1937).
(Courtesy of the Master and Fellows of Trinity College)

Albert Tyler (1906-1968) with sea urchins at Caltech (1966).
(Courtesy of the California Institute of Technology Archives)

Bob and Ruth Edwards at Borrego Springs, California (1958).
(Courtesy of the Edwards family)

Sir Alan Parkes at the Family Planning Association (1960s).
(Source: John Parkes)

"Bunny" Austin with Edwards in Cambridge (1960s).
(Copyright unknown, image courtesy of Edwards family)

Bob Edwards in the Marshall Laboratory with Barry Bavister,
Alan Henderson, and Richard Gardner (1969).
(Source: Barbara Rankin)

Edwards teaching a class in Cambridge (1968 or 1969).
(Copyright unknown, image courtesy of Edwards family)

M.C. Chang visiting Norfolk, Virginia (c. 1980).
(Source: Howard W. Jones, Jr.)

Howard and Georgeanna Jones with two IVF babies
in Norfolk, Virginia (1980s).
(Source: Howard W. Jones, Jr)

Garden view of Dr Kershaw's hospice in Royton (2017).
(Source: the author)

Patrick Steptoe with his operating theatre staff at Dr Kershaw's
hospital. Muriel Harris stands next to him (1978).
(Source: Barbara Rankin)

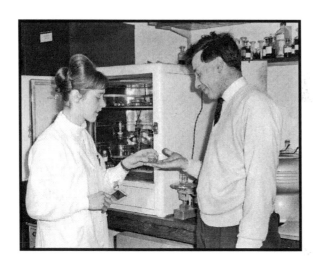

Jean Purdy with Bob Edwards in their laboratory at Dr
Kershaw's hospital in Royton (1970s).
(Source: Barbara Rankin)

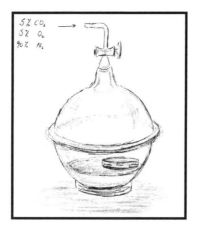

An impression of the desiccator used for IVF at "Boundary Park" hospital drawn by the director of medical photography. (Source: John Fallows)

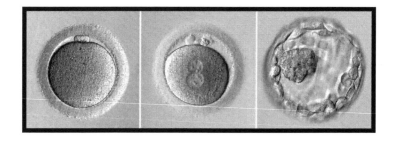

Human embryology: ripe ovum, fertilised egg, and blastocyst (left to right).
(Courtesy of Lucinda Veeck Gosden)

King's College Chapel and Clare College from the river.
(Source: the author)

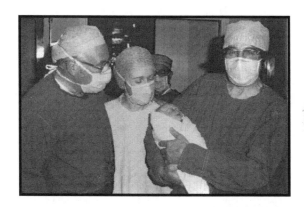

Patrick Steptoe, Jean Purdy, and newborn Louise Brown cradled
in the arms of Robert Edwards (1978).
(Courtesy of Bourn Hall Clinic)

The *Daily Mail* announcing the birth of Louise Brown (1978).
(Source: public)

Lesley and John Brown at home in Bristol celebrating Louise's
first Christmas (1978).
(Courtesy of Louise Brown family photos)

Bourn Hall, Cambridgeshire (2017).
(Source: the author)

Portacabins outside Bourn Hall (early 1980s).
(Courtesy of the Edwards family)

T

The first IVF conference (Bourn Hall, 1981). Seated on bench:
Edwards, Purdy, Steptoe, and Webster.
(Courtesy of Bourn Hall Clinic)

Edwards with Louise Brown and Alastair MacDonald at
Louise's 25th birthday celebration at Bourn Hall (2002).
(Courtesy of Bourn Hall Clinic)

Edwards posing beside a microscope (1980s).
(Courtesy of Bourn Hall Clinic)

Edwards and Steptoe receiving honorary doctorates
University of Hull (1983).
(Courtesy of the University of Hull and thanks to Professor
Henry Leese)

Rear view of Duck End Farm (2017).
(Source: the author)

The Edwards family gathered in Stockholm with friends and
colleagues for the Nobel Prize ceremony (2010).
(Courtesy of the Edwards family)

Further Reading

Laparoscopy in Gynaecology. Patrick C. Steptoe. Churchill Livingstone, 1966

A Matter of Life — The Story of a Medical Breakthrough. Robert Edwards & Patrick Steptoe. Hutchinson, London, 1980

Human Conception In Vitro. R.G. Edwards & Jean M. Purdy (eds.) Academic Press, London, 1982

Our Miracle called Louise — A Parent's Story. Lesley Brown. Grosset & Dunlap, London, 1984

Life before Birth — Reflections on the Embryo Debate. Robert Edwards. Hutchinson, London, 1989

Stealing Dreams — A Fertility Clinic Scandal. Mary Dodge & Gilbert Geis. Northeastern, 2003

Making Babies — Is there a Right to Have Children? Mary Warnock. Oxford University Press, Oxford, 2003

ESHRE — The First 21 Years. Simon Brown. Oxford University Press, 2005

Pandora's Baby — How the First Test Tube Babies Sparked the Reproductive Revolution. Robin Marantz Henig. Cold Spring Harbor Laboratory Press, NY, 2006

The Scientist as Rebel. Freeman J. Dyson. The New York Review Book Collections, 2008

The Fertility Doctor — John Rock and the Reproductive Revolution. Margaret Marsh & Wanda Runner. The Johns Hopkins University Press, Baltimore, 2008

Legal Conceptions — the Evolving Law and Policy of Assisted Reproductive Technologies. Susan L. Crockin & Howard W. Jones, Jr. The Johns Hopkins University Press, 2010

Robert Edwards — A Personal Viewpoint. Schulman, J. Self-published, 2010

Robert Edwards — the path to IVF. Martin H. Johnson. Reproductive Biomedicine Online 23, 245-262, 2011

IVF and Embryo Transfer — historical origin and development. John D. Biggers. Reproductive Biomedicine Online 25: 118-127, 2012

A Good Man — Gregory Goodwin Pincus. The Man, His Story, The Birth Control Pill. Leon Speroff. Self-published, 2012

Biology and Pathology of the Oocyte. Alan Trounson, Roger Gosden & Ursula Eichenlaub-Ritter. Cambridge University Press, 2013

Sir Robert Geoffrey Edwards, 27 September 1925 — 10 April 2013. Elected FRS 1984. Richard L. Gardner. Biographical Memoirs of Fellows of the Royal Society 1-22, 2015

Louise Brown — My Life as the World's First Test-Tube Baby. Louise Brown. Bristol Books, 2015

Essential Reproduction. Martin H. Johnson. Wiley-Blackwell, 8th edition, 2018

In-Vitro Fertilisation — The Pioneers' History. Gabor Kovacs, Peter Brinsden & Alan de Cherney. Cambridge University Press, Cambridge, 2019

In Vitro Fertilisation. Kay Elder & Brian Dale. 4th edition. Cambridge University Press, 2019

Robert Geoffrey Edwards
— career at a glance

Manchester Central High School for Boys (1936-1943)
British Army (1944-1947)
University College of North Wales, Bangor (1948-1951)
University of Edinburgh (1951-1957)
California Institute of Technology (1957-1958)
National Institute of Medical Research, London (1958-1962)
University of Glasgow (1962-1963)
University of Cambridge
    Ford Foundation Fellow (1963-1969)
    Ford Foundation Reader (1969-1985)
    First appointment at Churchill College (1974)
    Professor of Human Reproduction (1985-1989)
    Professor Emeritus (1989-2013)
Member of Cambridge City Council (elected 1973 & 1976)
Johns Hopkins Hospital (1965)
University of North Carolina, Chapel Hill (1966)
Scientific Director of Bourn Hall Clinic (1980-1990)
Founder-chairman of European Society for Human
    Reproduction & Embryology (1986-1988)
Founder-editor of Human Reproduction Journals (1986-2000)
Founder-editor of Reproductive Biomedicine Online (2000-
    2008)

Academic & honorary degrees
BSc (Wales, 1951)
Diploma in Animal Genetics (Edinburgh, 1952)

PhD (Edinburgh, 1955)

DSc (Wales, 1962)

Hon. DSc (Hull, 1983)

Hon. DSc (York, 1987)

Doctor Honoris Causa, Vrije Universiteit (Brussels, 1987)

Doctor Honoris Causa (Valencia, 1992)

Doctor Honoris Causa (Mons-Hainaut University, Belgium, 1992)

Doctor Honoris Causa (Timisoara University, Romania, 1999)

Hon. ScD (Cambridge, 2001)

Hon. Doctorate (Democritus University of Thrace, Greece, 2004)

Hon. Doctor of Medicine (Karolinska Institutet, Sweden, 2006)

Hon. Doctorate (University of Huddersfield, 2007)

Principal Honours & Awards

Fellow of the Royal Society of London (1984)

Fellow ad eundem, Royal College of Obstetricians and Gynaecologists, London (1985)

Commander of the British Empire (C.B.E.) (1988)

King Faisal International Prize for Medicine (1989)

Albert Lasker Award for Clinical Medical Research (2001)

"Pioneers of the Nation," Buckingham Palace (2003)

Chevalier dans l'Ordre National de la Légion d'Honneur (2007)

Nobel Prize for Physiology or Medicine (2010)

Knight Bachelor (2011)

Robert Edwards published 330 papers, apart from books and miscellaneous articles. The following is a list of eight landmark papers cited in his 2010 Nobel Lecture, delivered in his absence by Martin H. Johnson:

Cole RJ, Edwards RG, & Paul J. Cytodifferentiation in cell colonies and cell strains derived from cleaving ova and blastocysts of the rabbit. *Experimental Cell Research* 37, 501–504, 1965

Edwards RG. Maturation in vitro of human ovarian oocytes. *Lancet* 286, 926–929, 1965

Gardner RL & Edwards RG. Control of the sex ratio at full term in the rabbit by transferring sexed blastocysts. *Nature* 218, 346–349, 1968

Edwards RG, Bavister BD & Steptoe PC. Early stages of fertilization in vitro of human oocytes matured in vitro. *Nature* 221, 632–635, 1969

Steptoe PC & Edwards RG. Laparoscopic recovery of preovulatory human oocytes after priming of ovaries with gonadotrophins. *Lancet* 295, 683–689, 1970

Steptoe PC, Edwards RG & Purdy JM. Human blastocysts grown in culture. *Nature* 229, 132–133, 1971

Edwards RG & Sharpe DJ. Social values and research in human embryology. *Nature* 231, 87–91, 1971

Steptoe PC & Edwards RG. Birth after the reimplantation of a human embryo. *Lancet* 312, 366, 1978

Jamestowne Bookworks

Williamsburg, Virginia

Memoirs and history of reproductive science and medicine. Available in print and digital formats for online purchase from Amazon.

In Vitro Fertilization Comes to America (2014)
Howard W. Jones Jr.

A Surgeon's Story (2013)
Roger Gosden & Pam Walker

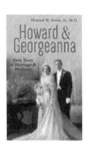

Howard & Georgeanna (2015)
Howard W. Jones Jr

Walter Heape, FRS (2016)
John Biggers & Carol Kountz

Index

Endnotes

1. Frankl, Viktor. Man's Search for Meaning. Introduction to Logotherapy. Beacon Press, Boston, MA, 2014 (first published 1946)

2. Elder K & Johnson MH. The Oldham Notebooks. Reproductive Biomedicine & Society Online 1: 3-70, 2015

3. Edwards, Robert & Steptoe, Patrick. A Matter of Life. Hutchinson, London, 1980

4. Rupert Brooke. The Old Vicarage, Grantchester (poem, 1912)

5. Milne EA. Ralph Howard Fowler, 1889-1944. Biographical Memoirs of Fellows of the Royal Society 61-78, 1945

6. Eve AS & Chadwick J. Lord Rutherford, 1871-1937. Biographical Memoirs of Fellows of the Royal Society 394-423, 1938

7. The nicknames of German and British troops in World War 1 were Fritz and Tommy, respectively

8. Wilfred Owen. Dulce Et Decorum Est (posthumous poem, 1920)

9. Alfred, Lord Tennyson. The Charge of the Light Brigade (poem, 1854)

10. A 60-year old soap opera by Granada TV filmed on the streets of Manchester

11. Manchester City Library Archives. Last lines of "Hush-a-bye, Baby" by T. Phadke

12. Manchester City Library Archives. Manchester High School for Boys. Letters

13. From a conversation with the author

14. Louis WR & Stookey RW. The End of the Palestine Mandate. University of Texas Press, Austin, 1986

15. Foetus is the customary spelling in Britain. Despite its apparent resemblance to British spelling of "oestrogen", the American form, "fetus", is probably more etymologically correct as the words have separate origins in Latin and Greek, respectively

16. Epigenetics is the notion of how a body of disparate cells is built from a totipotent egg, fashioned in time and space by methylation, acetylation, and protein binding of DNA (without affecting DNA sequence) to control gene expression

17. The word "egg" is used here for the female germ cell at fertilisation (or "zygote"). The immature female germ cell before fertilisation is called the "ovum" (plural ova) in place of the scientific term "oocyte"

18. Oestrogen is the original spelling of the female sex hormone (hence, oestrus, oestrone, etc.), deriving from the Greek "oestros" (for excitement, and "gen" for generation). In the Americas the word is usually contracted to "estrogen" to reflect phonetic pronunciation (like the change from oesophagus to esophagus), although the eminent American biologist Gregory Pincus who features in this book was still using the original spelling in his 1936 book, The Eggs of Mammals.

19. According to this hypothesis, the last formed ova are prone to chromosome errors and are the last to ovulate, hence explaining the link between maternal age and Down's syndrome. Despite extensive research it remains unproven, though not disproven

20. Article undated in the Papers of Conrad Hal Waddington. Edinburgh University Archives

21. Dyson, Freeman. The Scientist as Rebel. New York Review Books, 2006

22. Edwards Robert G. Conception in the Human Female. Academic Press, London, 1980

23. Hunter RHF. MC Chang—Reproductive biologist of distinction, 1908–1991. Human Fertility 16, 101-111, 2013

24. Nadya Suleman delivered her babies in 2009 from procedures not involving in vitro fertilisation

25. Papers of Robert Edwards. Archive Centre of Churchill College, Cambridge

26. Ibid. #25

27. Rothschild, Lord. Fertilisation. Methuen, London, 1956

28. Malthus, Thomas Robert. An Essay on the Principle of Population, 1803

29. Ehrlich PR. The Population Bomb. Ballantine, New York, 1968

30. Tyler A. Approaches to the control of fertility based on immunological phenomena. Journal of Reproduction & Fertility 2: 473-506, 1961

31. Gosden RG. The discovery of the mammalian ovum: lectures by Dr George W Corner. Biology of Reproduction 88: 1–11, 2013

32. The NIMR was absorbed into the new Francis Crick Institute in 2015 (https://www.crick.ac.uk/about-us/background/mill-hill-history/)

33. Polge C. Sir Alan Sterling Parkes, 10 September 1900 – 17 July 1970: elected FRS 1933. Biographical Memoirs of Fellows of the Royal Society 52, 263-283, 2006

34. Recorded conversation with Robert Edwards (2008)

35. Edwards RG. IVF and the history of stem cells. Nature 413: 349-351, 2001

36. Preimplantation Genetic Testing (PGT) is the new name for what was called Preimplantation Genetic Diagnosis/ Screening (PGD/PGS). It encompasses testing for aneuploidy (PGT-A), single gene defects (PGT-M), and structural rearrangements of chromosomes (PGT-SR)

37. Parkes AS. Sex, Science and Society. Oriel Press, Newcastle-upon-Tyne, 1966

38. Sellotape, known as Scotch tape in America

39. Extract of poem by Barbara Rankin, reproduced with permission. Archive Centre of Churchill College Cambridge

40. Quoted with permission from Sir Richard Gardner

41. Edwards RG. Maturation in vitro of human ovarian oocytes. Lancet 286, 926–929, 1965

42. Operating theatres in the UK are called operating rooms in North America

43. The first contraceptive pill combining an oestrogen and a progestin was sold as Enovid/ Enavid by GD Searle & Company after FDA approval in 1957 for menstrual disorders. Three years later it was being prescribed for contraception

44. Ibid. #3

45. Ibid. # 41

46. The catchy acronym for Gamete Intra-fallopian Tube Transfer (GIFT) was coined in America, where it was perfected. Earlier attempts by Steptoe and Edwards at Dr Kershaw's hospital were unsuccessful, which they called "Oocyte Recovery with Tubal Insemination" (ORTI).

47. Moor RM, Booth WD & Allen WR. A History of the Cambridge Animal Research Station, 1933-1986. R & W Communications, 2008

48. Catheter and cannula are interchangeable terms; only the former is used here

49. Chang's caution is still valid. There are babies conceived using in vitro maturation (IVM), but low efficiency has discouraged its use, and it is mostly offered to women with polycystic ovaries to avoid ovarian hyperstimulation

syndrome. Better results are obtained by initiating maturation with a hormone injection, including the first IVM baby reported by Lucinda Veeck at the Jones Institute in Virginia in 1983

50. Martin Johnson discusses in Reproductive Biomedicine Online (23, 245-262, 2011) how and when Edwards learned that Steptoe was using laparoscopy: probably from a review of Steptoe's book in the BMJ, which was acquired by the University Library the following March

51. Steptoe, Patrick C. Laparoscopy in Gynaecology. Churchill Livingstone, 1966

52. Edwards and Steptoe had different memories of their first encounter

53. The hospital is now called the Royal Oldham Hospital

54. Stanley Unwin (1911-2002) was a comic actor who mangled English words to make them sound humorous in a vernacular called Unwinese

55. Conditions that now seem obvious for cell survival were not well appreciated before. Brackett BG & Williams WL. Fertilisation of rabbit ova in a defined medium. Fertility & Sterility 19, 144-155, 1968

56. Edwards RG, Bavister BD & Steptoe PC. Early stages of fertilisation in vitro of human oocytes matured in vitro. Nature 221, 632-635, 1969

57. Papers of R Alan Beatty. Edinburgh University Archives

58. Ibid. #2

59. Biggers JD & Kountz C. Walter Heape, F.R.S. A Pioneer of Reproductive Biology. Jamestowne Bookworks, Williamsburg, VA, 2016

60. Kass LR. Making babies—the new biology and the old morality. Public Interest 26, 18-56, 1972

61. Edwards RG. Fertilization of human eggs in vitro: morals, ethics and the law. Quarterly Review of Biology 49, 3-26, 1974

62. Medawar PB. Induction and Scientific Thought. Methuen, London, 1969

63. Johnson MH, Franklin SB, Cottingham M & Hopwood N. Why the Medical Research Council refused Robert Edwards and Patrick Steptoe support for research on human conception in 1971. Human Reproduction 25: 2157-2174, 2010

64. The Edwards & Steptoe Research Trust continues to support research and education in the field of its founders (https://www.pdn.cam.ac.uk/other-pages/mjohnson/edwardsandsteptoefund)

65. Johnson MH & Elder K. The Oldham Notebooks—an analysis of the development of IVF 1969-1978. VI. Sources of support and patterns of expenditure. Reproductive Medicine & Society Online 1: 58-70, 2015

66. Arising from a meeting of the New York Obstetrical Society, 1958

67. Shettles LB. How to Choose the Sex of Your Baby. Doubleday (revised edition), 1989

68. By a quirk of history, the operating room for Mrs Del-Zio's procedure was later converted to an IVF laboratory for Weill Cornell Medical School

69. Rorvik DM. In his Image—The Cloning of a Man. Lippincott, 1978

70. Soupart P & Strong PA. Ultrastructural observations on human oocytes fertilized in vitro. Fertility & Sterility 25, 11-44, 1974

71. United States Department of Health, Education, and Welfare. Ethics Advisory Board. HEW Support of Research Involving Human In Vitro Fertilization and Embryo Transfer. Washington DC.
May, 1979

72. Johnson R & Walsh A. Camaraderie: One Hundred Years of the Cambridge Labour Party, 1912-2012. Cambridge Labour Party, 2012

73. Giono, Jean. The Man who Planted Trees. First published in 1953

74. Haldane JBS. Daedalus, or Science and the Future. Kegan Paul, Trench, Trubner & Company, London 1923, p. 44

75. Ian Brady and Myra Hindley were given life sentences for a spate of sadistic killings of children aged between 10 and 17 years old between 1963-1965 and buried their bodies on Saddleworth Moor

76. Leeton J. Test Tube Revolution—the early history of IVF. Monash University Publishing, 2013

77. Driscoll G. Fertility Society of Australia: A History. Edited by Douglas M. Saunders (self-published), p. 66, 2013

78. Bevis DCA. Embryo transplants. British Medical Journal 238, 27 July 1974

79. Borstal was a detention centre managed by HM Prison Service for reforming young people (abolished in 1982)

80. Lesley Brown (1947-2012) and John Brown (1943-2007). Not only did they die rather prematurely, but so did his daughter Sharon in 2013

81. Ibid. #25

82. Later she retook her maiden name, MacDonald, as she is known today

83. Now DMG Media

84. Steptoe and Son was a British TV comedy series about the rag-and-bone trade in the 1960s and 1970s. A parallel story about scavengers aired the other side of the Atlantic as Sanford and Son

85. Alias Subhash Mukhopadhyay

86. Anand Kumar TC. Architect of India's first test tube baby: Dr. Subhas Mukerjee (16 January 1931 to 19 July 1981). Current Science 72, 526-531, 1997. Bharadwaj A. The Indian IVF saga: a contested history. Reproductive Biomedicine and Society Online 2, 54-61, 2016

87. Freezing all embryos for singleton transfer after thawing is now common practice for the goal of singleton pregnancies (note the higher frequency of monozygotic twinning after IVF)

88. Eliot TS. The Waste Land (1922)

89. Jones Jr HW. In Vitro Fertilization Comes to America—Memoir of a Medical Breakthrough. Jamestowne Bookworks, Williamsburg, VA, 2014

90. Edwards RG & Purdy JM. Human Conception In Vitro (eds.) Academic Press, London, 1982

91. Ramsey P. Shall we "reproduce"? JAMA 220, 1346-1350 & 1480-1485

92. Dunstan GR. The Artifice of Ethics. SCM Press, London 1974, pp. 71- 83

93. Patrick Steptoe only treated married couples in the early years

94. See: The labs growing human embryos for longer than ever before. Nature 559: 19-22, 2018. Recent progress has been in the department where Edwards worked, now led by Magdalena Zernicka-Goetz

95. Hansard, House of Commons. Human Fertilisation and Embryology (Warnock Report) Volume 68. 23 November 1984

96. Quasi-Autonomous Non-Governmental Organisation

97. Hansard, House of Lords. Unborn Children (Protection). Volume 504. 8 March 1989

98. Now the Progress Educational Trust (https://www.progress.org.uk/)

99. A non-compete clause in a contract binds an employee not to enter the same profession or trade with another employer for a specified time. A common practice in business, its adoption in some IVF clinics (especially in America) was an early sign of a field embracing a business model

100. Funding for IVF in England is still contentious and unevenly distributed (sometimes called a postal code lottery)

101. Carroll, L. Through the Looking Glass, 1871

102. Ibid. #25

103. Since 2015, a blue plaque at Dr Kershaw's Hospice commemorates the work of Steptoe, Edwards, and Purdy, and in 2019 the Royal Oldham Hospital erected another plaque for Jean and Sister Muriel Harris (1923-2007). Jean's new headstone was dedicated on 20 July 2018 in the presence of Louise Brown, colleagues, friends, and her brother John who died 8 weeks later. See also: Gosden RG. Jean Marian Purdy remembered—the hidden life of an IVF pioneer. Human Fertility 21, 86-89, 2017. Although Jean didn't train as a scientist, she is gaining notice as a neglected woman in science, like Nettie Stevens (genetics), Rosalind Franklin (molecular biology), Jocelyn Bell Burnell (radio astronomy), and others

104. Taylor, P. An Irish Doctor in Peace and War (2015); An Irish Doctor in Love and at Sea (2017), Forge Books, Tom Doherty Associates, New York

105. The service opened by the late Ian Craft, a controversial pioneer who helped thousands of patients

106. Edwards RG. Human Reproduction 15, 2, 2000

107. Bob's journal office moved to Bourn Hall in 2018

108. Caroline Blackwell worked with Edwards for 30 years.

109. Gardner RL &, Johnson MH. Bob Edwards and the first decade of Reproductive Biomedicine Online. Reproductive Biomedicine Online 22, 106-124, 2011

110. See: Wellcome Trust Open Access publishing (https://wellcomeopenresearch.org/)

111. European data reveal how ICSI cycles have greatly overtaken standard IVF, yet there is no evidence of its superiority, except for severe male infertility. Overall success rates with the two techniques are comparable.

112. Picoult J. My Sister's Keeper. Atria Books, 2004

113. Spar DL. The Baby Business—How Money, Science, and Politics Drive the Commerce of Conception. Harvard Business School Press, Boston, 2006

114. Faddy MJ, Gosden MD Gosden RG. A demographic projection of the contribution of assisted reproductive technologies to world population growth. Reproductive Biomedicine Online 36, 455-458, 2018

115. Fishel S. Ruth Fowler (1930-2013). Reproductive Biomedicine Online 28, 3-4, 2014

116. Hamlet, Act I, Scene 2

117. Frost R. The Sound of Trees, 1916

118. Eliot, T.S. Four Quartets. Little Gidding, 1941

Made in the USA
Columbia, SC
29 August 2019